Business Guides on the Go

"Business Guides on the Go" presents cutting-edge insights from practice on particular topics within the fields of business, management, and finance. Written by practitioners and experts in a concise and accessible form the series provides professionals with a general understanding and a first practical approach to latest developments in business strategy, leadership, operations, HR management, innovation and technology management, marketing or digitalization. Students of business administration or management will also benefit from these practical guides for their future occupation/careers.

These Guides suit the needs of today's fast reader.

Michael Lewis
Fandom Analytics

Creating and Harnessing Consumer and Cultural Passion

Michael Lewis
Goizueta Business School
Emory University
Atlanta, GA, USA

ISSN 2731-4758 ISSN 2731-4766 (electronic)
Business Guides on the Go
ISBN 978-3-031-65924-9 ISBN 978-3-031-65925-6 (eBook)
https://doi.org/10.1007/978-3-031-65925-6

© The Editor(s) (if applicable) and The Author(s), under exclusive license to Springer Nature Switzerland AG 2024

This work is subject to copyright. All rights are solely and exclusively licensed by the Publisher, whether the whole or part of the material is concerned, specifically the rights of translation, reprinting, reuse of illustrations, recitation, broadcasting, reproduction on microfilms or in any other physical way, and transmission or information storage and retrieval, electronic adaptation, computer software, or by similar or dissimilar methodology now known or hereafter developed.

The use of general descriptive names, registered names, trademarks, service marks, etc. in this publication does not imply, even in the absence of a specific statement, that such names are exempt from the relevant protective laws and regulations and therefore free for general use.

The publisher, the authors and the editors are safe to assume that the advice and information in this book are believed to be true and accurate at the date of publication. Neither the publisher nor the authors or the editors give a warranty, expressed or implied, with respect to the material contained herein or for any errors or omissions that may have been made. The publisher remains neutral with regard to jurisdictional claims in published maps and institutional affiliations.

This Springer imprint is published by the registered company Springer Nature Switzerland AG
The registered company address is: Gewerbestrasse 11, 6330 Cham, Switzerland

If disposing of this product, please recycle the paper.

Mike combines a statistician's keen eye for the telling detail, a marketing scientist's knack for identifying key societal trends, and a lifelong sports fan's enduring love of the game. He's crafted that rarest of books—both entertaining and educational.

—Jay Busbee, Senior Writer, Yahoo Sports

Fandom Analytics is a game changer for anyone who wants to understand the intersection of art and science within sports and entertainment fandom. Mike helps make sense of the cultural phenomenon that is sports, offering an engaging exploration that we can all relate to.

—David Elgin, Senior Vice President, Analytics Atlanta Hawks & State Farm Arena

The definitive guide for understanding fandom! Dr. Lewis distills decades of research into an actionable framework useful for brands inside and well beyond traditional sports—to create fandom, cultivate extreme loyalty, and dominate the marketplace.

—Todd Harris, CEO of Skillshot Media and Ghost Gaming

Mike's vast experience of fandom across multiple domains come together beautifully here to provide an insightful and compelling understanding of how we think as humans and how the business world can strategize around it. A fascinating read for the fandom newbie or experienced professional!

—Lucy Rushton, General Manager, Bay FC

Mike has created an insightful framework that reveals how fan culture shapes the marketing landscape and how marketing, in turn, reshapes the fan experience.

—Justin Watkins, Vice President, Strategy, Atlanta Braves

Preface

Welcome! The book you are now beginning (or considering) reading represents the culmination of the last two decades of my professional life. I've started to think of my career as a three-act play. This work is the apex of the second act.

I started my intellectual journey as a quantitative marketer with multiple degrees in optimization and statistics. I spent the first 15 years of my business school professor career working on topics like yield management, dynamic pricing, and consumer loyalty programs. My work on these topics often used dynamic optimization models of consumer behavior. The goal was always to optimize the value of some asset, whether it was a consumer relationship, inventory, or a brand. It was complicated mathematics applied to explain and improve decisions related to consumers. I think of this as my first act: a marketing scientist specializing in the dynamic analysis of customers and other marketing assets.

The best thing about academia is the freedom. Marketing analytics is a worthy field, and dynamic models of consumer behavior are important, but I started to get a little bored. It was time to start something new. I began to spend more time on an underappreciated part of marketing: how marketing impacts society and culture. Developing an algorithm for setting prices to maximize customer lifetime value or setting shipping fees to optimize customer spending is worthwhile. Still, this type of work is mainly interesting to firms trying to improve their bottom line.

To me, the part of marketing that really matters is where marketing touches culture and inspires passion. Consumer loyalty matters to brands, but the loyalty we see in the grocery store pales compared to the passion we witness in people interested in sports, entertainment, politics, and other categories that make up our culture. I define fandom as the passion for some cultural entity. For my second act, I decided to apply my skills in customer analytics to topics in sports and culture (there has also been some work on politics, movies, and fashion). I think of this work as Fandom Analytics.

My second act has been an easy transition. Customer lifetime value models are not that different from models of player performance. Models of brand equity can be applied to baseball teams or soft drinks. I've worked on various topics ranging from on-field performance metrics to brand equity analysis for sports clubs. My second act involved combining my academic skills with my lifelong love of sports to develop a portfolio of work focused on sports and fandom analytics. It's been a passion project that has allowed me to stay interested and to keep learning.

A short book to an author can feel like a long book to a reader or student. When I think about the classes I've taken and the books I've read, things can usually be boiled down to a couple of paragraphs and maybe a key figure or two. It's just how we learn; we store a high-level summary of the material, and this map is there to bring us back to the source material when we need the details. What are the key takeaways from "Fandom Analytics"?

- The foundational argument of the book is that fandom is a critical part of human behavior that impacts both marketing results and the cultures we live in. The brands that create fans dominate the marketplace, and the cultural entities (sports, entertainment, politics, gaming, etc.) that inspire fandom define our societies.
- The Fandom Analytics Framework in Fig. 2.1 provides a tool for structured thinking about fandom creation and management. The framework provides the roadmap for the book and is the critical concept I want readers to gain from the book.
- Fandom Analytics requires an interdisciplinary approach that considers stories' roles in subcultures, fandom's psychological identity benefits, and the marketing concepts of brand and customer equity. The core of fandom analytics should be sports analytics techniques that identify great players and create outstanding teams.

* The chapters on "Fandom Beyond Sports" and "The Future of Fandom" are about generalizing the book's ideas to think beyond our main context of sports and beyond what fandom looks like at the moment. The book studies the critical concept of fandom in the realm of sports, but the material can be extended to all sorts of cultural products.

I've spent a lot of time thinking about and researching issues related to fandom. When it came time to put this thinking into a book, a bunch of decisions needed to be made to keep the presentation concise. I would like to mention three of these decisions.

The first decision was whether to ground the book in the single category of sports or to take a more general approach to the topic and discuss fandom across multiple categories. This was a real dilemma. A book about just sports feels a little limiting, but a book about all of fandom would probably require multiple volumes. I've attempted to split the difference and write about primarily sports fandom with selected material that extends the work to other categories.

Second, a challenge in writing a book about fandom is the balance between examples and theory. Examples are more powerful for most readers, but theory is more enduring. Given that the book is about fandom, I decided to err on the side of more examples and less academic theory. As the book is written in the second half of 2023 from my location at Emory University in Atlanta, the examples frequently feature names like Taylor Swift and Lionel Messi. As a side note, even coming up with examples is fairly challenging. There are very few shared cultural references these days, so I try to keep it to the big names.

The third predicament is the issue of technical content versus accessibility. Analytics can quickly become complex. But the goal is not to write a book on statistics, so I have kept equations and mathematics to a minimum. I have provided selected references for the more adventurous analyst. The goal is to provide the structure and perhaps motivation rather than a technical treatment. Given the breadth of the topic, a technical treatment would require a much more extensive and complicated book.

The folks offering the preceding comments about the book deserve a special shout-out. The folks include top marketing analytics executives at the Atlanta National Basketball Association (NBA) and Major League

Baseball (MLB) teams, an e-sports evangelist, a sportswriter who has written about National Association for Stock Car Auto Racing (NASCAR), and a woman who was the first female general manager in Major League Soccer (MLS). I've included these folks as they have been frequent sources of information and inspiration. These folks are passionate sports pros who work in very different functions, but at the core, they are all in the business of fandom. There is nothing better than when the professor learns something, and I'm grateful to know them.

Finally, I also want to mention a few folks from "within" the academy who contributed to the project. Doug Battle is my podcast producer and cohost. He is a great fan and provided my indirect source material. Jonathan Fineman and Jesse Bernstone were my teaching assistants and helped massively with figures. Last but certainly not least, Manish Tripathi, a former faculty at Emory, was an amazing partner during the early days of the sports analytics project.

Emory University
Atlanta, GA, USA

Michael Lewis

Contents

1	**Fandom: The Business of Cultural Passion**	1
	1.1 The Power of Fandom	1
	1.2 Defining Fandom	4
	1.3 Examples	8
	1.4 Monetizing Fandom	12
	1.5 Plan and Purpose	13
	1.6 Insights and Connections	15
	References	16
2	**Fandom Analytics Framework**	19
	2.1 Marketing Analytics to Fandom Analytics	19
	2.2 Fandom Analytics Framework	24
	2.3 Interdisciplinary Perspectives	26
	2.4 Fandom Management	32
	2.5 Non-sports Fandom Analytics	33
	2.6 Insights and Connections	35
	References	36
3	**Stories and Narratives**	37
	3.1 Shared Sports Memories	37
	3.2 Roles of Shared Stories in Fandom	38

	3.3 Fandom as Subculture	41
	3.4 Excitement and Persuasion	43
	3.5 Knowledge and Experience Transmission	45
	3.6 Community Structure and Hierarchy	47
	3.7 Current Trends	48
	3.8 Organizational Perspectives	51
	3.9 Insights and Connections	56
	References	57
4	**Fandom Communities and Fan Identity**	61
	4.1 Public Displays of Fandom	61
	4.2 Fandom Benefits	63
	4.3 Relationships	65
	4.4 Community	67
	4.5 Identity	68
	4.6 Analytics Challenges	70
	4.7 Insights and Connections	72
	References	73
5	**Fan Attitudes and Survey Research**	75
	5.1 Fan Motivations, Attitudes, and Behaviors	75
	5.2 Next-Generation Fandom Survey	78
	5.3 Fandom Attitudes	82
	5.4 Fandom Motivations	86
	5.5 Fandom Behaviors	90
	5.6 Extensions, Limitations, and Data Integration	93
	5.7 Insights and Connections	95
	References	96
6	**Fandom Equity**	99
	6.1 Economic Value of a Fandom	99
	6.2 Sports Value Proposition	100
	6.3 Fandom Equity	103
	6.4 Measuring Fandom Equity	105

	6.5 Measuring Fandom Equity in Major League Baseball	107
	6.6 Fandom Equity Alternatives and Limitations	111
	6.7 Insights and Connections	112
	References	114

7 Fan Lifetime Value — 115
- 7.1 What is a Fan Worth? — 115
- 7.2 Economic Value of Fans — 117
- 7.3 Customer Lifetime Value — 119
- 7.4 Fan Retention and Revenue — 122
- 7.5 Fan Base Valuation — 123
- 7.6 Challenges and Extensions — 127
- 7.7 Insights and Connections — 129
- References — 131

8 Sponsorships and Fandom Transference — 133
- 8.1 Sports Sponsorships — 133
- 8.2 Sports Entities and Sponsoring Brands — 135
- 8.3 Awareness — 138
- 8.4 Associations — 139
- 8.5 Community — 142
- 8.6 Analytical Challenges — 144
- 8.7 Insights and Connections — 147
- References — 148

9 Sports Analytics: Player Evaluations and Game Decisions — 151
- 9.1 Sports Analytics — 151
- 9.2 Sports Analytics and Fandom — 154
- 9.3 Player (People) Analytics — 156
- 9.4 Game (Strategy and Tactics) Analytics — 165
- 9.5 Cognitive Biases and Sports Decisions — 169
- 9.6 Insights and Connections — 173
- References — 175

10 Sports Analytics: Leagues, Teams, Players, and Fans 177
- 10.1 Winners and Losers 177
- 10.2 League Organization 179
- 10.3 Competitive Balance 181
- 10.4 Interventions 183
- 10.5 Analysis Issues 193
- 10.6 Insights and Connections 194
- References 195

11 Fandom Beyond Sports 199
- 11.1 The Swifties 199
- 11.2 Fandom Dimensions: The WILD Categorization Scheme 202
- 11.3 W: We Win 203
- 11.4 I: Influences 205
- 11.5 L: Life-Cycle 207
- 11.6 Display 209
- 11.7 WILD System 211
- 11.8 Insights and Connections 214
- References 216

12 The Future of Fandom and Fandom Analytics 219
- 12.1 Evolving Sports Fandom 219
- 12.2 Current Trends Impacting Fandom 222
- 12.3 Demographics 225
- 12.4 Technology 228
- 12.5 Marketing 233
- 12.6 Fandom Focused Organization 243
- 12.7 Organizational Capabilities 249
- 12.8 Final Thoughts 253
- References 256

1

Fandom: The Business of Cultural Passion

1.1 The Power of Fandom

Fandom is one of the most potent forces in society. Sports, for instance, can animate and unify communities. What other force besides college football can regularly get more than 90,000 people to coordinate outfits and show up in small cities like University Park, Pennsylvania, or Athens, Georgia, during fall weekends? Whole countries can come together over sports. Five million people celebrated in Buenos Aires following Argentina's 2022 World Cup victory (Young, 2022). Beyond sports, Taylor Swift's Eras tour has captivated a significant portion of Millennial and Generation Z women and is estimated to have led to $5 billion in consumer spending (Kopstein & Espada, 2023). Like sports, Taylor Swift fans are passionate and unified, dressing in costumes inspired by their favorite albums, from classic country-style outfits for the *Fearless* era to neon and glitter for the *1989* era. What besides fandom can inspire towns, countries, and generations to come together in coordinated outfits to passionately cheer for a shared interest?

The notion that fandom drives sports and entertainment categories is not controversial, but fandom also influences diverse contexts, such as political elections, educational choices, and product success. Fans are ultimately consumers of sports, entertainment, and other cultural products. While fandom is usually found in cultural categories like sports, movies, and music, any organization trying to persuade consumers or impact society can readily understand fandom's appeal. It is rare that consumer products achieve the status of having fans, but brands like Coke, Tesla, Lululemon, Apple, and a few others certainly inspire a degree of fandom. The critical differentiator between fans and ordinary consumers is that fans possess a passion, engagement, and devotion that ordinary consumers lack. The intense passion of fans means that fans are especially valuable customers. The passion of fans relative to ordinary consumers also suggests that fandom may have different foundations than ordinary brand loyalty.

This book is primarily about sports fandom. Sports fandom is an especially potent form of fandom that can last from early childhood through old age. Sports fandom also often has a community aspect, as teams and fandoms are often explicitly linked to locations. The linkage to a community is critical because it facilitates sports fandom to be a uniting force that unifies cities or nations. Sports fandom also transcends cultures. Americans love their NFL, Europeans and South Americans are fixated on soccer, and Indians are obsessed with cricket.

Sports fandom is not just about the love of sport; fandom is also embedded in personal and national identities. At the individual level, whether someone is a Dallas Cowboy or Manchester City fan is a frequent element in describing a person. At the societal level, baseball was known as America's national pastime; the All Blacks might be New Zealand's most recognized organization, and most of Europe and South America are obsessed with their national soccer teams. Sports fandom frequently becomes part of how people and societies build their identities and describe others.

The importance of fandom to people is illustrated by the desire of brands to attach themselves to sports. Major international tournaments like FIFA and the Olympics are sponsored by some of the most famous brands from around the globe. FIFA's 2022 sponsors included Coca-Cola, Adidas, Visa, and Hyundai, while the Tokyo Olympics sponsors included Coca-Cola, Toyota, Intel, and Samsung. Formula 1 racing cars are covered by famous brands. For instance, the Red Bull 2023 car included Oracle, Honda, and Red Bull logos.

The economic power of fandom is obvious, as the monetization of fandom has helped create several multibillion-dollar sports leagues. For instance, the NFL generates $12 billion in annual revenue (Ozanian, 2023), while the EPL generates £5.5 billion (Buckingham, 2023). Any team, celebrity, politician, or brand knows the power of supporters becoming fanatics. Fans will pay premium prices, are fiercely loyal, and act as evangelists. The mystery is how to create, manage, and leverage fandom. At the heart of managing fandom is understanding fandom. Fandom is complicated because the emotions are more profound, and the role of community is more substantial than in ordinary consumption. Fandom is also a topic that reveals the limitations of traditional marketing and the importance of creating special or extraordinary products, services, and experiences.

The power of fandom also transcends commerce. Fans are quick to defend their favorite teams. The intensity and passion of fans can lead to blind devotion and violence. In European soccer, extreme fandom is at the core of hooliganism, which has led to on-field disruptions and violent clashes with opposing teams' fans (Reyass, 2017). Following one of the worst scandals in collegiate sports, a contingent of Penn State football rioted in support of the embattled football program and coach (Boylan, 2012). In settings as different as Donald Trump's MAGA rallies, the #FreeBritney movement, and the revolt of the Swifties against Ticketmaster, fans come together to protect the objects of their affection.

The book is intended as a resource for those interested in building and managing fandom in sports and other cultural categories. This is primarily accomplished through a Fandom Analytics Framework that provides a fandom management roadmap. The foundation for this fandom management roadmap involves a deep exploration of where fandom comes from, the value it provides people, and how it can be managed. When an organization's core customers are "Fans," traditional approaches to marketing will have substantial deficiencies. Fandom-driven organizations need broader thinking, interdisciplinary approaches, and different types of analytics to maximize the value of their customer bases. The goal is to provide definitions, frameworks, and perspectives that clarify the nature and challenges of managing fandom and guidance that can improve results.

1.2 Defining Fandom

Fandom is a trait that we all recognize but seldom think about precisely defining. We all know people who describe themselves as fans and can all recognize instances of fandom. However, we probably do not think about what separates a fan from a non-fan or when preference becomes so intense that it becomes fandom.

Academics in a variety of social science fields have attempted to define fandom, and several consistent themes emerge. First, fandom involves extreme preferences. According to Sandvoss (2005), fans are characterized by intense enthusiasm, passion, and dedication towards their chosen subject. Second, there is a community or social aspect to fandom. A fandom is a group of individuals who share a common interest in a specific subject or object such as a sports team, musician, or movie. Third, fandom involves engaging in fan-specific behaviors. Fans are known to engage in multiple activities to express and celebrate their fandom, such as attending conventions, creating fan art, writing fan fiction, or participating in online discussions (Hills, 2003). Generally, fandom can be described as a subculture that involves a strong sense of belonging and connection among its members (Bennett, 2001).

Several themes emerge across these perspectives. First, fandom is about intense positive attitudes towards some entity. Second, fandom includes a group component as a subculture evolves around the object of fandom. The intense positive emotions of fans drive individuals to engage in fan behaviors such as wearing clothes that reveal fandom and create fandom communities. Third, being a part of a fan group provides some utility to fans. Fandom involves monetary and time costs, so participating in fandom must also provide some benefits. Fourth, fandom is not domain-specific. Fan subcultures may be most common in sports, but fandom can occur in many categories.

For the purposes of this book, I define fandom in simple terms:

- Fandom is the expression of individual and shared passion, engagement with, and interest in some cultural entity.

My definition is intentionally broad. Fandom is something that we observe in many categories and to varying degrees. A more precise but limiting definition of fandom is less helpful as it may constrain what classifies as fandom. My definition includes three key elements that are relevant to fandom:

1. Fandom operates at the group and individual levels. Fandom requires a group or subculture to exist. Individuals (Fans) must gain some value from being a part of the group (The Fandom).
2. Fandom requires intense emotions that drive behavioral engagement.
3. Fandoms form around entities that are culturally relevant. Sports, entertainment, politicians, and even brands define the culture.

An expansive definition of fandom is also chosen because there is significant variation in terms of how fandom manifests across people and categories. In particular, fandom operates along a continuum as the levels of engagement may vary substantially across people who all classify themselves as fans. Additionally, the different structures of categories tend to change the character and expression of fandom across categories.

1.2.1 Fandom Continuum

Fandom is not an either-or phenomenon. Even within a stadium, there may be "die-hard" fans who show up with faces painted in the team colors and experience every win or loss as a personal victory or defeat, but there might also be casual fans who put on a team jersey and enjoy being part of the crowd for a few hours. Both forms of fandom are valid. Fandom may vary from intense to casual, and an individual's level of fandom may vary over time.

Recognizing that the degree of fan passion may vary across a fan community is relevant in several ways.

A fan community may include a variety of fan types ranging from the hardcore fan who knows the detailed history of the team and never misses a game to the peripheral fan who likes to attend when the team is vying for a championship or when friends are attending a match. The intense fans may be the bedrock of the community, but fans with lesser interest may also make important contributions to the group. At the level of the individual, fandom may change over time. Individuals may begin as casual fans and evolve to become intense fans. Fandom involves a relationship between the team (or athlete) and the consumer. Based on the fan's evolving knowledge and interests, this relationship may change over time. An individual may evolve from a casual fan to an expert fan whose fandom is critical to their self-concept. The organization needs to consider segment differences when creating marketing plans and content.

From the team or cultural entity that is the object of fandom, the notion of a fandom continuum is also critical in terms of the possible degree of passion that can be created. A sports team in an established and popular league can generate intense fandom—face painting, shared songs, or collecting behaviors. In contrast, a new team in a less established or popular league may struggle with generating fandom and may need to pursue awareness or build interest. An NFL football team with 75 years of history has very different fandom possibilities compared to a new lacrosse team in a brand-new league.

1.2.2 Category Differences

As I have mentioned, our focus in this book is primarily on sports fandom. Sports fandom is, in many ways, the gold standard for fandom, but fandom exists across a range of categories. Figure 1.1 highlights several categories that play important roles in culture and inspire fandom: sports, entertainment, arts, games, cultural institutions, products, and politics. Thinking about fandom in different categories may provide value as it highlights different forms of fandom and reveals what is possible. A movie franchise or automaker may gain insights by comparing their fandoms to what exists in sports. Fandom has universal aspects that are shared across categories but also idiosyncratic elements that vary across categories. The idiosyncratic differences may be due to the nature of given products and each category's role in society. Fandom is about passion for the things that make up a culture, so a category's history and traditions matter. A category like sports might have a tradition of public spectacle like wearing

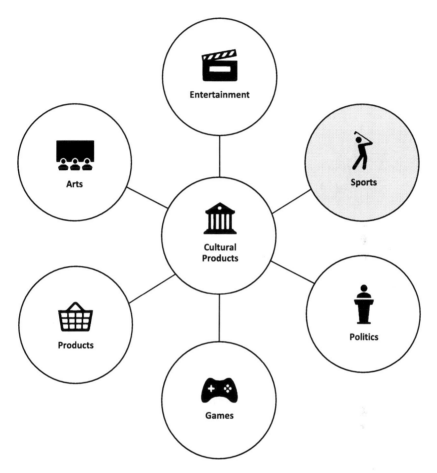

Fig. 1.1 Fandom categories

team jerseys and verbal chants, while the norms of classical music performances would lead its fans to dress in formal attire and restrained applause.

One fandom dimension that often varies across categories is the length of the fandom life-cycle. For example, sports fandom has traditionally been an almost lifelong trait. Being a lifelong sports fan is more than just supporting a team or athlete. It is a way of life that brings people together, creates memories, and provides a sense of belonging. For many, it is a family tradition passed down from generation to generation. In contrast, entertainment fandom is often fleeting. For example, the music industry has a long history of One-Hit Wonders or artists who have a single mass-market hit, such as "Mickey" by Toni Basil and "Come on Eileen" by Dexys Midnight Runners. Fandom for these artists tends to be brief rather than enduring. There are counterexamples of musical artists with multi-decade careers, like Elton John and Cher, who have maintained fan bases for 50-plus years. Nevertheless, even this type of enduring fandom is different in character from what occurs in sports. Fandom for a musical artist is centered on a person who ages, and because musical tastes constantly change, the artist's fanbase often ages with the artist. In contrast, sports teams and leagues are constantly renewing fanbases and may be viewed as institutions.

Fandom also varies across categories in terms of fans' willingness to publicly express or demonstrate fandom. The "clothing test" is a quick way to categorize fandom. The idea of the clothing test is to consider how willing and eager people are to wear a brand's logo. Sports fandom may be the ultimate example of success on the clothing test. At almost any arena across the globe, you can find fans wearing team colors and often team-branded clothing. The clothing test illuminates category fandom differences. Musicians frequently sell concert t-shirts, while probably only the most rabid political supporters are willing to wear a shirt that features a political candidate. The critical insight is that the level and character of fandom that can be built differs across categories, so the strategies and metrics used should also be adapted.

1.3 Examples

The book will use numerous examples of fandom and fan behaviors to illuminate concepts. However, a challenge in discussing fandom is that full appreciation of any instance of fandom requires a shared cultural background. We began the chapter with quick examples from American collegiate football, Argentinian soccer, and Taylor Swift. These are all powerful and popular fandoms, but they are not universal. College football is enormously popular but is strictly a US sport. The Argentinian

World Cup championship team and Lionel Messi are a global phenomenon, but soccer lags other sports in the United States. Taylor Swift is a global force in music, but her popularity varies across generations. It is hard for SEC football fans to appreciate Argentinian's love for their national soccer team and hard for Argentinians to grasp the importance of the annual Iron Bowl game featuring Alabama and Auburn.

A book about fandom needs examples. Fan behavior and emotions are fascinating and relatable, but examples do not mean much unless the reader has enough familiarity to appreciate the intensity and details of a fandom. Our examples in the book will try to focus on exceptionally well-known instances of fandom. Two of our recurring examples will be Michael Jordan and Formula 1. These are both global fandoms and the subjects of recent documentary programming: *The Last Dance* on ESPN (Hehir, 2020) and *Drive to Survive* on Netflix (Gay-Rees & Martin, 2019-present).

1.3.1 Michael Jordan

Michael Jordan is a global superstar with numerous basketball accolades. Jordan's basketball exploits, such as multiple NBA championships and the Olympic Dream Team, have created an almost legendary aura around him. Michael Jordan is a great source material for a book on fandom because his exploits are familiar, and his career has created many illustrative examples of the power and intricacies of fandom. Jordan's career has included being the primary ingredient in building basketball fandoms in Chicago and North Carolina through on-court excellence, being associated with an Olympic team that redefined international sports, transcending sports to become a movie star, and even in retirement being such an iconic figure that a show about his final NBA championship became ESPN's most viewed documentary (Thorne, 2020). Jordan's athletic accomplishments and resulting fandom show the powerful link between excellence and sports fandom.

In addition, Jordan's popularity is so extensive that he has also become one of the most important figures in sports marketing. Foremost among Jordan's marketing successes is the Air Jordan brand. The Air Jordan brand has become a household name in the world of sneakers. In 1984, Michael Jordan signed a deal with Nike to create his own line of shoes. The first Air Jordan shoe, the Air Jordan 1, was released in 1985, and it had an immediate impact. The shoe included a bold design and use of the now-iconic "Jumpman" logo. The shoe was also banned by the NBA because it did not meet the league's strict uniform regulations, which only added to its mystique and appeal. Despite the ban, the Air Jordan 1 quickly became a hit among basketball players and sneakerheads alike. The Air Jordan line has exhibited staying power as the brand continues to release new models and special editions into the 2020s. Air Jordan's cultural impact is so significant that the story of the Air Jordan became the source material for a Hollywood movie *Air*, (Affleck, 2023).

The Air Jordan story is significant as it illustrates the power of marketing within fandom. The success of the Air Jordan is driven by its association with Michael Jordan. Jordan's spectacular skills are associated with the shoe, making the shoe more desirable. However, the associations and marketing benefits go both ways. As the Air Jordan line became a favorite of collectors and sneaker aficionados, the brand acquired its own unique following. To younger audiences, their introduction to Michael Jordan may be through exposure to the Air Jordan line. The success of the shoe and the resulting Air Jordan fandom has added additional layers to the story of Michael Jordan.

1.3.2 Formula 1

Formula 1 is a global "open wheel" racing organization with a rich history and a modern approach to creating fan loyalty. The foundation of Formula 1 popularity is the combination of cutting-edge technology, iconic circuits, and superstar drivers. Formula 1 is known for gripping racing powered by advanced technologies that result in racing involving extreme G-forces and top speeds exceeding 200 mph. Formula 1 also features iconic circuits across the globe. Monaco is known for its tight corners, narrow streets, and glamorous setting. The Circuit de Spa-Francorchamps in Belgium is a classic track, with its fast corners and unpredictable weather making it a challenge for drivers. Silverstone in the

United Kingdom is also highly regarded, with its high-speed corners and history dating back to the first-ever F1 race in 1950. The uniqueness and challenges of each track inspire fandom for individual races.

Formula 1 also has fascinating human faces that inspire and attract fans. From the past, drivers like Ayrton Senna and Michael Schumacher remain etched in the minds of fans as legends of the sport. Senna won three world championships before his tragic death in 1994, while Schumacher held the record for the most world championships with seven titles until Lewis Hamilton tied the mark in 2020. Since 2010, Hamilton and Max Verstappen have dominated the sport and become international celebrities. The combination of amazing technology, iconic locations, and global stars is a potent mix for building fandom.

Another driving force behind Formula 1's popularity is the level of sponsorship that the sport receives. Major corporations worldwide invest heavily in the sport, providing the necessary funding to keep the races and teams running. This has enabled Formula 1 to attract some of the best drivers and teams in the world, making it one of the most competitive and exciting racing sports on the planet. Perhaps, Formula 1's most important marketing partnership is with the streaming platform, Netflix. The Netflix series *Drive to Survive* (Gay-Rees & Martin, 2019-present) offers an inside look at the sport, showcasing the drama, rivalries, and behind-the-scenes action that takes place both on and off the track. The show has helped to bring new fans into the sport, providing a glimpse into the world of Formula 1 that was previously inaccessible to many. *Drive to Survive* has also profiled disputes between drivers, team principles, and the legal troubles of a team owner (Trivedi, 2022). These conflicts add drama to the racing action.

Formula 1 fandom is a unique and exciting community that offers a sense of camaraderie, expertise, and thrilling experiences. Formula 1 also highlights the roles of marketing and the power of sports stories. Formula 1 teams have a symbiotic relationship with sponsors by providing platforms for non-sports brands in exchange for investments that fund technological innovations and racing success. Formula 1 and *Drive to Survive* also showcase the power of sports stories in building fandom.

1.4 Monetizing Fandom

The preceding definitions and examples reveal the importance of fandom in modern culture. Fandom can provide structures and communities that allow people to interact and connect. Sports fandoms have a natural structure, with fans building networks or subcultures around teams, players, and leagues. Historically, sports fandoms arose around the local club. However, in the modern era, fandom does not just happen. Even if fandom comes from the grassroots and develops organically, the value of fandom is quickly recognized and monetized. Fandom is big business.

The examples of fandom reveal something important about modern fandom. The teams or cultural entities that attract fan communities are often actively managed and marketed as brands. The fans that comprise these fandom communities are often high-value customers. Nike's Air Jordan and Red Bull are consumer brands that are promoted and positioned to appeal to consumers using sports. The fandom that is created around these brands is a valuable economic asset.

The genesis of the success of Air Jordan shoes was largely driven by fans' passion for and associations with Michael Jordan. Jordan himself can also be considered a brand cultivated over decades. The foundation for the Jordan brand is Jordan's exceptional talent, but the Jordan brand has also been built through his history of winning, partnerships with brands, crossovers into film, and compelling personality. Even two decades after retiring, the Jordan brand drives sneaker sales and is the fodder for popular content like *The Last Dance* docuseries and the feature film *Air*.

The ability of Nike and Hollywood to monetize the Jordan brand highlights the role of fandom in modern marketing. Fan passion is something that firms and individuals can leverage to create profitable opportunities. Modern fandom is not the organic or naturally occurring passion that builds around shared cultural entities. In past eras, passion for a national, collegiate, or hometown club likely evolved almost organically, with the local or national community coming together to support their team. The key point is that in the past, community belonging often preceded or was the basis for a team's following. Games were covered in the local media, but brand marketing was an afterthought. Sports and entertainment brands are now recognized as economically valuable brands that merit active management.

The customers or fans of sports brands like Air Jordan and Formula 1 are also increasingly viewed as economically valuable assets that merit active management. Air Jordan shoes are often priced at about $100 per pair. Neglecting inflation, an average Air Jordan loyalist purchasing a new pair every 2 years has provided Nike with about $2000 in revenue since the launch of the brand. However, a superfan who avidly collects Jordans may have spent considerably more in retail channels and sneaker exchanges like StockX. As a point of reference, in 2023, a signed, game-worn pair of Air Jordans sold for more than $2.2 million (Tarmy, 2023).

Formula 1 also highlights the value of brands and fans. The teams are often automobile manufacturers (Mercedes, Ferrari) or consumer product brands (Red Bull). An exciting, high-performing car provides valuable associations to a car maker like Mercedes or an energy drink like Red Bull. Formula 1 markets itself aggressively through its races and programming partnership with Netflix. Formula 1 has become a marketing platform allowing non-sports brands to reach consumers. The more successful Formula 1 is in building its brand (fandom), the more lucrative it is as a marketing platform.

1.5 Plan and Purpose

My goal for this book is ambitious, especially given that it is a short book. The intention is to tell a story about the importance of fandom and how fandom can be understood in the current culture. The intent is also to provide a reference: a book that can sit on the shelf of professionals in sports, entertainment, and other cultural categories where fandom is the key to success. I would also like it to sit on the shelf of brand marketers who recognize that inspiring consumer passion to the level of fandom is the ultimate in customer loyalty.

The goal of the introductory chapter has been to make a case for the importance of fandom and to provide a working definition of the fandom construct. Fandom is vitally important to society because fandom defines cultures. The American culture of the 1960s was largely defined by baseball, muscle cars, rock and roll, and television. The America of the 2020s is fixated on the NFL, Hip-Hop, social media, and streaming. These are very different societies. Patterns of fandom largely define our day-to-day environment. Where fandom exists determines the sports on television, the shows on streaming services, the content suggested by social media algorithms, and the music on the radio. Fandom also defines generations. Baby Boomers still listen to classic rock, and Millennials will be listening to grunge into their 70 s. Looking across generations, baseball remains one of the favorite sports of Baby Boomers while the game struggles to attract Generation Z. Cultural preferences and fandoms seem to be largely defined during youth and can persist for decades.

The importance of fandom today and into the future means that fandom is also a big business. Fandom is not unique to sports. Actors, musicians, fashion designers, politicians, social media personalities, and even cultural institutions like museums and universities frequently inspire the intense passion and enthusiasm that we associate with fandom. The size of the global entertainment industry estimated to be about $2.3 trillion in 2022 (PWC, 2023) reveals the economic importance of fandom.

The cultural and economic importance of fandom-based industries means that there is significant interest in actively growing and managing fandom. This book is designed to satisfy this interest. My premise is that the key to successfully managing fandom is an interdisciplinary approach to fandom analytics. The book begins with a Fandom Analytics Framework that considers (1) where fandom comes from, (2) how fandom provides value to fans, (3) how fandom fits into modern marketing concepts, (4) the possibilities of transferring fandom across categories, and (5) the role of sports analytics in fandom. This framework provides a structured approach to fandom management and a road map for the book.

Subsequent chapters delve deeply into each element of the framework. Chapter 3 considers the role of storytelling in fandom. Chapter 4 considers the psychological foundations of fandom. This is an investigation into how and why being a fan provides value to people. Chapters 5, 6 and 7 focus on the application of marketing analytics to fandom. Chapter 5 discusses traditional marketing research surveys. Chapter 6 discusses brand equity analytics. Chapter 7 discusses the economics of individual fan relationships. Chapter 8 highlights one of the distinctive aspects of sports fandom, the ability of sports brands to attract sponsors from brands in other industries.

Following the material focused on consumers and marketing, we review key principles of sports analytics. Sports analytics are a foundational part of fandom because fandom for a team or player is usually directly tied to athletic success. Chapter 9 focuses on concepts related to player evaluation and game strategy. Chapter 10 examines the consequences of league design and structure on fandom.

The book concludes with material that generalizes the concepts beyond sports and looks into the future of fandom. Chapter 11 generalizes the discussion of fandom beyond sports with a typology that compares different categories on several fandom dimensions. Chapter 12 examines current demographic, technology, and marketing trends to predict how fandom-focused categories will evolve over the next several years. Chapter 12 also considers the challenges of creating a fandom-focused organization.

1.6 Insights and Connections

Each chapter will conclude with a section titled Insights and Connections. The goal of this section will be to summarize each chapter's key concepts and to highlight the most salient connections to previous and following material. The theme of Chap. 1 is that fandom is a critical element of modern society. Fandom is about cultural passion, which means fandom dictates what we watch, talk about, and spend money on. The market also responds to consumer passion, so fandom dictates what sports are shown on television, what movies are made, what fashion looks like, and more. Fandom is the engine that makes a society interesting and moves culture forward.

As we begin the discussion of fandom analytics, this chapter was primarily about motivating the topic's importance and describing the book's approach. The starting point for fandom analytics is a definition of fandom.

- Fandom is the expression of individual and shared passion, engagement with, and interest in some cultural entity.

This definition is intentionally broad because fandom and passion are relevant across a wide range of categories. The flexibility of the definition also allows fandom to be something that varies across categories and that can exist on a continuum. The face-painted season ticket buyer for the local football team and the person who watches every episode of a Netflix series are both fans but with different behaviors and intensity levels.

The goal of Chap. 1 has been to highlight fandom's relevance and cultural importance. The discussion and examples also reveal that fandom is a valuable asset that is increasingly actively managed. Fans are hyper-loyal and economically valuable consumers who present challenges and opportunities to organizations. The next chapter lays out a framework for systematically analyzing and managing fandom. This framework then serves as the roadmap for a comprehensive discussion about analyzing fandom.

The book is mostly about sports but with occasional detours into other entertainment categories. The detours are included because sometimes lessons about sports fandom are best illuminated by using a wider scope of examples. Other times, non-sports examples are included to illustrate how lessons from sports fandom can inform thinking about other categories. Sports is the foundation and the focus but not a limiting rule.

References

Affleck, B. (2023). Air [Film]. *Amazon Studios, Skydance Sports, Mandalay Pictures.*
Bennett, A. (2001). *Cultures of popular music.* McGraw-Hill Education.
Boylan, J. (2012). Penn State football scandal: Now we know Joe Paterno knew. *Bleacher Report.* Accessed December 2, 2023, from https://bleacherreport.com/articles/1256931-penn-state-football-scandal-now-we-know-what-joe-paterno-knew
Buckingham, P. (2023). Premier league generated £5.5 Billion in 2021–22, more than La Liga and Bundesliga combined. *The Athletic.* Accessed November 13, 2023 from https://theathletic.com/4610513/2023/06/14/premier-league-revenue-football-finance/

Gay-Rees, J. & P. Martin (Producers). (2019-present). Formula 1: Drive to survive [TV Series]. *Netflix*. https://www.netflix.com/

Hehir, J.. (2020). The last dance [Documentary series]. *ESPN Films*.

Hills, M. (2003). *Fan cultures*. Routledge.

Kopstein, J. & M. Espada (2023). The staggering economic impact of Taylor Swift's eras tour. Time Magazine. Accessed December 2, 2023, from https://time.com/6307420/taylor-swift-eras-tour-money-economy/

Ozanian, M. (2023). NFL National Revenue was Almost $12 billion in 2022. *Forbes*. Accessed November 11, 2023, from https://www.forbes.com/sites/mikeozanian/2023/07/11/nfl-national-revenue-was-almost-12-billion-in-2022/

PWC. (2023). Perspectives from the global entertainment & media outlook. *PWC*. Accessed January 16, 2024, from https://www.pwc.com/gx/en/industries/tmt/media/outlook/insights-and-perspectives.html

Reyass, C. (2017). 10 Most Feared Soccer Hooligan Gangs. Cleats.com. Accessed December 2, 2023, from https://vocal.media/cleats/10-most-feared-soccer-hooligan-gangs

Sandvoss, C. (2005). *Fans: The mirror of consumption*. Polity.

Tarmy, J. (2023). Michael Jordan sneakers sell for a record $2.2 million. Los Angeles Times. Accessed January 8, 2024, from https://www.latimes.com/business/story/2023-04-11/michael-jordan-sneakers-sell-for-a-record-setting-2-2-million

Thorne, W. (2020), "Last Dance": Michael Jordan series finishes as most-viewed ESPN documentary ever. *Variety*. Accessed December 2, 2023, from https://variety.com/2020/tv/news/last-dance-michael-jordan-docuseries-espn-tv-ratings-1234610101/

Trivedi, U. (2022). Ex-billionaire Vijay Mallya gets four month jail term in India. *Bloomberg*. Accessed December 6, 2023, from https://www.bloomberg.com/news/articles/2022-07-11/ex-billionaire-mallya-gets-four-month-jail-term-in-india

Young, R. (2022). Millions of Fans Pack Buenos Aires to Celebrate Argentina's World Cup Win. *Yahoo.com*. Accessed November 1, 2023 https://sports.yahoo.com/millions-of-fans-pack-buenos-aires-to-celebrate-argentinas-world-cup-win-210136865.html

2

Fandom Analytics Framework

2.1 Marketing Analytics to Fandom Analytics

Sports fandom is one of those things that is easy to identify but can be challenging to describe or analyze. A Green Bay Packers fan wearing green face paint and a cheese head hat while standing in his basement full of memorabilia is obviously enthusiastic about the team, but there is a lot that we do not know. Why does the fan love the Packers? What behaviors does the fan engage in? What is the fan worth to the team?

These types of questions may be asked about any consumer product, but in categories like sports, the analysis challenges are deeper, and the opportunities that come from understanding are more lucrative. Fan analysis is more complex than standard customer analysis because the factors and influences that lead to passion and fandom are usually embedded in community belonging, family traditions, and individual identity rather than just preferences for particular product attributes. The value in understanding fandom is also often greater than in most consumer categories because fandom results in extraordinary loyalty and behaviors.

Fandom for the local football (American or International) team may have been passed down through multiple generations and possess its own lore and legends, and in each new generation, we find fans who identify as (almost) members of the team who are willing to face paint, wear the team's jersey, and spend substantial money on the team. The connections between the fans and teams are deep and complex, resulting in extreme devotion and significant spending. We seldom see similar influences and behaviors for a person's favorite grocery store, soft drink, or cellular provider.

While fandom may be a next level form of customer loyalty, the analysis of consumer behavior is something that marketers have done for decades. So, the question is, how do we need to adapt and extend standard approaches to marketing analytics when we consider fandom-oriented categories like sports?

2.1.1 Marketing Analytics

The first matter to consider is that while marketing analytics has a long tradition, it is also an ever-evolving field. The most significant factors driving this evolution are data availability and communications technologies. Analytics have revolutionized much of the marketing world from the local grocery store to online and mobile retailers. Ever-increasing data allows marketing analytics professionals to continually refine firms' understanding of customers and to implement improved marketing tactics.

The data available to support and improve marketing decisions has steadily increased over the past several decades. Scanner data allowed grocery stores to analyze sales promotions and develop brand choice models (Blattberg et al., 1995). Travel reservation systems provided airlines and travel companies with opportunities to create yield management systems for optimizing the value of inventory. Travel industries also led the development of loyalty programs that created longitudinal data that would become the basis for customer relationship management systems.

The e-commerce revolution created further opportunities to track and analyze customer behavior. The Internet environment allowed analysis of browsing and search behaviors through click stream data (Bucklin et al., 2002). The combination of search with purchasing behavior enabled recommendation systems that leveraged customer data to customize product offerings. The ability of e-commerce sites to be customized to individual customers (Khan et al., 2009) has also allowed firms to engage in simple to advanced experimentation. Social media data provides a revolutionary ability to monitor and engage with consumers. Firms can "listen" to consumers on social to understand the real-time impact of marketing and other firm activities. Social also provides new avenues for understanding promotion, as engagement with influencers can be tracked and analyzed at a granular level.

Machine learning and artificial intelligence systems appear to be the next stage in the marketing analytics story (Huang & Rust, 2021). These techniques leverage massive amounts of data to garner new insights. For example, generative AI may have the potential to improve customer experience and automate many sales functions. The ultimate impact of AI and other marketing analytics tools is yet to be determined, but the trends seem clear. The amount and types of data are growing, and analytics tools will continue to improve in terms of capabilities and speed. Future marketers will inevitably have greater access to data and more advanced analytics tools.

2.1.2 Sports Marketing Analytics

The sports industry has adopted many of the analytics techniques developed in other industries. Like other industries, sports organizations have invested in analytics based on specific category factors and data availability. Sports organizations often can track purchase and usage data for years, but they also often lack visibility of fan behaviors outside the arena.

For example, sports organizations share similarities with travel organizations in terms of inventory. In the airline industry, a unit of inventory is a seat on a flight between two destinations, while a unit of inventory for a sports franchise is a seat. A critical similarity is that inventory is perishable since an empty seat on a flight or during a game becomes worthless. Another critical similarity is that seats have different values depending on factors like the day of the week or time of day. The primary goal of travel industry revenue management systems is to optimize inventory value, such as a flight's seats or rooms on a cruise ship, rather than to sell out the inventory.

Revenue management and dynamic pricing are increasingly common in sports. Lionel Messi's signing with Inter Miami was one of the major sports stories of 2023. Messi brought massive publicity and his own fandom to the team, and these factors created opportunities for applying revenue management techniques. Prior to Messi joining, the lowest Inter Miami ticket price was $29, and average attendance in the team's 21,000-seat arena was about 12,000 (Baldi, 2023). By acquiring Messi and his massive fan base, Inter Miami found itself with a larger potential audience that was far less price-sensitive. Using dynamic pricing techniques, Inter Miami was able to set prices from $220 to $280 for a mid-week Leagues Cup game against the Atlanta United (Cardenas, 2023). Interestingly, this pricing did not yield a sellout. The insight is that the addition of Messi and his fans enabled the club to use analytics to set prices and manage inventory to maximize game revenues. A complexity in fandom management is that there may be significant value in emphasizing both attendance and revenue since having a fan in the arena creates an opportunity for the fan to have a memorable loyalty-building experience, and bigger crowds may create energy and excitement.

The marketing analytics revolution is global, and European soccer clubs have also used analytics to understand their fans better and tailor their marketing strategies to better engage with them. For example, FC Barcelona has leveraged social media analytics to connect with fans and grow its global fandom. The team has emphasized storytelling and authenticity supported by analytics to identify the most effective content (Spotify, 2023).

The richness and extensiveness of sports fan data, such as decades of information on ticket buying and other behaviors, lead to new opportunities for customer relationship management. Teams may track customer relationship warning signals, such as not using or selling tickets, and may intervene with retention efforts. Customer-level data may also be used to customize marketing offers related to add-on sales or upselling. As data becomes more available and technology creates more opportunities, analytics will increasingly drive market decisions in sports.

The examples of dynamic pricing, social media analytics, and CRM marketing represent the application of marketing analytics practices developed in other industries to the sports category. However, while sports organizations share similarities with standard marketing organizations that build brands and manage customers, in sports, the level of consumer loyalty, engagement, and passion often far exceeds loyalty in most categories. This difference creates opportunities for sports organizations. For example, sports organizations are often able to attract lucrative sponsorships and partnerships with non-sports businesses.

However, data and analytics are not a panacea in sports and other cultural categories. These "fandom" categories are special in two key respects. One key differentiator is that fandom involves intense emotional connections between brands and consumers. The relationships between cultural brands are further bolstered by extensive histories, community factors, and psychological needs. Standard insights and approaches to customer retention may be irrelevant to fan-team relationships. Fans have such deep connections to teams that they are willing to overlook almost any slight or failure if the team wins. Furthermore, while sports can benefit from marketing analytics tools and marketing concepts, the role of marketing is often drastically different in sports than in most consumer categories. Marketing often has the primary responsibility of building brands and managing customer relationships. In sports, the marketing department is clearly not the primary creator of fandom. The great players and championship teams are what create fans. Marketing and marketing analytics play more of an enhancing than a leading role in building fandom.

These distinctive elements make it useful for rethinking marketing analytics and developing a new approach to fandom analytics. Fans' relationships with sports organizations are deeper and are based on a complex mix of personal experiences, community influences, and media narratives combined with individual-level psychological traits. The complex drivers of and psychological importance of fandom make it necessary to go beyond data and models to understand and manage fandom.

2.2 Fandom Analytics Framework

Fandom is a complex topic that has its foundations in fundamental human needs and leads to extraordinary levels of loyalty to the object of the fandom. Fandom is also distinctive as it often has value beyond the specific category of sport or entertainment through sponsorships. When put in these terms, fandom sounds like the marketing department's responsibility. In marketing parlance, fandom is about creating consumer loyalty of such intensity that customers act like fanatics and brand equity that is so aspirational that it is transferable to something else.

Yet, fandom management is something beyond standard marketing practice. Creating fandom often seems to require something mysterious or magical. There needs to be a special or aspirational something at the core of the fandom. Fandom occurs when teams win championships or communities form around a musician or movie franchise. The primary role of marketing is to excel in the activities surrounding the special team, performer, or brand that is the core of the fan community, not to create the specialness. However, while marketing is less relative to building fan passion, analytics is playing an increasingly critical role. In sports, analytics are increasingly used to select the players and tactics that win games and create the magic at the heart of fandom.

Figure 2.1 displays the Fandom Analytics Framework that maps out the factors that create fandom and the outcomes that result from fandom. The framework is displayed as a circle with a core to highlight that fandom creation and monetization is a continuing process supported by rigorous analytics. We briefly describe each element of the framework before covering each in detail.

The top of the figure is labeled "Foundations: Stories and Narratives." The foundations of fandom are fans' memories of their favorite teams. Fans remember and often mythologize the championships, last-second wins, and heroic performances of teams and athletes. These stories are the basis for enduring loyalty and interest in a team or player. The action fades, but the memories last.

The second element is labeled "Benefits: Community and Identity." Fandom is different than most consumer loyalty in the degree of commitment. For consumers to commit to this degree, their commitment must

2 Fandom Analytics Framework

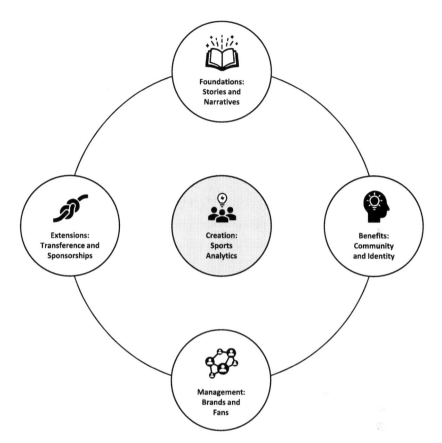

Fig. 2.1 Fandom analytics framework

provide some value or benefits. The crucial point of differentiation is that fans use affiliation with teams as a building block for their self-concepts and communities. Fandom is about belonging to something. The importance of fandom for identity construction and community membership implies that fandom satisfies vital psychological and social needs. Managing fandom requires understanding these psychological drivers.

The bottom of the figure is labeled "Management: Brands and Fans." Fandom involves a powerful relationship between the fan and some entity like a team or athlete. The fan relationship can be conceptualized as a brand-consumer relationship. The value of the fan relationship can be considered in terms of teams' or celebrities' brands or the value of customers' future contributions. When the brand is the unit of analysis, we can use concepts and tools for brand equity measurement. When the fan is the unit of analysis, concepts like customer equity and lifetime value may be relevant.

The bubble on the left is labeled "Extensions: Transference and Sponsorships." A notable aspect of fandom is that its power extends beyond the direct object of the fan's love. When fans love a team or a player, they have positive feelings and associations with the club or athlete. These feelings and associations are often so strong that transferring some of the positive associations to a product in another category is possible. The growth of social media and influencer marketing magnifies the importance of fandom in marketing.

At the center of the figure, the core process is labeled "Creation: Sports Analytics." Creating content that inspires fandom requires building something special and aspirational as fandom usually comes from excellent and memorable performances. One reason to focus on sports for a general study of fandom is that the quality of performance in sports is more objectively measured than in other performing arts and consumer markets. It is also abundantly clear that the key to creating sports fandom is to build a winning team, and in the modern world of sports, balancing analytics and intuition is the key to achieving excellence. Perhaps no industry has as direct a link between using analytics to construct a high-quality product and creating communities of fans.

2.3 Interdisciplinary Perspectives

The Fandom Analytics Framework provides a structure for evaluating and managing fandom businesses and assets. The framework is designed to be systematic as it considers fandom in terms of multiple stages. The framework begins with fandom's foundational elements and proceeds through fandom's economic outcomes. This consideration of multiple stages requires the application of multiple disciplines and multiple forms of analytics.

The term analytics is usually associated with fields like data science, statistics, machine learning, and artificial intelligence. Analytics driven by data and computational techniques has become the norm in numerous business sectors and functions. Regardless of the underlying technique, the trend is unambiguous. As computer systems advance and can process increasing amounts of information, data and analytics will increasingly influence decision-making in myriad contexts.

Sports analytics is a high-profile example of analytics practice (Lewis, 2004). Sports analytics is the practice of using data to gain insights into decisions about training, team composition, and game strategy. The increasing emphasis on data and statistical analysis in the on-field side of sports should motivate questions about the application of analytics to the fan or consumer side of sports. Suppose the ultimate goal of sports business is to create a robust and valuable fandom through winning. If this is the case, sports analytics is connected to fandom through its impact on team performance.

Considering analytics in the context of sports highlights a vital issue in the use of analytics in decision-making. Analytics and data rarely tell the whole story in sports analytics. Data limitations always cause analytics to tell an incomplete story about the right player to select or game strategy to employ. Analytics is best viewed as a compliment to human experts with deep, holistic understandings of their particular sports. Analytics are helpful for identifying gaps or biases in experts' judgments.

The limitations of data and analytics are especially pronounced when studying fans and fandom. Fandom involves multifaceted but partially observable activities that are driven by psychological needs and community factors. The complex factors that drive fandom mean that existing data sets are insufficient to understand fan behavior completely. The limitations of data and statistics necessitate two important adjustments to how fandom-oriented organizations utilize analytics.

1. Analytics are best viewed as decision-support tools rather than decision-automating tools.
2. The definition of analytics should be broadened to involve a multidisciplinary perspective.

Fandom analytics is best accomplished through an interdisciplinary approach that includes the skills of the anthropologist, the psychologist, the marketing scientist, the economist, and the statistician.

2.3.1 Anthropology

A foundational tenet of fandom analytics is that fandoms are groups or subcultures that are centered around sports organizations, teams, or players. These fandom subcultures possess shared interests, rituals, and hierarchies. As anthropology is the study of human societies and cultures, the tools and perspectives of the anthropologist should be part of the fandom analytics tool kit. Anthropologists use a variety of research methods, including participant observation, interviews, and archival research, to gather information about the customs, beliefs, and practices of the people they study.

Ethnographic research is especially relevant to the study of fandom. Ethnographic research is a qualitative research approach that aims to understand people's behaviors and culture within a specific context. It involves observing and interacting with participants in their natural setting to gain insights into their beliefs, values, and practices. The research often involves extended periods of fieldwork and data collection through interviews and participant observation. Holt (1995) provides an example of an ethnographic study of fandom through a 2-year study of Chicago Cubs fans in their "habitat" of the Wrigley Field's bleachers.

One particularly relevant aspect of culture or community is the importance of shared stories. Anthropologists believe that stories are a fundamental part of human communication and serve various purposes. Some stories are meant to entertain, while others are meant to educate or transmit cultural values. Anthropologists have sought to understand the role of storytelling in different cultures and how it has evolved over time. Sports fandoms are subcultures with their own sets of stories, rituals, and hierarchies. To understand the fandom, the approach and insights of the anthropologist are the right starting point.

2.3.2 Psychology

While fandom communities are best understood using methods to understand a community or subculture, psychology is the applicable discipline at the level of the individual fan. An individual's fandom cannot be fully understood through observing a fan's behavior or recording a fan's transaction history. Fandom is often an essential aspect of a person's personality or identity. The skills of the psychologist or consumer behavior specialist are vital for understanding fandom's emotional and attitudinal components.

Fandom's role in social identity is an essential aspect of fandom analytics. Social identity is a crucial component of our sense of self, and psychologists are interested in understanding how it develops and influences our behavior. Social identity refers to the groups we belong to and the ways in which we define ourselves in relation to those groups. This can include factors such as our race, ethnicity, gender, religion, and social class. It can also include being a Chelsea F.C., Dallas Cowboys, or Michael Jordan fan.

A critical implication of fandom being used to construct social identity is that being a fan must provide some psychological benefits or social utility. Understanding these noneconomic benefits is also in the skill set of the psychologist. For example, Cialdini et al. (1976) investigated the benefit of "Basking in Reflected Glory" by examining the increased propensity of college students to affiliate with winning teams publicly.

2.3.3 Marketing Science

The analytical foundation for the "management" portion of the framework is found in the marketing discipline. Marketing is itself an interdisciplinary discipline. Marketing leans heavily on fields like economics and psychology to conceptualize problems while statistics and operations research techniques are used to solve empirical challenges. The tools of marketing analytics are increasingly relevant to fandom because team brands and fans are now recognized as valuable marketing assets. While fandom has traditionally been something that organically developed, fandom is now something that is aggressively managed using the tools of marketing.

Relevant tools for studying fan-team relationships include Customer Surveys, brand equity measurement (Ailawadi et al., 2003), and Customer Lifetime Value Analysis (Lewis, 2010). Customer Surveys are useful for quantifying fans' emotional and attitudinal connections to teams. Brand equity is a vital concept because teams can be thought of as brands. Brand equity is the notion that brands have economic value. Customer Lifetime Value Analysis recognizes that customers are the ultimate source of a firm's revenues. In the case of sports, fans are the source of direct revenues and indirect revenues. Fans provide direct revenues through tickets, and indirect revenues are the reason that teams can sell media rights and attract sponsors.

Sponsorship analytics is another aspect of the framework that is driven by marketing perspectives. Teams can attract sponsorships because they offer a platform that drives awareness and because sponsors want to associate their brands with teams and athletes that fans love. Sponsorship decisions involve marketing principles related to the fit between sponsoring brands and endorsing sports organizations. Sponsorship valuation also presents significant analytics challenges.

2.3.4 Statistics and Analytics

At the core of the Fandom Analytics Framework is Sports Analytics. It is an uncontroversial notion that team performance in terms of winning games and acquiring star players significantly impacts fandom. Sports analytics is the application of analytic techniques to questions about roster composition and game strategies, but sports analytics can be more generally be thought of as a specialized version of performance analytics.

Winning games and selecting top players is fundamentally about improving quality and performance. Improving quality is fundamental to creating brand equity in almost all categories. While brand equity management may nominally be the responsibility of the marketing department, the reality is that having great products and quality is the key to creating customer loyalty and fandom. Apple's slick user interface,

Porsche's driving performance, and the Laker's 17 NBA championships have more to do with each organization's brand strength and customer fandom than anything done by their respective marketing departments. The relationship between analytics, performance, and fandom is more apparent in sports than in most categories. For example, if data and analytics can support better drafting and free-agent acquisitions that result in more wins, then player analytics directly impact fandom.

The analytics revolution in sports has been the subject of substantial media attention. Baseball enthusiasts often attribute the origin of sabermetrics to the work of Bill James, a baseball writer and statistician. His work popularized the use of advanced metrics in baseball analysis, and his contributions have revolutionized modern baseball thinking. The practice of sabermetrics, specifically, and sports analytics, generally, was introduced to the public through Michael Lewis' book *Moneyball* and its subsequent film adaptation (Lewis, 2004). Some of the most commonly used statistical techniques in sports analytics include regression analysis, data visualization, and machine learning. These techniques allow analysts to identify patterns and trends in large data sets, providing valuable insights that can be used to make informed decisions and gain a competitive edge.

2.3.5 Economics

The previous intellectual disciplines are useful for analyzing fandom at the organizational level. The focus is on how individual fans and fan communities relate to a sports organization. However, fandom analysis can occur at multiple levels. Fandom can also be considered at the league level. As the world becomes more interconnected via the Internet and smartphones, fandom is becoming less tied to geography, and the leagues are increasingly competing for fans. The decisions of leagues and governing associations are increasingly impacting sports fandom. In particular, league structures related to how teams compete in terms of talent acquisition and retention can influence teams' incentives and decisions and thereby impact fan preferences. Economics expertise may be useful for designing league structures that facilitate rather than reduce fandom.

One of the complexities of sports is that the economic incentives faced by individual teams may conflict with the goals of an overall league. Neale (1964) referred to these conflicting incentives as "the peculiar economics of sport." At the core of these peculiar economics is that sports teams and leagues operate with contradictory incentives. Teams optimize revenues as they win at a higher rate. However, the sports product requires cooperation as a game or match is co-produced by two competing teams. Specifically, teams cooperate to co-produce an exciting, competitive matchup. A league with persistent competitive imbalances is potentially a problem if some teams are chronically uncompetitive. The always victorious team may develop a robust fan base, but fandom may suffer in markets with teams that never win.

To alleviate competitive imbalances, leagues operate as collectives with guidelines defining off-field competition rules related to player acquisition, free agency, salary caps, etc. The concern is that a league's operating structure can influence a league's ability to attract and maintain fans. Economic frameworks and perspectives are useful for considering how a league's rules create incentives for teams that may either enhance or degrade overall fandom.

2.4 Fandom Management

Business frameworks can be valuable tools for an organization through a structured approach to problem-solving, decision-making, and goal setting, which can help businesses achieve their objectives more effectively. By following a framework, businesses can identify areas for improvement, set clear goals and objectives, and allocate resources more efficiently. Additionally, business frameworks can help organizations stay competitive in their industry by providing a standardized approach to problems and a structure for benchmarking competitors. The Fandom Analytics Framework provides a structure for evaluating fandom from its sources to its financial value.

The purpose of the Fandom Analytics Framework is to help structure how sports organizations conceptualize and approach fandom management. The framework is intentionally broad in terms of organizational functions and explicitly interdisciplinary. Fandom is a powerful human trait that can be of immense economic value, but fandom is difficult to create and manage. Fandom almost seems to require a bit of magic as we transition from standard marketing with the objective of convincing a consumer to buy a product to situations where the goal is to develop so much enthusiasm that people cover their bodies in team logos, decorate their homes in team colors and memorabilia, and are willing to endure decades on waiting lists. The goal is loyalty beyond reason that is driven by a complex mix of product quality, community influences, and psychological needs. However, trying to create and manage passion can feel like trying to harness magic as fandom may appear illogical or excessive. An intense fan may seem like a crazy person rather than a rational consumer. A detailed and comprehensive framework that structures the analysis to include where fandom comes from, the benefits fandom provides, and the economic value of fandom is what is needed to manage fandom-oriented businesses.

2.5 Non-sports Fandom Analytics

The Fandom Analytics Framework is generalizable to other fandom contexts but with the caveat that category differences may alter the importance of the various framework elements. Ultra-passionate and engaged fans exist in categories, such as movies, music, politics, and fashion. There is a natural question of whether the framework extends to other categories. The answer is yes, but there needs to be consideration of how category history and structure vary.

For example, the importance and structure of storytelling varies across cultural products. In sports, the stories are both the product and how consumers and media interpret the product. Sports has an ongoing record of its product as statistics from every season are archived. In entertainment, often the product is the primary story. Star Wars films or Taylor Swift's music are stories that new generations can share or discover. In sports, the stories result from competition, while in entertainment, stories are scripted products. As such, the sports organization needs more of a focus on how to archive and package their histories and current stories.

The entertainment organization needs to think through the fandom implications before constructing its stories. The importance of social identity might also vary. Sports fans are well-known for wearing the jerseys or colors of their favorite teams. Fans of classical music or a soft drink are less likely to wear clothing or logos from their favorite symphony or cola brand. A favorite composer or soft drink can still be a part of the individual's social identity, but the way the fan expresses fandom differs across categories.

Applying brand and customer management tactics also varies across categories because of institutional differences and data collection capabilities. Sports leagues are essentially permanent institutions, so sports teams are ongoing concerns that can invest in brand building and monitoring over multiple years. A movie not designed for multiple sequels may come and go in a month or two with no opportunity or purpose for brand building. Likewise, sports organizations can collect details data on customer transactions by ticket buyers while the movie company relies on distribution channels (theaters and streamers) that traditionally do not provide data to the film production company.

The role of analytics may be the most significant differentiator between sports and other fandom analytics. Sports produce detailed performance data and objective outcomes. Evaluating other cultural entities tends to be far more subjective. Analytics may still play a role in improving performance, but using data to select a point guard or striker is far more feasible than using models to select a lead actress or trombone player.

The Fandom Analytics Framework also has value as it provides insight into how brands can aspire to create fans even in categories where fandom is not common. The concept of building a subculture based on consumers' experiences or shared stories with a brand may be prohibitively challenging in many categories, but it is the path to creating fans. The framework provides a comprehensive structure that can be adapted based on industry realities.

2.6 Insights and Connections

Fandom is an extraordinary type of customer loyalty. Fandom is about extreme passion for sports or other types of brands, and fans are valuable economic assets. Yet, fandom is more than just customer loyalty. Fandom is driven by emotional connections and community dynamics. Fandom is also exceedingly valuable because it can be used to market products in unrelated categories. Furthermore, at the core, fandom is overwhelmingly created by a non-marketing set of analytics related to creating winning teams and selecting talented players.

Sports and other types of fandoms are fascinating and financially important topics that can be best understood through interdisciplinary analytical approaches. Psychological and ethnographic analysis can highlight the foundational elements of fandom. Marketing analytics can value sports brands and fan relationships. Statistics and economics can be used to analyze players and predict the impact of league design decisions. Fandom may feel like a fuzzy topic, but it is something that merits rigorous, interdisciplinary analytical approaches.

Beyond sports, fandom is a critical concept in many categories and for society itself. This chapter presents a framework that helps structure the analysis of sports and other types of fandoms. The emphasis is on understanding where fandom comes from, how it can be measured, and how it can be monetized.

* The Fandom Analytics Framework provides a structure for evaluating and managing sports fandom.
* The Framework highlights the importance of an interdisciplinary perspective for fandom management.
* The Framework is flexible and applicable to non-sports categories. However, category differences in fandom need to be considered.

The framework also provides a visual roadmap to the remainder of the book. The book proceeds along the figure's outer loop and then comes to the topic of sports analytics. The later chapters provide context related to organizational design, a generalized view of fandom across categories, and future trends.

References

Ailawadi, K. L., Lehmann, D. R., & Neslin, S. A. (2003). Revenue premium as an outcome measure of brand equity. *Journal of Marketing, 67*(4), 1–17.

Baldi, R. (2023). "I'm Happy. I have friends who are not": What Inter Miami lost with Messi. *The Guardian.* Accessed November 29, 2023, from https://www.theguardian.com/football/2023/nov/28/im-happy-i-have-friends-who-are-not-what-inter-miami-lost-with-messi

Blattberg, R. C., Briesch, R., & Fox, E. J. (1995). How promotions work. *Marketing Science, 14*(3_supplement), G122–G132.

Bucklin, R. E., Lattin, J. M., Ansari, A., Gupta, S., Bell, D., Coupey, E., et al. (2002). Choice and the Internet: From clickstream to research stream. *Marketing Letters, 13*, 245–258.

Cardenas, F. (2023). Why Messi's arrival doesn't mean guaranteed sellouts at Inter Miami's stadium. *The Athletic.* Accessed November 1, 2023, from https://theathletic.com/4748102/2023/08/04/inter-miami-ticket-prices-messi/

Cialdini, R. B., Borden, R. J., Thorne, A., Walker, M. R., Freeman, S., & Sloan, L. R. (1976). Basking in reflected glory: Three (football) field studies. *Journal of Personality and Social Psychology, 34*(3), 366.

Holt, D. B. (1995). How consumers consume: A typology of consumption practices. *Journal of Consumer Research, 22*(1), 1–16.

Huang, M. H., & Rust, R. T. (2021). A strategic framework for artificial intelligence in marketing. *Journal of the Academy of Marketing Science, 49*, 30–50.

Khan, R., Lewis, M., & Singh, V. (2009). Dynamic customer management and the value of one-to-one marketing. *Marketing Science, 28*(6), 1063–1079.

Lewis, M. (2004). *Moneyball: The art of winning an unfair game.* WW Norton & Company.

Lewis, M. (2010). *Customer relationship management: Maximizing customer lifetime value.* Wiley Encyclopedia of Operations Research and Management Science.

Neale, W. C. (1964). The peculiar economics of professional sports. *The Quarterly Journal of Economics, 78*(1), 1–14.

Spotify. (2023). FC Barcelona social media fan engagement campaign. *Spotify.* Accessed November 1, 2023, from https://newsroom.spotify.com/2023-10-18/fc-barcelona-social-media-fan-engagement-campaign/

3

Stories and Narratives

3.1 Shared Sports Memories

One of the most iconic moments in Michael Jordan's career came during the 1989 NBA playoffs when he hit "The Shot" to eliminate the Cleveland Cavaliers in the first round. With just a few seconds left on the clock and the Bulls trailing by one, Jordan drove to the basket and hit an incredible jump shot over Craig Ehlo, securing a 101–100 victory for the Chicago Bulls. The image of Jordan pumping his fist in celebration has become one of the most enduring images in NBA history, and "The Shot" remains one of the defining moments of Jordan's illustrious career.

For Bulls fans, Jordan's exploits, like "The Shot," are a shared memory. Millions of fans watched "The Shot" live, and many millions more saw highlights on broadcast and cable television. ESPN eventually produced a 3-min video package that featured game footage and interview comments from Kevin Durant, Scottie Pippen, and LeBron James. "The Shot" was an instant story that could be shared among current NBA fans, and ESPN's treatment immortalized the story for future generations.

At the time, "The Shot" did not win the Bulls a title, as the Bulls lost to the Detroit Pistons in the conference championships. Nevertheless,

"The Shot" became a shared story for Bulls and NBA fans alike. The Shot was viewed by millions, was reinforced by media coverage, and made an important social moment through talk in offices and schools. In the immediate aftermath, Jordan's exploits fueled Bull's fans' hopes for the future, and in the long term, the event was a building block in the legend of Michael Jordan.

"The Shot" is just one Michael Jordan story. Bulls and Jordan fans have a multitude of stories about Jordan's and the Bulls' exploits. Jordan's rookie playoffs against the Celtics in 1986 is still one of the most talked-about moments in NBA history. Despite the Chicago Bulls losing the series, Jordan's impressive performance set the tone for his future success in the league. Larry Bird, an all-time great Celtic player, famously said of Jordan, "That was God disguised as Michael Jordan." This quote is fascinating as it positions Jordan as equivalent to a legendary or mythical figure, a god of basketball.

Another one of Jordan's greatest games occurred during the 1997 NBA Finals, where the Bulls faced off against the Utah Jazz. In Game 5, with the series tied 2–2, Jordan put on a show for the ages. Despite battling the flu, he scored 38 points, including a critical three-pointer in the game's final minutes. He also contributed seven rebounds, five assists, and three steals, leading the Bulls to a 90–88 victory. This game has since become known as the "Flu Game." The story again adds to the Jordan lore as an example of Jordan's resilience and determination in the face of adversity.

These stories are what connect fans to the Bulls, Michael Jordan, and each other. The action fades, but the stories and narratives remain for decades. Bulls fans can instantly connect with each other by talking about games that took place decades ago. They have an archive of stories about Michael Jordan being the Greatest of All Time (GOAT) and can rehash the Bulls' rise from also-rans to champions. It is a body of knowledge that almost serves as a password or key to the Bulls fandom community.

3.2 Roles of Shared Stories in Fandom

Stories and narratives play a vital role in sports fandom. These stories and narratives are like the shared history and beliefs that underlie a nation or community—they are what fans have in common. The Michael Jordan stories in the preceding section are just a particularly vivid example that is widely known across the world, but every fandom has its own body of stories.

Sports fandom revolves around narratives based on shared memories, current competitions, and future hope. A noteworthy thing about sports is that fans start the season with their loyalties in place. While each new season is a fresh start for teams, fans begin each season with their fandom firmly established. These fixed preferences are associated with the past achievements of the team and its players. These achievements are not raw data for fans but rather stories of past championships, amazing performances, or soul-crushing disappointments. Sports fans also go into each new season with the hope that this will be the year their beloved team wins a championship. Maybe the team is projected to be a winner, and the hope is that the team meets expectations. Alternatively, maybe the team is an underdog, and the hope is for a miracle. Hope is another noteworthy element of fandom (MacInnis & De Mello, 2005) because fan hopes are usually grounded in a narrative. The narrative might be "the team will be great because a new free agent will fill a gap in the roster" or "our new coach is going to inspire a winning attitude."

Without a body of stories, a sports organization is just another name, logo, and set of colors. The stories are the foundation for what the team means to its fans. Without the stories, a sports brand is, at best, an interesting concept or maybe something that people hope catches on. This is why new sports leagues tend to struggle. There is no foundation, only curiosity and maybe hope.

Figure 3.1 provides a conceptual diagram of the role of stories and narratives in fandom. This figure's center is the set of shared stories labeled as the Shared Foundation of fandom. In our context, it is the shared foundation for a specific sports fandom community or subculture. For example, Michael Jordan fandom's shared foundation might include stories of his national championship at North Carolina, Portland's decision to bypass Jordan in the 1984 draft, "The Shot," his six NBA championships, the Olympic Dream Team, and his initial retirement from basketball to play minor league baseball.

The figure also includes three circles that represent how shared stories create and reinforce fandom. The first circle is labeled "Excitement and

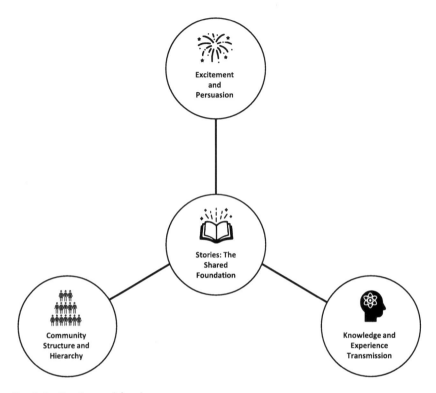

Fig. 3.1 Stories and fandom

Persuasion." Stories play an important function as they provide an archive or record of excitement. Excitement is critical because it creates an environment that induces or persuades consumers to become fans.

The second circle is labeled "Knowledge and Experience Transmission." Fandom, particularly sports fandom, has a community or network structure where fans are connected to and communicate with fellow fans. Sharing knowledge or stories of a team's current activities or reminiscing over past events is a cornerstone of fan communications.

The third circle is labeled "Community Structure and Hierarchy." The third role of stories is that they provide a currency of knowledge that facilitates fan hierarchies. Fans can range from the super fan who knows seemingly everything about a sports organization to the casual fan who likes to be a part of the crowd. Hierarchies matter as they provide structure to communities and may provide an incentive for fans to want to learn more.

3.3 Fandom as Subculture

It is useful to define fandoms as subcultures before discussing the roles of stories in fandom. A subculture can be roughly defined as a group of people who share common interests, values, beliefs, and behaviors that distinguish them from society's dominant culture. A fandom is one type of subculture. Fandom subcultures can be focused on myriad objects ranging from TikTok stars to celebrity scientists. Members of subcultures often express their identity through their clothing, language, and social interactions. An individual dressed in a Star Trek uniform at a "Trekkies" convention unambiguously expresses their identity as a Star Trek fan (McArdle, 2016). Likewise, a decked-out New York Knicks fan at Madison Square Garden or a Brazilian soccer fan in a yellow and green jersey are identifying as members of specific fan subcultures.

Fandoms share a great deal: experiences, traditions, symbols, and knowledge. Sports fans watch the same games, participate in established stadium traditions, wear the team's colors and jerseys, and often have detailed knowledge about the team's past, present, and future. Every sports fandom is a unique subculture, as the fandom is passionate about a specific team or sport. Even something with as broad an appeal as the NFL or FIFA attracts a minority of the US or global population. These unique sports fandoms each have a distinct set of stories and narratives.

Shared stories help to establish and reinforce a subculture's identity and provide a sense of continuity within the community. Stories can be passed down from generation to generation or from peer to peer, connecting members of a group to a subculture's history and traditions. Stories can educate new members about the group's customs and defining moments. Additionally, shared stories can be a source of inspiration to learn or participate more in the subculture community. Ultimately, shared stories help to create a sense of unity and belonging within the subculture, strengthening the bonds between members and fostering a sense of community.

Anthropologists have stressed the importance of stories to preserve cultural traditions and history. They serve to transmit knowledge, values, and beliefs across generations. Stories have the power to create emotional connections, elicit empathy, and shape our understanding of the world around us. According to Bruner (1990), "Narrative is a mode of thought as well as a mode of communication, and the two are inseparable." In other words, stories convey information and shape how we think about that information. These tales provide information about teams and athletes, yes, but they also provide the structure for how fans think about those teams and athletes. The stories about Michael Jordan's exploits define Jordan as a dominant cultural figure and perhaps the greatest NBA player ever.

Anthropologists have also looked at the psychological and social functions of storytelling. For example, some have suggested that stories are a way to cope with anxiety or stress. They argue that stories allow people to explore difficult emotions or experiences in a safe and controlled way. Others have suggested that stories are a way to build social bonds and create a sense of community. By sharing stories, people can connect with one another and create a shared sense of identity. Fans can bond over a championship season, but fans also can bond over the shared disappointments of a heart-breaking defeat or years of futility. Dallas Cowboy and Manchester United fans can bond over stories of championships, while Buffalo Bills and Tottenham fans can commiserate over feelings of being cursed by the sport's gods.

Anthropologists have also studied how storytelling has changed over time. For example, in some cultures, storytelling has evolved from oral to written traditions. This has led to new forms of storytelling, such as novels or movies. In other cultures, storytelling has adapted to new technologies, such as social media or video games. It is an interesting question how these changes have affected the way stories are told and how they are received by audiences. Modern sports leagues grew to prominence with media channels like the daily newspaper and network television. As the media evolves to social media and streaming platforms, the way sports stories are told and processed will inevitably change. Social media has already led to a market for condensed stories that can be told in seconds before the audience swipes to the next piece of content.

Stories are not just a means of communication but a fundamental aspect of human culture. They allow groups to pass down knowledge from one generation to the next, preserving histories, traditions, and values. Stories are also a fundamental aspect of sports fandom and sports brands. The stories are the web that connects fans and the substance of sports brands.

3.4 Excitement and Persuasion

The top of Fig. 3.1 is a circle with the words Excitement and Persuasion. A critical role of stories for a sports fandom is to create an environment that stimulates current fans and attracts prospective fans. The component of sports stories that fulfills this role is excitement. Excitement provides direct utility and may help enhance future fandom by making sports consumption more impactful. An important element of sports events is that they create excitement and psychological arousal. Sports stories can amplify the power of this excitement of live events by triggering the memories of exciting events.

More generally, surprising and exciting events create a state of arousal. Arousal is a state of physical and mental activation that prepares an individual for action or response to stimuli. Arousal can be triggered by a variety of factors, including external events, internal thoughts and emotions, and physiological needs. It is often accompanied by increased heart rate, respiration, and blood pressure, as well as heightened attention and alertness to the environment. These traits sound a lot like what a fan experiences in the closing moments of a tight, hard-fought game.

Sports, by their very nature, create excitement and arousal. Sports fans regularly see spectacular plays, stunning comebacks, and surprising victories by underdogs. The sports events also naturally create stories in their aftermath. The participating teams or athletes are natural protagonists and antagonists. The action is often dramatic and can contain plot twists, naturally mirroring the structure of a well-written story. The excitement embedded in sports becomes part of sports stories. The context of "The Shot" is Michael Jordan's late-game heroics and last-second shot. It is impossible for a sports fan not to be excited by the competitiveness of the game and Jordan's spectacular athleticism. "The Shot" is a perfect example of a sports moment that became a sports story as it embodies sport's ability to thrill and excite an audience.

The key mechanism for how excitement impacts fandom is persuasion. Arousal plays a significant role in persuasion. Studies have found that emotional arousal can enhance the persuasive effectiveness of messages (Petty & Cacioppo, 1986). For example, researchers have found that celebrity endorsers are more persuasive when individuals are psychologically aroused (Sanbonmatsu & Kardes, 1988). These findings suggest that understanding and utilizing arousal levels can be crucial in creating persuasive messages that influence attitudes and behaviors more effectively. The linkage of sports fandom to exciting stories is fairly direct. When sports stories, live or archived, create excitement, the potential fan is more likely to be persuaded to develop positive feelings for a team or athlete.

The power of stories has been recognized since ancient times, and philosophers have tried to understand why stories matter. Aristotle's rhetoric is a classic concept dealing with the practice of persuasion (Kennedy, 2006). Persuasion is an integral element of fandom, as the potential fan must be converted or induced to become a member of a fandom subculture. Aristotle emphasized the importance of three types of rhetoric or content: logos, ethos, and pathos. Logos is the use of logic and reason to appeal to an audience's intellect and rationality. Pathos appeals to an audience's emotions and feelings. Ethos is the use of credibility and authority to persuade an audience. Ideally, persuasive communications will include all three elements. These concepts are widely used in everything from advertising to political speeches.

Academic literature across a spectrum of disciplines supports the notion of logos, pathos, and ethos in persuasive storytelling and communication. For instance, Moyer-Gusé (2008) found that using pathos in storytelling can help create a stronger emotional connection with the audience and increase engagement with the narrative. Deighton et al. (1989) found a similar result in the context of emotionally engaging drama being used in advertising. Phillips and McQuarrie (2010) found that narrative transportation (being carried away by a story) enhances persuasion by intensifying brand experiences. These findings highlight the importance of emotional connections in persuasion. Sports stories often have all the ingredients for effective persuasion.

Sports can be especially effective in arousing emotions and triggering excitement that enhances persuasion. The memory of an amazing shot or great play can activate memories of excitement. A video of a past play or a vivid piece of writing can inspire excitement in a new audience. Sports can be emotionally arousing, therefore eliciting pathos, and the excitement can be contagious and make people want to be a part of fandom.

Sports also have a built-in advantage related to credibility, translating to ethos. Professional sports leagues and elite international competitions like the Olympics are explicitly competitions among the best available athletes. The drop-off in interest between major leagues and minor leagues is likely due to fan's desire to see the best or most credible competition. The lack of perceived credibility may be a factor that limits the appeal of new and minor leagues.

Logos or logic may be less directly relevant to the process of persuading people to become fans. However, sports competitions and leagues are built around logical structures. The competitions are fair, and leagues have an implicit logic of being structured to identify the best teams each season. Sports stories do not make a rational case for why someone should be a fan, but sports stories feature elements that clearly provide consumer utility. Fair, uncertain, and exciting competitions provide entertainment value (Rottenberg, 1956).

3.5 Knowledge and Experience Transmission

As we have discussed, shared stories are the common language and common experiences that allow fans to connect. The collection of stories generated over seasons also represents an archive of knowledge about the team or athlete. This archive of knowledge is important within the fandom community as it provides a common set of knowledge across the fan base and knowledge base that future fans can explore.

The archive of Michael Jordan stories is extensive. Michael Jordan won six NBA championships with the Chicago Bulls. Jordan's championship credentials also include leading the US men's 1992 Olympic "Dream

Team" to a gold medal and the North Carolina Tar Heels to the 1982 NCAA Championship. He is also a ten-time NBA scoring leader and a five-time NBA MVP. Jordan has also acted as a spokesperson for brands such as Nike, Coca-Cola, Chevrolet, Gatorade, McDonald's, and Ball Park Franks. These accomplishments and pursuits are well-known by Bulls and Jordan fans. Knowing these facts is like knowing the language of the Michael Jordan fandom subculture.

On the other end of the spectrum, a potential fan might be unfamiliar with the details of Jordan's career until being recommended *The Last Dance* (Hehir, 2020) documentary by a streaming service algorithm. Once an interest is peaked by the excitement embedded in *The Last Dance*, the new fan has an immense amount of source material related to Jordan's championships, records, commercials, and documentaries. As new fans explore, they can communicate with the established fan community. Older Jordan fans may love the opportunity to tell stories about the Bulls' glory days. Learning the lore or stories of a fandom is a necessary and enjoyable part of becoming a member of a fandom subculture.

A similar story could be told about F1 fandom. F1 fandom has grown dramatically as Netflix's *Drive to Survive* series (Gay-Rees & Martin, 2019-present) has exposed new audiences to the drama and personalities of Formula 1 (Adler, 2022). A new fan of the series is quickly exposed to the current key players but is also exposed to racing teams like McLaren and Ferrari with rich legacies and circuits like Silverstone and Monaco with deep histories. The current stories about Max Verstappen and Red Bull are an entry point to a sport with decades of history filled with other tales of drivers, cars, and tracks.

The prevalence of sports stories leads to an environment where learning about a team or player is easy and accessible. Research has also shown that stories can be an effective tool for learning and memory retention. For example, Green and Brock (2000) found that participants were able to recall significantly more details (words) when the information was presented within a narrative rather than a list. Stories can help us remember information by providing a context and structure for the information to be stored. Sports information is almost always delivered in the form of stories, making the content especially memorable.

Sports may be the ideal category in terms of generating a body of content for fans to discover, collect, learn, and share. The key is that sports have a structure that creates memorable stories. The audience is highly engaged, which leads to heightened cognitive attention, and the structure of sports (a fixed timeline, uncertain outcomes, heroes and foes, etc.) results in a product that naturally creates impactful narrative. Increasingly, these stories are archived in multiple formats and across platforms. A Formula 1 fan can watch documentary content on Netflix, live racing on cable television, read articles on the Internet, and follow teams and drivers on social. Formula 1 is not unique in this respect, as sports are increasingly generating a constant stream of new content or stories. This is material for current fans to enjoy and for future fans to discover.

3.6 Community Structure and Hierarchy

The collection of stories that surround a team also provides a basis for hierarchies within fandom communities. A fandom community consists of fans that vary based on engagement, knowledge, and status levels. For instance, Edlom and Karlsson (2021) use the term "superfans" in the context of music to recognize fans who are particularly engaged and committed to fandom. Superfans exist in all categories and are especially common in sports. The face-painted, jersey- or costume-wearing fan with strong opinions about the coaches and referees is widespread across sports and geographies.

There is a common belief among fans that being a true fan requires more than just rooting for a team. It takes knowledge and dedication to understand the game and the players. True fans know the history of the team and can recite stats and facts about individual players. Having expert knowledge about the team requires a commitment to the team and the sport, and this commitment conveys status. In fandom-based communities, knowledge of the focal entity is often critical in determining fan hierarchies. The fan with the most knowledge of the organization's stories achieves status as an expert. The fan who knows the narratives about the current players and also the stories of past greats achieves a special status within a fan community.

Groups naturally evolve hierarchies and leadership structures as a means of organization and coordination. According to a study by Cheng et al. (2010), social hierarchies emerge in groups due to the need for coordination and cooperation, with individuals naturally assuming leadership roles based on their skills and expertise. Hierarchy is reinforced through communication patterns and social interactions, with those in leadership positions often receiving more attention and respect from group members. Hierarchy and leadership structures are a natural aspect of group dynamics, and their presence can contribute to group effectiveness and success. The role of hierarchy in sports fandoms is often more subtle, as sports fandoms tend to lack formalized organizational structures. Sports fandom hierarchies create roles like expert storytellers, game tacticians, or fans with encyclopedic knowledge about players.

The existence of the expert superfan has been memorialized in popular culture. *Saturday Night Live*'s Bill Swerski's "Superfans" sketch featured several Chicago Bears superfans dressed in homage to former Bears coach Mike Ditka discussing Chicago sports and making predictions about upcoming games (Siegel, 2018). The skit ran from 1991 to 1997. The sketch resonated with people because of the commonality of the expert, overly committed, and engaged sports fan.

Hierarchies naturally develop and play important roles in communities. Expert fans can act as educators, while excessively engaged face-painting fans may provide color or personality to the group. Fan group leaders may also play an important role in new fan acquisition. Fandom hierarchies can also provide utility as more knowledgeable fans may enjoy a form of status by being the "top" fan.

3.7 Current Trends

The evolving media environment of the 2020s has highlighted the critical nature of sports stories. Sports fandom is built on shared memories, current competitions, and future hope. These three elements create a unique bond between fans and their team, and they help to create a sense of belonging to a community. Without these elements, sports fandom would lose an important part of its identity and history. These three elements are also the basis for most sports stories and narratives.

The importance of storytelling and story archives is demonstrated by NFL Films (Tanier, 2015). Founded in 1962, NFL Films has created an archive of dramatically told stories of NFL games and personalities. The NFL Films archive provides a collection of stories that can be fodder for established fans to reminisce or provide an entry point for new fans.

The impact of NFL Films in the rise of the NFL to being the dominant American sports league is debatable, but there are no MLB Films or NBA Films. NFL Films turned the collection of games into high-quality, creatively produced stories that could be readily shared across generations. Because NFL Films exist, there are hundreds of hours of full-color, brilliantly edited, meticulously preserved testaments to the wonder of professional football and the glory of its superstars during the NFL's rise to prominence in the 1960s and 1970s. NFL Films has spent over five decades making ordinary games look legendary and making legendary games feel and look fresh and vivid to new generations. Because of NFL Films, professional football history is made into vibrant, compelling content and is not limited to columns of statistics in old newspapers.

Other leagues and organizations are trying to create content that both captures the current audiences and builds an archive of content. For example, the previously discussed *The Last Dance* documentary is a captivating and revealing account of Michael Jordan's life and career (Hehir, 2020). The series features interviews with Jordan himself, as well as his teammates, coaches, and rivals, which shed light on the many stories and controversies surrounding the basketball legend. The documentary covers Jordan's rise to fame, battles with opponents and teammates, and remarkable comeback in the late 1990s. It also explores Jordan's commercial success during his career, such as his hugely successful shoe line and endorsement deals with major brands. *The Last Dance* offers a fascinating insight into one of the most iconic athletes of all time, but it also explicitly creates an archive of stories about Michael Jordan and the Chicago Bulls.

The Last Dance documentary's success highlights the power of sports narratives. There was no mystery as to the outcome of the games and series featured in the series, but millions of viewers eagerly watched it.

The crucial insight from *The Last Dance*'s viewership is that fans are interested in the stories and narratives surrounding Jordan, not just his basketball skills. There is an appeal of nostalgia as the series recounts events from a previous generation, and there is also the appeal of new, in-depth interviews that provide details and personal reflections about the famous moments. A vital aspect of the Last Dance is that these and other stories are now archived in a single, easily accessible location. The Last Dance also provides a set of stories that can attract a new generation of Michael Jordan fans and reinforce the existing fandom.

As mentioned, Netflix's *Drive to Survive* is a documentary series that provides a behind-the-scenes look into the world of Formula 1 racing. The series delves into the lives of drivers, team owners, and mechanics and showcases the extreme risks they take in pursuit of victory. The show highlights the human element of the sport, and viewers get a sense of the intense passion and dedication it takes to succeed in one of the world's most dangerous and competitive sports.

Like *The Last Dance, Drive to Survive* uses sports as the source of narrative storytelling. The on-track action is the continuing thread that provides the motivations for the human actors. Viewers watch the rise and fall of drivers and teams. The focus on individuals' struggles and triumphs creates emotional connections that strengthen the impact of winning and losing. Drive to Survive changes the product from a helmeted driver decked out in sponsors' logos winning a race to a story about a real human overcoming challenges to achieve lifelong goals.

Drive to Survive has also enjoyed significant commercial success and had an impact on F1 fandom. The Athletic reported that F1's US TV viewership (Shea, 2023) has grown from 538,000 per race in 2017 to 1.21 million in 2022. Market research from the Morning Consult (Silverman, 2022) also found that 53% of F1 fans attribute *Drive to Survive* as a cause of them becoming F1 fans.

Drive to Survive represents an explicit attempt to use storytelling to develop fandom. Rather than have stories organically created via the action on the field being featured and interpreted by traditional media, the F1 organization has taken control of the storytelling function. Via the

Netflix platform, the organization can provide narratives about the rise of a driver, Max Verstappen, or the intrigue surrounding team owners, like the criminal charges against Vijay Mallya (Trivedi, 2022). Simply by watching the series, viewers acquire a knowledge base that can facilitate emotional connections between the fan and drivers and allows the fan to be a part of the F1 conversation.

NFL Films was created more than 60 years before this book, but the sports and entertainment industries are still gaining an appreciation for the importance of storytelling. The success of sports documentaries like *Drive to Survive* and *The Last Dance* has spurred additional interest in sports storytelling. As social media creates an ability for sports organizations and personalities to act directly as media companies, this trend will likely accelerate. Athletes are already using Instagram and TikTok to reclaim their stories, and the future is likely to see even more sophisticated and longer form content production by individual teams and athletes.

3.8 Organizational Perspectives

The importance of stories to fandoms and the importance of fans to sports organizations means that sports organizations need to have an explicit focus on creating stories and narratives surrounding their team and players. For organizations to effectively consider storytelling and content development, new perspectives and skills may be needed.

The notion that brands have their own stories is not new (Brown et al., 2003), but the shift from consumer brands to sports personalities and organizations magnifies the importance of stories. There are only so many stories about a soft drink or car model, while sports organizations potentially write a new chapter every time they play a game, fire a coach, or acquire a player. As sports and other cultural organizations increase their emphasis on story creation, academic perspectives and practitioner experiences may be useful for thinking about how existing organizations may be adapted to a future where defining narratives and telling stories is paramount.

3.8.1 Academic Perspectives

The value in considering stories from an academic perspective is that academic researchers strive to uncover the fundamentals of how storytelling influences people. In fact, storytelling is a phenomenon that is of great interest to multiple academic disciplines. Researchers and scholars from fields such as psychology, literature, sociology, and anthropology are all intrigued by the power of narratives to shape our understanding of the world and ourselves. The findings from these disciplines are relevant to the phenomena of fandom as they illuminate the fundamental power of stories to groups and subcultures. Generally, the study of storytelling can provide insights into the human psyche, social dynamics, cultural values, and historical events. Sports fandoms are a little bit different from most subcultures as they are actively managed by teams and organizations. The active management of fandoms means that marketing is the most applicable academic field to fandom, as subcultures are not only studied but also shaped and monetized.

Within marketing, consumer culture theory is the most relevant sub-discipline for understanding several aspects of fandom. Fandom is different from many marketing phenomena because it has richness and complexity that is difficult to capture using survey or transaction history data. Consumer culture theory encompasses a broad range of research topics related to consumer behavior and marketing. According to Arnould and Thompson (2005), CCT seeks to "explore the cultural, social, and historical contexts of consumption, and to understand how these contexts shape the meanings, practices, and experiences of consumers." This approach emphasizes the importance of understanding the social, cultural, and economic factors that influence consumer behavior, as well as the ways in which consumers use products to express their individual and collective identities.

Ethnographic research is a qualitative research method that involves studying people in their natural settings and observing their behavior, beliefs, and attitudes. Ethnographers immerse themselves in the culture they are studying and gather data through observation, interviews, and other methods. This style of research aims to understand the cultural context in which people live and make sense of their experiences. The ethnographer is uniquely positioned to catalog and analyze the stories that animate a consumer subculture, like a fandom.

Holt (1995) conducted ethnographic research on fans by spending multiple seasons with Chicago Cubs fans in the Wrigley Field bleachers. Spending a summer with fans in the Wrigley Field bleachers provides an opportunity to understand the content and nature of fan communications. What current players are discussed? How much do fans complain about team management? What past teams and players still animate and excite fans? Listening to fans to see what stories are of current interest and which are at the core of the fandom community is a critical step for sports brands.

Direct observations and interviews should be a primary tool for organizations interested in exploiting the power of storytelling. Organizations need to understand how fans collect, organize, and use stories within the fandom community. These insights can guide the organization's selection of story topics and formats. The issue of what stories mean to fans should also be considered. Stories may be about great performances, but they may also focus on fleshing out the human side of players. Great performances might be inspirational, while stories about personalities might help build relationships by humanizing the team. By using ethnographic research, marketers can gain valuable insights into the needs and desires of their target audience and develop marketing strategies that are better aligned with the cultural and social context of sports consumption and fandom.

3.8.2 Managerial Challenges

For sports organizations, storytelling provides opportunities and nuanced challenges. The importance of storytelling is intuitive. Sports has a long history of its most exciting moments being turned into stories and narratives by sports media. Technological innovations are disrupting the relationship between sports organizations and media partners. Social media and other technological innovations are allowing individuals and organizations to develop platforms and tell their own stories.

Sports storytelling also comes with significant challenges. Like most business challenges, the key to success is in acquiring the right talent and creating the right organizational structures and incentives. In terms of types of talent, the world is changing quickly, and multimedia storytellers are needed. The organization may wish to tell stories in formats ranging from 15-second TikTok clips to book-length treatments.

Storytelling is probably not the task of the public relations or communications professionals. These functions are still needed, but the shift from traditional media to social media relocates the responsibility of building narratives to internal resources. The goal of storytelling is not awareness or incrementally moving brand equity metrics. The goal of storytelling is to have an emotional impact on current and potential fans. In terms of storytellers themselves, the need is for insightful, talented artistic professionals who can create content that affects fans. A challenge is that these types are not concentrated in any single discipline. Storytellers can come from any walk of life.

Storytelling should become a core function that accesses outside resources when needed. In particular, the organization should be the driver of what stories are told. The organization best knows its fans and history, so it should be well suited to selecting the people and moments that will resonate most powerfully. Related to this, organizations must adopt a long-term perspective and consider content as a library or archive. Storytelling should not be one-off or opportunistic. Stories should be selected strategically to create a record or archive of the team's history or to motivate interest in the team's future.

The biggest challenge is that organizations are constrained by their team's successes. A team with prime-age Michael Jordan and a fascinating supporting cast is a story generator. Likewise, a Red Bull racing team with a generational talent in Max Verstappen supplanting Mercedes at the top of F1 is prime storytelling fodder. In contrast, a struggling team that is not close to the post-season or a racing team always stuck at the back of the grid is a more challenging endeavor.

Netflix's *Drive to Survive* illustrates how storytelling can generate interest even for non-winners. The challenges of a struggling team or even an owner, Vijay Mallya, facing criminal charges can also make for compelling content. A key insight from *Drive to Survive*'s coverage of non-winners and even failures is that emotional connections can be built from stories of sports' losers as well as their winners.

Managing a storytelling function is challenging as compelling storytelling is an art and even the greatest directors and producers have projects that are disliked by critics and audiences. Selecting the right topic and creating the right production can be difficult. A unique aspect of sports fans is that they enjoy stories about the past and future as much as they do about the present. A documentary about a long-retired Michael Jordan or Jackie Stewart may be as equally or more compelling than features on current Chicago Bulls players or F1 drivers.

A crucial insight into organizational storytelling is that stories should not be viewed as independent pieces. Fans possess many stories in their heads. The organization should strive to understand common stories across the fan base. Older fans have decades of stories, while younger fans may have a minimal appreciation of a team's history.

The archive of stories about a team should be designed strategically. Stories about great seasons, special moments, adversity, or even the mascot can be told. Notre Dame is the most storied college football program. The history of Notre Dame football includes coaches with legendary status like Knute Rockne, 11 national championships, and seven Heisman Trophy winners. Notre Dame lore also includes moments when the team switched uniforms at halftime against USC in 1985 and the story of Rudy Ruettiger, the inspiration for the 1993 film *Rudy* who became famous for his perseverance and determination to play for the Fighting Irish (Anspaugh et al., 1993).

From the perspective of the sports organization, two key points emerge. First, storytelling is an art that should be included in-house. Narrative selection and storytelling must be core functions of the modern sports organization. As a core function, it is dangerous to outsource entirely. Second, sports organizations should think of their histories as collections of stories. From this perspective, the organization can think of itself as both a content producer and archivist. The organization should think in terms of the collection of stories in addition to thinking about the story of the moment.

3.9 Insights and Connections

The stories and narratives held in common by a team's fans are the foundation of that team's fandom subculture. Stories are the main points of connection that unite fandoms, whether it is a quick recap of last night's game or a reminiscence about a past championship season. The key points from this chapter include the following:

- Stories are the key to transmitting fandom across individuals and generations.
- Stories create excitement that enhances fan attitudes and feelings towards a team or player.
- The accumulated stories about a team or franchise represent a knowledge base that allows fans to become experts.
- Fandom-oriented brands should be considered from anthropological or Consumer Culture Theory perspectives. Fandom-oriented brands have complex relationships with their fans that are best understood using methods to study cultures.
- Fandom-driven organizations need to develop competencies related to content creation. These competencies include storytelling and story selection.

Looking ahead, the idea that a player's or team's stories are the foundation of fandom is related to the notion that sports stars and teams are brands. In this conception, the shared stories of teams or athletes are how fans know these brands. Michael Jordan's spectacular athleticism and fierce competitiveness are the core elements of the Jordan brand. The stories of Jordan's 63 points versus the Celtics, the dominance of the Olympic Dream Team, and 6 NBA championships are what support these core brand elements.

Sports create stories and memories naturally through competition. These competitions involve athletes who frequently become heroes and role models. Fans often enjoy "relationships" with their sports stories and enjoy stories about their on-field achievements and off-field lives. These stories become the foundation for the sports brands that consumers love.

The casting of a fandom subculture as a brand community may seem like a meaningless renaming, but an essential aspect of modern fandom analytics and management is that fandom becomes something that is actively managed and monetized. The idea that sports fandoms are brand communities that provide meaning to fans is the key idea for the next several chapters.

References

Adler, D. (2022). Netflix, drive to survive, and the new cult of F1 fandom. *Vanity Fair*. Accessed on November 19, 2023, from https://www.vanityfair.com/style/2022/03/netflix-drive-to-survive-and-the-new-cult-of-f1-fandom

Anspaugh, D., Goldsmith, J., Courage, A. M. (1993). Rudy [Film]. *TriStar Pictures*.

Arnould, E. J., & Thompson, C. J. (2005). Consumer culture theory (CCT): Twenty years of research. *Journal of Consumer Research, 31*(4), 868–882.

Brown, S., Kozinets, R. V., & Sherry, J. F., Jr. (2003). Teaching old brands new tricks: Retro branding and the revival of brand meaning. *Journal of Marketing, 67*(3), 19–33.

Bruner, J. (1990). *Acts of meaning: Four lectures on mind and culture (vol. 3)*. Harvard University Press.

Cheng, J. T., Tracy, J. L., & Henrich, J. (2010). Pride, personality, and the evolutionary foundations of human social status. *Evolution and Human Behavior, 31*(5), 334–347.

Deighton, J., Romer, D., & McQueen, J. (1989). Using drama to persuade. *Journal of Consumer Research, 16*(3), 335–343.

Edlom, J., & Karlsson, J. (2021). Keep the fire burning: Exploring the hierarchies of music fandom and the motivations of superfans. *Media and Communication, 9*(3), 123–132.

Gay-Rees, J., & Martin, P. (Producers). (2019-present). Formula 1: Drive to survive [TV Series]. *Netflix.*. https://www.netflix.com/

Green, M. C., & Brock, T. C. (2000). The role of transportation in the persuasiveness of public narratives. *Journal of Personality and Social Psychology, 79*(5), 701.

Hehir, J., Burdett, J., Jordan, M., Jordan, Y., Jordan, L., Jordan, D., … & Wilkes, C. (2020). The last dance: A 10-part documentary event [TV series]. *ESPN Films*.

Holt, D. B. (1995). How consumers consume: A typology of consumption practices. *Journal of Consumer Research, 22*(1), 1–16.

Kennedy, G. A. (2006). *On rhetoric: A theory of civic discourse*. Oxford University Press.

MacInnis, D. J., & De Mello, G. E. (2005). The concept of hope and its relevance to product evaluation and choice. *Journal of Marketing, 69*(1), 1–14.

McArdle, M. (2016). This is how star trek invented modern fandom. *GQ Magazine*. Accessed on December 30, 2023, from https://www.gq.com/story/this-is-how-star-trek-invented-fandom

Moyer-Gusé, E. (2008). Toward a theory of entertainment persuasion: Explaining the persuasive effects of entertainment-education messages. *Communication Theory, 18*(3), 407–425.

Petty, R. E., & Cacioppo, J. T. (1986). *The elaboration likelihood model of persuasion* (pp. 1–24). Springer.

Phillips, B. J., & McQuarrie, E. F. (2010). Narrative and persuasion in fashion advertising. *Journal of Consumer Research, 37*(3), 368–392.

Rottenberg, S. (1956). The baseball players' labor market. *Journal of Political Economy, 64*(3), 242–258.

Sanbonmatsu, D. M., & Kardes, F. R. (1988). The effects of physiological arousal on information processing and persuasion. *Journal of Consumer Research, 15*(3), 379–385.

Shea, B. (2023). F1's "Drive to survive" effect: Inside the show's ratings and its impact on race viewership. *The Athletic*. Accessed November 15, 2023, from https://theathletic.com/4402239/2023/04/13/f1-formula-one-drive-to-survive-ratings/

Siegel, A. (2018). Da story of da bears: How an "SNL" sketch defined sports fandom. *The Ringer*. Accessed on November 8, 2023, from https://www.theringer.com/tv/2018/9/27/17907760/da-bears-saturday-night-live-george-wendt-robert-smigel

Silverman, A. (2022). Formula 1 fandom in the United States is up 33% since 2020, thanks in part to Netflix series. *The Morning Consult*. Accessed December 6, 2023, from https://pro.morningconsult.com/instant-intel/f1-fandom-netflix

Tanier, M. (2015). Visionary artistry of Ed Sabol's NFL films remains unrivaled and irresistible. *The Bleacher Report*. Accessed November 8, 2023, from https://bleacherreport.com/articles/2359615-visionary-artistry-of-ed-sabols-nfl-films-remains-unrivaled-and-irresistible

Trivedi, U. (2022). Ex-billionaire Vijay Mallya gets four month jail term in India. *Bloomberg*. Accessed December 6, 2023, from https://www.bloomberg.com/news/articles/2022-07-11/ex-billionaire-mallya-gets-four-month-jail-term-in-india

4

Fandom Communities and Fan Identity

4.1 Public Displays of Fandom

Sports fandom often includes very public displays. We have already noted several times that fans wear team jerseys, paint their faces in team colors, share songs and cheers, follow teams and players on social media, and decorate their homes with team flags. These are not just indicators of fandom; these are open exhibitions of fandom. Fandom leads many fans to proclaim their passions to the world.

College fandom in the United States also includes significant demonstrations of fandom and even coded language whereby fans of schools self-identify. Football fans across the globe are known for their in-stadium displays. Penn State University has a storied football program with a passionate fan base. The Penn State "White Out" game was created in 2004, and the school now regularly gets over 100,000 fans to show up to the "White Out" game dressed in white shirts (Wogenrich, 2023). The "White Out" is a marketing achievement as tens of thousands of fans coordinate outfits—in this case community is built in the fan base through being in uniform. The "tifo" culture in Europe fully embraces the public display of fandom. Tifos are large, elaborate displays created by fans before matches, often using thousands of pieces of colored paper or fabric to create intricate designs and images. These tifos are typically unfurled just before the match begins, creating a stunning visual display that can cover entire sections of the stadium. Tifos are a way for fans to show their creativity and passion for their team, and they have become an integral part of soccer culture in Europe. Many tifos, such as Barcelona FC's 12th Man and Borussia Dortmund's Yellow Wall, have become iconic examples of fandom.

Public displays and acknowledgment of fandom also occur outside of arenas through fandom-specific rituals and communications. The University of Illinois has only enjoyed moderate athletic success over the past few decades. Nevertheless, the fanbase is still passionate about broadcasting their allegiance. The ILL-INI chant is a popular tradition among University of Illinois fans. It is often heard at sporting events and rallies, with half of the arena chanting I-L-L and the other responding with I-N-I (Cohn, 2017). The chant becomes more than an in-arena cheer as Illinois fans might use the cheer as a greeting to strangers who happen to be wearing Illinois-branded apparel. Seeing an Illinois logo, the first fan might shout out "I L L" with the recipient hopefully returning an "I N I." If the second half of the chat is received, there is an immediate connection between the two and the start of a conversation. University of Illinois fandom is not unique in this level of fandom. Wearing team colors and logos is often an invitation to start a conversation between strangers.

Sometimes, public displays extend beyond sports. Part of the spectacle surrounding the Barbie movie of 2023 was that fans spontaneously and in mass decided to wear pink while attending screenings (Kuo, 2023). This behavior was an act of self-labeling by fans. Fans were proclaiming their participation in the Barbie moment. Dressing up in pink said that the film was important and inspirational. Dressing in pink also made it easy to be found by other fans.

The important thing connecting tifos to matching white outfits and ritualistic chants is that fans self-identify. This is a critical insight, as it reveals that fans want to be recognized as fans and to connect with other fans. Fandom is not a solitary activity but rather a social or group activity. How this social aspect provides benefits to fans is the next important building block in analyzing fandom.

4.2 Fandom Benefits

Public displays of fandom are fascinating in their frequency and underlying motivation. It is obvious that sports fans are driven to identify themselves as fans of their beloved players and teams, but this motivates a question of why. Why do sports fans want to identify themselves as fans? What value do fans gain from being recognized as fans?

Fans, of course, get value from watching games. Sports provide entertainment through the impressive physical feats and skillful abilities of athletes working in coordination. Sports also provide excitement through competitive contests with back-and-forth action and uncertain outcomes. Nevertheless, sports fandom is about more than just the actual games. Fans root for the same team year after year, even though the players change. A reviled opposing player can become a fan favorite when trade or free agency removes him from a hated rival and places him on the hometown team's roster wearing the home team's jersey.

Fandom often involves an enduring relationship with a team or organization. The relationship between team and fan is only one aspect of the social role of sports fandom. Sports fandom is also about being a part of a community that shares the same passion for a team or player. These communities have structures, traditions, and stories that members know and love. Watching a favorite team's games among thousands of other cheering fans in a cherished arena or with dozens of other fans in a pub provides something that watching an informal game in the local park lacks.

At the level of individuals, encountering a stranger who happens to be wearing a beloved team's jersey on a train or airplane often provides a conversation starter. Two strangers wearing the same team apparel can bond over the current players, past victories, or upcoming schedule. This bonding opportunity occurs because being a fan means being a part of something. Many fans are proud to be a part of a fandom. In the United States, fandoms even refer to themselves as nations. The Pittsburgh and Las Vegas NFL fans refer to themselves as the Steelers (Guidotti, 2024) and Raiders Nations (Trezevant, 2024), respectively. Just about every college fandom does the same (Gator Nation at Florida, Dawg Nation at Georgia, Longhorn Nation at Texas, etc.). The "Nation" descriptor is

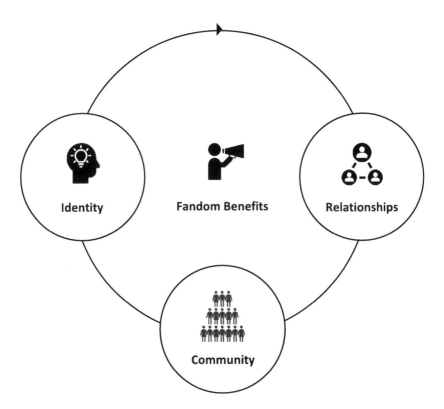

Fig. 4.1 Fandom benefits

interesting as it reveals a desire of the fandom to be separate and significant.

The preceding observations imply that fandom provides significant social and relationship benefits. Figure 4.1 provides a diagram highlighting fandom's "non-sport" benefits. This diagram does not include the utility of seeing athletic performances but rather focuses on the structure and benefits of the fan communities that collectively support sports organizations. The figure shows a circular process where "Relationships" create "Community" and "Community" enables "Identity" benefits.

The first element of the process is labeled "Relationships." Relationships are the foundation of fan communities and a primary source of fandom benefits. Sports have an amazing ability to connect people, so they are natural relationship builders. Sports provide the foundation for two types of relationships. The first is a relationship between fans and some sports entity, like a team or athlete. The second is relationships between fans.

The second part of the process is labeled "Community." Connection to others is a vital aspect of fandom; the individual relationships between fans collectively create a network or community of fans. Communities of fans become shared subcultures with bodies of knowledge, hierarchies, and traditions. Human beings are social animals, and fandom provides a valuable social group.

The final aspect of the process is labeled as "Identity." At the individual level, being a fan is being a part of something. Being part of something like a fandom is often deeply felt and may become important to the person's self-perception. The implication is that fandom provides value through recognition as a community member and social identity signaling. Social identity, in particular, is a critical aspect of fandom. People have many interests and preferences, but what makes fandom special is that fans often use fandoms to construct their social identities.

4.3 Relationships

Relationships are an essential aspect of fandom. Fans have a critical but asymmetric relationship with their favorite teams and athletes. Fans also have relationships with other fans where fandom can play a defining or supporting role. A useful structure for considering the nature of fandom relationships is the four conditions outlined by Hinde (1995). Hinde (1995) suggests that interpersonal relationships require four properties. First, relationships involve reciprocity between independent partners. Second, relationships must involve purposeful engagement and meaning. Third, relationships are multidimensional and may take multiple forms. Fourth, relationships are process phenomena that evolve over time and multiple interactions.

The core relationship in sports fandom is the relationship between the fan and the team or player. The idea of a fan-team relationship may seem odd to many observers. In common vernacular, relationships are between two people who know and interact with each other. A relationship between a person and an intangible entity like a team or brand may seem artificial. Even the case of a fan relationship with an athlete may seem like a stretch as the player is usually unaware of the fan's existence.

The notion of a relationship between fans and team (or athletes) brands is a specific case of a consumer-brand relationship (Fournier, 1998). However, an important aspect of team-fan relationships is that they are likely to be much stronger and more meaningful to fans than most brand-consumer relationships. Like consumer products, the relationships are typically one-sided, but from the fan's perspective, the relationship with the team possesses the four relationship elements. There is a form of reciprocity as the fans' treatment of the team may change with winning and losing. The team wins, and fans show up, but if the team loses, the fans stop attending, and maybe the team fires the coach. The relationship often has a deep meaning to the fan. The relationship can be multidimensional as the relationship can provide meaning, excitement, camaraderie, and other aspects. The relationship is also dynamic and can change over the fan's life-cycle.

In contrast to standard brand-consumer relationships, sports relationships probably involve far more passion and commitment. The difference in relationship intensity is a vital aspect of the relationships between fans that are the basis for community building. Unlike most categories, the fans are passionate about the team and eager to share their passions with like-minded individuals. In addition, sports fandom can both create and enhance human relationships. In existing relationships within families or between friends, shared fandom provides something that can create or strengthen bonds. Sharing stories about and communal viewing of sports events provides opportunities for interactions between fans.

Sports fandom also provides a common interest that can facilitate new relationships with other fans. Common clothing, communal knowledge, and known rituals provide connections and shared experiences across fans. Self-identifying through apparel can initiate a dialog, and the archive of team stories and activities of current players can create easy and friendly conversations.

4.4 Community

In common terminology, fandoms are groups or communities. Dallas Cowboys fans, Manchester United supporters, and Scuderia Ferrari Formula 1 racing team enthusiasts are all communities with shared interests and knowledge. The intensity and formality of fan groups varies across sports organizations, geography, and time, but there is almost always some underlying community. Fandom almost always includes a social or community element.

Sports fandoms are essentially subcultures focused on a team or player, but unlike many subcultures, sports fandoms are actively managed. Part of this active management involves treating the team or organization as a brand. As teams and players operate as brands, fandoms are a form of a brand community. Muniz Jr and O'guinn (2001) defined brand community as a community "based on a structured set of social relations among admirers of a brand." Muniz and O'Guinn also claim that brand communities exhibit shared consciousness, rituals and traditions, and a sense of moral responsibility. The idea of shared consciousness, rituals, and traditions is incredibly consistent with sports fandom, as fandoms share a passion for their team's success, rituals like matching clothing for games, and a body of stories about the team.

Of course, sports fandoms existed before modern marketing as these fandoms, with their shared values and rituals, developed naturally around local clubs. As sports organizations progressed from local clubs to nationally or internationally prominent organizations with millions of fans and massive revenues, marketing concepts, like branding, necessarily increased in relevance. A challenge to managing fandom communities is that fans generally want to be part of a community devoted to something pure rather than something managed as a brand. Fans overwhelmingly want to view their teams as sports enterprises devoted to winning rather than consumer brands devoted to profits. The issue of the motivation of the team begs the question of how fandom communities provide value to fans. A community focused on the purity of sport and winning titles for the hometown feels very different than a community focused on a profit maximizing brand.

There is also a fundamental question about the value that being a part of a community provides. Group membership can also provide psychological and practical benefits. For instance, fans may enjoy the shared traditions and being a part of physical crowds rooting for the same team. An established psychological benefit of sports fandom is the value of "basking in reflected glory" (Cialdini et al., 1976). The idea is that people seek to be affiliated with successful sports teams. Cialdini et al. found that students were more likely to wear school-identifying clothing and use the word "we" in relation to their school following a victory by the school's football team relative to a loss.

Groups may also provide more concrete or even political benefits. The world of sports in the 2010s and 2020s has been increasingly focused on political issues, and sports stars like Colin Kaepernick and Megan Rapinoe have become famous as social activists focused on racial and gender issues. The politicization of sports impacts fans by changing the perception of teams and athletes. The US Women's National Soccer Team became as recognized for gender equity issues as for soccer prowess (Das, 2022). Survey data has also found that most fans support players speaking out on social justice issues (Beer, 2020). Fans may derive value if their groups advocate for issues they care about. The danger for teams and players is that fans may be split on these issues and advocacy can negatively impact fans with contrary viewpoints.

Generally, being a part of a community provides benefits. "Basking in reflected glory" is a benefit through association. Fans can connect themselves to a successful team, and that connection provides utility. The term "reflected glory" suggests that the winning or success of the team becomes associated with the fan. The finding that fans use the term "we" more after a victory is also instructive. The term "we" suggests that fans want to associate or identify as members of the team more closely.

4.5 Identity

Fans can benefit from being a part of a fandom that helps create relationships and affiliations with a sports organization centered community. Relationships and community should be viewed as related aspects of fandoms. Specifically, relationships are the connections in the community network. Fan relationships create fandom communities, and being members of fandom communities often becomes a core aspect of how people define themselves.

Social identity theory (Tajfel & Turner, 2004) is an important psychological concept about how individuals define themselves based on their memberships in social groups. Social identity theory suggests that people derive their sense of self from their social identities, such as nationality, gender, race, religion, occupation, and interests such as fandoms. This theory proposes that people not only identify with certain groups but also tend to compare their groups (ingroup) with others (outgroup). According to social identity theory, group membership is a crucial aspect of self-concept that shapes behaviors, attitudes, and beliefs. It explains why people often perceive members of their ingroup as similar and favorable while they view members of outgroups as different and inferior. This phenomenon, known as ingroup bias, can have significant implications in various contexts, including politics, intergroup relations, and organizational behavior.

The discussion of ingroup preferences and outgroup biases readily translates to sports fandom. Sports fans have a common cause and an inclination to be friendly with other fans. Sports fans also view rival fans negatively, perhaps playfully but sometimes aggressively. European soccer has a tradition of fanatical soccer fans known as Ultras. Ultras are amazingly passionate fans known for using musical instruments and fireworks within stadiums but also engaging in hooliganism and violence against rival fans. For example, Red Star Brigade's ultras and Dinamo Zagreb's ultras history of conflict and riots is related to a combination of soccer rivalry and conflicts between Serbians and Croatians (Mullaney, 2011). The Dinamo-Red Star Riot of 1990 resulted in over 60 injuries and is credited as one of the causes of the Croatian War for Independence (Dinamo–Red Star Riot, 2023).

The importance of self-concept in consumer behavior has been studied extensively in marketing (Reed, 2002; Bhattacharya & Sen, 2003). In marketing, the context is typically how brand usage or loyalty is related to social identity. The notion of brand community is a related concept since having explicit interactions with others related to loyalty to a brand suggests that the brand plays an important role. Several of our previous examples, such as Penn State fans dressing in unison for "White Out" games or international soccer fans participating in elaborate in-stadium displays, suggest that fans are eager to identify with their teams.

Identification with a team can also take the form of feeling so closely connected that the team's wins feel like the person's wins, and the losses feel like personal defeats. This level of connection is common across sports and is illustrated by the frequent existence of fan groups explicitly linked to the actual team. The 12th Man tradition of the Texas A&M collegiate football team may be the most famous example of fans being explicitly honored as a member of the team (Lomax, 2016). American football teams include 11 players on the field, so the idea of the 12th Man is that the fans in the stands are equal members of the team. The level of passion and connection also appears in fan's behavioral reactions to wins and losses. The previous section noted Cialdini et al.'s (1976) finding that winning team fans are more likely to use the word "we" when discussing their team. On the other side of the won-loss result, researchers have found that fans of losing teams cope by eating more saturated fat and calories (Nuwer, 2013).

4.6 Analytics Challenges

Belonging to a fandom subculture or brand community is a voluntary choice. This is a salient observation as it suggests that engaging with these communities provides value that exceeds the effort and cost of participating. Research suggests that brand communities create value for consumers (Schau et al., 2009; Muniz Jr & O'guinn, 2001) through knowledge creation and emotional connections. These general results are partially relevant to fandom-oriented categories. The knowledge creation discussed by researchers (Schau et al., 2009; Muniz Jr & O'guinn, 2001) is about product knowledge from shared experiences that leads to improved product usage. This aspect is probably of minimal importance to sports fans.

However, the emotional connection aspects of brand communities are extra relevant. The emotional connections between fans and teams far exceed the emotional intensity of the connections between consumers and brands. Fan communities are the pinnacle of brand communities in terms of the intensity of the brand-fan relationships and their role in fans' social identities. Major sports franchises have fandoms eager to identify as fans with public displays and traditions.

The challenge in understanding the value that fandom provides fans is that the relationships are intangible, and the communities are frequently informal. This creates data challenges and limits the role of traditional analytics. The existence of relationships between fans, the structure of fan communities, and the importance of fandom to social identity are all vital information that is unlikely to be observable to an analyst.

The marketing analytics revolution has been primarily prompted by growing amounts of consumer data. Sports fandom has also seen growth in data availability as customer data warehouses, digital tickets, secondary ticket markets, and other technology-driven innovations have arisen. These developments have led sports marketers to focus on the problems that the data can address. Prices can be optimized by analyzing patterns in demand in primary and secondary ticket markets (Lewis et al., 2019). Customer attendance and transaction data can be used to create retention policies (Lewis, 2005). However, the psychological benefits of belonging to a fandom are not observable from transaction data.

The difficulty for fandom analytics is that emotions, feelings, and memories are the key factors that influence fandom. Fandom is not about the response to a discount or a targeted offer; fandom is about belonging, connections, and passion. This is an essential message for fandom analysts as it highlights the need to use interdisciplinary approaches and leverage multiple types of data. Fans will respond differently to marketing offers than non-fans, but these are downstream effects of fan's emotional and attitudinal components. We can often observe behaviors suggesting fandom's benefits, such as wearing team apparel or sharing fan rituals. However, to fully understand fandom, it is necessary to survey consumers directly. Figure 4.1 delineates the benefits of fandom as three overlapping categories: relationships, community, and identity. To measure and separate these benefits, carefully designed survey data is needed.

4.7 Insights and Connections

Fandom requires effort. Fans may have passion for a team, which may be a labor of love, but fandom requires time, mental effort, and often economic sacrifice. For fandom to make sense, fans must gain some benefits or value that exceeds their investments. In this chapter, our focus is on the social value of being a fan. Three words are prominent in this discussion: Relationships, Community, and Identity.

- Fandom is the focal point for meaningful relationships between (1) fans and teams and (2) fans and other fans.
- Sports fandom provides benefits from being a part of a community. These benefits can be directly related to easy communication and connections between fans or indirect when fans gain psychological benefits from being associated with a team or player.
- Social identity is at the core of the most intense segment of sports fans. These ultra-intense Fans often use fandom as a defining trait of their self-conception and feel their team's wins and losses as personal victories and defeats.

These benefits of being a part of a fandom are closely related and overlapping. The relationships between fans have value and create a fandom community. The fandom community provides value by transferring positive associations and social identity benefits. The coolness of being a part of the group then leads to more interest in fan relationships.

This chapter leverages the preceding material related to the role of stories in subcultures. The stories of a team or athlete reinforce the connections of the relationships that build fandom communities. Sports fandoms have a foundation of stories and narratives shared by networks of fans who derive identity benefits from being fans. This rich, complex, and largely unobservable set of factors does not lend itself to data analysis. An important observation at this point is that the first elements of fan analytics are not under the purview of the statistician, and a broader view of analytics is needed. A formally trained anthropologist or psychologist may not be needed, but the skill sets and orientation for understanding the role of subculture and social identity are critical.

The discussions about relationships, community, and identity in this chapter are the starting point for the next chapter, which features detailed fandom survey data that quantitatively investigates the benefits that motivate fandom.

References

Beer, T. (2020). Over 70% of sports fans support players speaking out on social justice issues, survey finds. *Forbes*. Accessed January 13, 2024 from https:// www.forbes.com/sites/tommybeer/2020/08/13/over-70-of-sports-fans-support-players-speaking-out-on-social-justice-issues-survey-finds/

Bhattacharya, C. B., & Sen, S. (2003). Consumer–company identification: A framework for understanding consumers' relationships with companies. *Journal of Marketing, 67*(2), 76–88.

Cialdini, R. B., Borden, R. J., Thorne, A., Walker, M. R., Freeman, S., & Sloan, L. R. (1976). Basking in reflected glory: Three (football) field studies. *Journal of Personality and Social Psychology, 34*(3), 366.

Cohn, S. (2017), Pulse of Illini Nation: I-L-L, I-N-I chant, *Champaignroom. com*. Accessed on November 19, 2023, from https://www.thechampaignroom.com/2017/9/12/16294868/pulse-of-illini-nation-chant

Das, A. (2022). U.S. soccer and women's players agree to settle equal pay lawsuit. *New York Times*. Accessed January 26, 2024, from https://www.nytimes.com/2022/02/22/sports/soccer/us-womens-soccer-equal-pay.html

Dinamo—Red Star Riot. (2023, October 30). In Wikipedia. https://en.wikipedia.org/wiki/Dinamo%E2%80%93Red_Star_riot

Fournier, S. (1998). Consumers and their brands: Developing relationship theory in consumer research. *Journal of Consumer Research, 24*(4), 343–373.

Guidotti, R. (2024). What's on the menu for Steelers Nation for Sunday's playoff parties? *CBS News*. Accessed January 13, 2024, from https://www.cbsnews.com/pittsburgh/news/whats-on-the-menu-steelers-nation-playoff-parties/

Hinde, R. A. (1995). A suggested structure for a science of relationships. *Personal Relationships, 2*(1), 1–15.

Kuo, C. (2023). Pretty (devoted) in pink: 'Barbie' hordes spill into theaters. *New York Times*. Accessed January 13, 2024, from https://www.nytimes.com/2023/07/23/movies/barbie-fans-outfits.html

Lewis, M. (2005). Research note: A dynamic programming approach to customer relationship pricing. *Management Science, 51*(6), 986–994.

Lewis, M., Wang, Y., & Wu, C. (2019). Season ticket buyer value and secondary market options. *Marketing Science, 38*(6), 973–993.

Lomax, J. (2016). The 12th man tradition. Texas Monthly. Accessed November 5, 2023, from https://www.texasmonthly.com/the-daily-post/12th-man-tradition/

Mullaney, P. (2011). European football: The 10 craziest ultras groups. *Beacher Report*. Accessed January 13, 2024, from https://bleacherreport.com/articles/937447-european-footballs-craziest-ultras-groups-we-countdown-the-top-10

Muniz, A. M., Jr., & O'guinn, T. C. (2001). Brand community. *Journal of Consumer Research, 27*(4), 412–432.

Nuwer, R. (2013). Football team losses make fans eat their feelings. *Smithsonian Magazine*. Accessed January 13, 2024, from https://www.smithsonianmag.com/smart-news/football-team-losses-make-fans-eat-their-feelings-1478271/

Reed, A. (2002). Social identity as a useful perspective for self-concept–based consumer research. *Psychology & Marketing, 19*(3), 235–266.

Schau, H. J., Muñiz, A. M., Jr., & Arnould, E. J. (2009). How brand community practices create value. *Journal of Marketing, 73*(5), 30–51.

Tajfel, H., & Turner, J. C. (2004). The social identity theory of intergroup behavior. In *Political psychology* (pp. 276–293). Psychology Press.

Trezevant, E. (2024). A letter to raider nation: The importance of AP at HC. *Sports Illustrated*. Accessed January 13, 2024, from https://www.si.com/nfl/raiders/news/las-vegas-raiders-antonio-pierce-mark-davis-demeco-ryans-champ-kelly

Wogenrich, M. (2023). How the Penn State white out became the greatest show in sports. *Sports Illustrated*. Accessed November 19, 2023, from https://www.si.com/college/pennstate/football/how-the-penn-state-white-out-became-the-greatest-show-in-sports

5

Fan Attitudes and Survey Research

5.1 Fan Motivations, Attitudes, and Behaviors

We can observe many outcomes of fandom. For instance, we can visually identify a fan from the clothing they wear, and observation can even help us assess the degree of fandom. We can make an educated guess that the person decked from head to toe in team gear with accompanying face paint is an especially intense fan. The Penn State fans dressed in white or Dortmund Borussia fans in yellow are likely to be passionate supporters. We can also identify a fan from secondary data such as a team's ticket sales transaction database. A fan might purchase season tickets for years and buy apparel from the stadium vendors. Another individual might be in the database as a prospect or maybe as a buyer of only a single ticket. The behaviors of the season ticket buyer suggest that the individual is a fan of the team, while we know little about the preferences of the second individual.

Nevertheless, identifying a fan via behaviors can be challenging as data is often incomplete. For example, team-branded clothing purchased from an independent retailer or watching a game at a pub is difficult or impossible to track. Fan data is especially a difficult marketing data because many fan behaviors do not have directly observable economic consequences for the object of fandom. In most consumer categories, the economic value of a customer is almost entirely represented by purchases of the focal product, but in sports, fan behaviors like watching games on television provide value to teams through media rights deals. Unfortunately, teams themselves usually cannot track individual television viewing. Fan activity on social media may also be problematic, as linking social media handles to customer databases may be an intractable problem.

Observable fandom data is also incomplete in terms of the inferences that can be made regarding fans' passion and preferences. While we can make a reasonable inference about the fandom of the face-painted, jersey-wearing game attendees, there may be many intense fans in the population of non-season ticket buyers. Fans can be passionate but lack the time or financial resources to become season ticket buyers. For instance, the Penn State fan in white could be a guest whose clothing was suggested by the ticket provider, or the season ticket holder could be a businessperson who buys tickets solely to entertain clients. Conversely, the non-ticket buyer in the database could be a rabid fan with limited discretionary income. The analyst can make inferences, but the attitudinal component of fandom is at least a partial mystery to the outsider.

The fact that fandom is only partially observable creates challenges for sports organizations. Observable data can be illuminating and may be monetarily valuable when the team can conduct individual-level marketing (Blattberg & Deighton, 1991; Peppers & Rogers, 1993). Detailed data on tickets purchasing and usage may be used for targeted marketing promotions. However, behavioral data has shortcomings because many important aspects of fandom cannot be observed. The critical issue is that fandom behaviors are the product of fans' loyalty and passion for their teams. While fandom behaviors are incredibly important as they are the actions that are rewarded in the marketplace, fandom behaviors are downstream of the emotional attachments that fans have for their favorite teams and players. To wholly understand fandom, it is necessary that we understand the attitudes and motivations that underlie fandom.

5 Fan Attitudes and Survey Research

Attitudes and motivations are internal, unobservable psychological traits. An attitude can be roughly defined as the feelings and beliefs for a specific entity. Attitudes encompass the affective, cognitive, and behavioral components that influence an individual's response to the object of their attitude. Fans have a favorable attitude for a favored team and negative feelings for hated rivals. Attitudes are developed and evolve through personal experiences, social interactions, and exposure to media messages. Attitudes play a central role in shaping behaviors and decisions. The attitude towards a team or player is the central measure of fandom. When we talk about the love or passion for a team, we are talking about the attitude about the team.

Motivation can be defined as the driving force behind an individual's behaviors. Motivation is the internal or external stimulus that inspires an individual to achieve a goal or objective. Motivation can be influenced by factors such as personal values, social norms, and environmental conditions. In the context of fandom, motivation is related to how and why individuals gain utility from being a fan. The fundamental question is, why does someone choose to be a fan?

The preceding chapter focused on the value an individual gains from identifying with a fan community. Being a fan requires effort, attention, and maybe economic sacrifices. The effort may be unconscious as the pull of fandom is sufficiently strong that going to a game or decorating a room with team collectibles is a labor of love, but effort is still required. Fans must have some inner motivation to be fans. Figure 5.1 shows the process of fandom. The left circle is labeled "Motivations." Motivations speak to the reasons why an individual is interested in being a fan. This is the why of fandom. The center circle is labeled fandom attitudes. Fan attitudes are the person's emotions and feelings for the team or athlete. The last node is labeled behaviors. Behaviors are the activities that result

Fig. 5.1 Motivation, attitude, and behavior chain

from fandom such as buying tickets, watching games on television, and wearing team clothing.

The diagram is presented as a process. Motivations are the impetus for individuals to develop feelings for a team. Motivations lead to becoming part of a fandom, and a positive attitude towards the team is the result of becoming a part of the fandom. Behaviors are the way that a fan's attitudes are expressed.

Measurement of motivations and attitudes is essential for fandom analytics. Understanding motivations is critical because how well a team performs on dimensions related to an individual's fandom motivations likely impacts the intensity of fandom that develops. Suppose an individual or segment is motivated by being affiliated with a prestigious group, then teams that are highly respected may attract the segment's fandom more than a team that wins while featuring controversial players. As motivations are satisfied, fans develop positive attitudes towards the team that lead to fan behaviors. The more intense the fan attitudes, the more prevalent the economically valuable fan behaviors will be. Motivations may also influence fan behaviors. A fan motivated by being identified as part of a group is more likely to wear apparel that identifies them as a fan. A comprehensive analysis of fandom requires an investigation of complicated forces such as innate differences in psychological tendencies and individual differences in experiences.

5.2 Next-Generation Fandom Survey

From the perspective of the analyst, much of the fandom process in Fig. 5.1 is invisible. Motivations and attitudes are not directly observable, and behaviors are usually only partially observable. The analysis of fandom motivations and attitudes requires research techniques that directly measure these constructs. Consumer surveys that directly ask consumers about their preferences, needs, and wants are a vital element of a complete fandom analytics program.

Consumer surveys are a foundational element of marketing research (Kumar et al., 2018) across a wide range of industries. Survey research involves multiple steps, such as sampling strategy (who to survey) and survey design (what to ask). Consumer survey research is a broad and important topic, but for our purposes the key point is that they can be a direct attempt to understand consumers' motivations and attitudes. Surveys provide an opportunity to directly ask consumers or fans about the motivations and attitudes that underlie consumer loyalty and passion. This is the key aspect of survey research: the survey can directly ask about what is happening in the fan's head. For an emotionally driven product like sports, where passions can be intense, directly asking about fans' motivations and attitudes is essential. Surveys can also include questions about behaviors and segmentation variables, which we will discuss in a moment. This enables the analysts to link motivations to attitudes to behaviors.

An important aspect of consumer and fan research is segmentation. There are various ways to segment consumers, and each method has its own advantages and disadvantages. One of the most common ways to segment consumers is by demographics, such as age, gender, income, education, and occupation. This method makes it easy to collect and analyze data. Another way is to segment by psychographics, such as personality, values, interests, and lifestyles. This method is more complex and subjective, but it can provide deeper insights into the motivations and behaviors of consumers. Segmentation by behavior, such as purchasing history, brand loyalty, and usage rate, can be a useful way to identify the most profitable and loyal customers. In practice, different segmentation methods are useful for different managerial goals. For example, a sports league interested in growing its fan base might break the market into demographic segments to identify potential growth opportunities. A team interested in maximizing revenues might segment based on a measure of customer profitability like customer lifetime value (Jain & Singh, 2002; Lewis, 2005) so that it can develop strategies that attract and retain high-value customers.

Surveys do have systematic problems, such as biased samples and demand effects. Samples may be biased as the population willing to answer surveys may be systematically different from the general population. Demand and other effects occur when subjects are biased by the act of taking a survey (Weber & Cook, 1972). For example, demand effects occur when subjects respond to surveys based on inferences about the goals of the survey. For example, in a survey about fandom, it is possible that subjects might overestimate their level of fandom because they want to be more relevant to the researcher or because being a fan has a positive connotation. However, the limitations of surveys do not disqualify surveys as a vital research tool as all methods possess limitations. Surveys have limitations and biases but can gather information about feelings and attitudes inaccessible through other methods. A critical feature of fandom analytics is that interdisciplinary approaches are needed to assess different fandom aspects. A combination of approaches and data types is also useful for triangulation as alternative analytical approaches have different strengths and weaknesses.

The Next-Generation Fandom Survey is an annual sports and cultural fandom survey conducted by Professor Michael Lewis and the Emory Marketing Analytics Center (Lewis, 2023). The survey is designed to assess the current state of fandom for sports and various entertainment categories. The 2023 survey was conducted using a sample of 2468 Americans evenly distributed across the Generation Z, Millennial, Generation X, and Baby Boomer cohorts. The survey assesses the current state of fandom and is also designed to delve into the underlying motivations that drive fandom. The survey includes a range of questions related to fandom motivations, attitudes, behaviors, and market segmentation.

An important characteristic of the next-generation survey is that it is designed from the premise that being a fan means being part of a group. Definitions of fandom frequently include "membership in a subculture" as a distinguishing element of fandom. Fandom can be a casual affiliation that is seldom mentioned or an explicit over-the-top relationship that includes team logos on clothing, public displays of memorabilia, and thousands of dollars spent on live attendance.

A critical insight that arises from identifying fandoms as groups is that being part of a fan group or subculture must provide some value to fans related to group membership. Being a member of a fan community may provide multiple types of benefits. For example, being a fan may give a sense of belonging and community. Fans may feel a kinship with other cheering fans at a stadium or feel knowledgeable when discussing the latest game with friends. Being a fan can provide significant social benefits by providing a point of connection between individuals.

5 Fan Attitudes and Survey Research

Fandom can also provide a means to communicate personality traits and interests. Sports organizations attempt to be exciting and successful while emphasizing community involvement. Identifying as a fan of a successful and respected team can be a means to linking oneself to an admired and influential organization. As noted in the previous chapter, the area of psychology most relevant to the psychological benefits of fandom to individuals is social identity theory. Social identity theory is a psychological theory that explains how people form and maintain their identities within a social context. According to this theory, individuals define themselves based on the groups they belong to, such as their family, friends, and colleagues. These social groups provide a sense of belonging and identity, and people tend to associate themselves with groups that share similar beliefs, values, and characteristics. Fandom may provide social identity benefits that help a person define and express their self-concept.

However, as noted, while fandom membership must provide value, the cornerstone of a fandom survey needs to be an assessment of fandom attitudes. At the core, sports fans are passionate and loyal consumers of a brand. However, rather than a consumer brand like Toyota or Coca-Cola, the object of the loyalty is a sports club or athlete. Brand loyalty is a well-studied construct in marketing, and multiple attitudinal metrics are used to gauge loyalty to a brand. Attitudinal metrics are essential tools for measuring brand loyalty. The simplest way to analyze sports fans and fandoms is to survey individual fans about how they feel about sports, teams, and athletes. We can ask whom someone roots for or how much they like different teams and players. We can ask if they are willing to wear the jersey of a team or if they would follow an athlete on social media. We can ask how much they are willing to spend on a ticket or how far they would travel to see a match.

This quick list begins to reveal the value and challenges of fan surveys. There are lots of ways to ask about fandom. We can ask a simple yes-no question about whether someone is a fan, or we can ask the subject to rate their preference on a scale from, say, one to seven for a variety of teams or leagues. We could ask for the fan to put teams in categories or rank from most favorite to least. Of course, "preference" is a neutral term that might not capture important aspects of fandom. Maybe the survey should use phrases such as "How passionate are you about ____?" or "How much do you love ____?"

Measures of preference are attitudes. Attitudes are a set of beliefs, feelings, and opinions that shape a person's behavior and perception towards a particular subject or situation. They can be positive, negative, or neutral and can be influenced by personal experiences, culture, and social norms. Thinking about fandom as an attitude can be helpful as it provides a metric that captures a feeling at a given point in time and because it points to additional areas of inquiry. For example, the relationship between fandom attitudes and behaviors can be illuminating. Sports fandom is about passion and preference for a team or sport, but what makes fandom economically valuable is that it leads to behaviors like buying tickets or merchandise. Behaviors are the downstream effects of attitudes. Investigating the factors that create passion for a team can also be useful. Winning is the key ingredient to developing fandom, but myriad factors can influence the effects of winning. For example, teams and athletes can be viewed as having different personalities.

The next three subsections of this chapter present results from the 2023 edition of the next-generation survey. The presentation is intended to demonstrate the roles of attitudes, motivations, and behaviors in fandom, not to be an exhaustive review of US fandom in 2023.

5.3 Fandom Attitudes

Fandom is the enthusiasm, passion, and preference for a sports team, athlete, or other aspect of culture. However, while we can observe many manifestations of fandom, fandom is primarily something that is felt within a person: an attitude that we cannot directly observe. As an attitude, fandom is also something that does not occur on an easily definable scale. Fandom is unlike temperature or weight with defined and standard units. Questions about fandom attitudes require subjects to make subjective evaluations about their feelings towards a team or league. Surveys of fandom are, therefore, best interpreted as relative values best used for comparisons between sports entities rather than absolute measures of fandom strength.

The Next-Generation Fandom Survey includes questions about how much each respondent is a fan of sports in general and fandom for specific sports. The survey sample is American teenagers and adults, so the specific sports are Football, Basketball, Baseball, Hockey, and Soccer. The survey also asks about fandom in sports categories like Esports and the Olympic Games and in a broad range of entertainment categories. The primary fandom question asked respondents to rate their fandom on a scale of 1 to 7, where 7 indicates intense fandom and 1 indicates no interest. For the results that follow, a "Fan" is defined as someone rating their fandom a 6 or 7 on the 7-point scale, and an "Apathetic" is someone rating their fandom a 1 or a 2.

Figure 5.2 shows the percentage of the 2023 Next-Generation Fandom Survey sample that are "Sports Fans" and "Sports Apathetics." The data suggests that about 40% of the American population considers themselves sports fans, and 21% are apathetic towards sports. The data is informative as it suggests that sports fandom is widespread and nearly double the rate of sports apathy. However, the data is also limited and inspires many questions. What was sports fandom like prior to 2023? How does sports fandom compare to fandom for other categories like movies or music? What results would be given by alternative definitions of fandom, such as a rating of 7 on the 7-point scale? What results would be obtained from alternative measures that ask about preference,

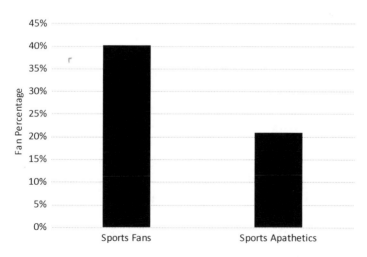

Fig. 5.2 US sports fandom and apathy in 2023

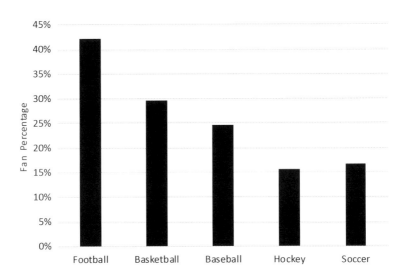

Fig. 5.3 US fandom by sport in 2023

enthusiasm, or passion? These are interesting questions that highlight the richness of fandom attitudes and the challenges in reporting fandom data. In this chapter, we report results that highlight the motivation-attitude-behavior process in Fig. 5.1, and our attitudinal measure of fandom is individuals' self-rating on the 7-point fandom scale.

Figure 5.3 shows fandom for the five specific sports: Football, Basketball, Baseball, Hockey, and Soccer. The results are not surprising. Football shows the greatest strength, with 42% of the sample indicating they are football fans. Basketball is second at 30%, and baseball finishes third at 25%. Hockey and soccer are at 16% and 17%, respectively.

The results show the comparative preferences for each sport. Notably, football scores are higher than in the general sports category. This result suggests that college and professional football may transcend the general category of sports and be viewed as something relevant to the broader American culture. The results also raise questions. The NFL's Super Bowl regularly attracts about 100 million viewers. This number is not radically different than what would be expected if we multiplied the 42% fandom rate by the size of the US population. However, the viewership of the other sports' championships falls far below the product of the fandom rates in the figure and the US population. This suggests that fandom can be something casual that does not lead to regular viewing. The sport-specific data also highlights the importance of collecting data at regular intervals. The figure shows attitudinal data in 2023 but does not speak to any underlying trends. Is basketball narrowing the gap with football? Is baseball falling over time? What are the trends for hockey and soccer?

The comparison of fandom rates across sports shows the relative popularity based on self-reported fandom attitudes of each sport in the US market. This market-level analysis is useful as it reveals the fandom attitudes across the overall population, but the analysis can also be conducted at a segment level. There are, however, numerous possible segmentation variables. A simple demographic segmentation variable is gender. Gender is potentially useful as sports have historically been male-oriented. Examining fandom differences across genders reveals the extent to which fandom is still related to gender and can provide valuable intelligence to sports organizations wishing to expand in the female segment.

Figure 5.4 shows the percentage of male and female respondents who identify as Fans and Apathetics. Sports fandom is much higher for the male segment, with 53% of the sample indicating fandom and only 14% showing apathy. In contrast, 29% of females surveyed were classified as fans, and 27% were labeled Apathetics. In relative terms, sports fandom is 82% more prevalent in the male segment compared to the female

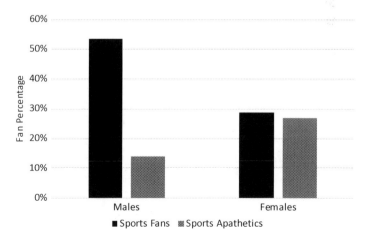

Fig. 5.4 US sports fandom in 2023: Males versus females

segment, while the apathy rate is almost double in the female segment versus the male segment. An initial observation is that there is more opportunity to grow fandom in the female segment. However, what the analysis lacks is information about what drives fandom across the genders. If the motivations or wants of the genders are different, then different approaches may be needed to target each segment.

The preceding results are mainly intended to provide a baseline for fandom attitudes at a specific point in time. Individuals are asked to directly state their fandom level for the overall sports category and several specific sports. This data shows the relative rates of fandom attitudes across different sports. Other data is collected about different demographic traits, such as gender. This information allows the analyst to get a sense of how fandom attitudes vary across consumer segments.

This data on fandom attitudes fits into the center of the diagram in Fig. 5.1. Starting in the middle of the fandom process disregards the ordered structure of the diagram, but the fandom attitude is the core of fandom as it is based on the relationship between the fan and a sports entity. The fan-team (or other sports entity) relationship reflects the fan's loyalty, preference, and engagement with a team or athlete. The next questions are as follows: (1) What are the motivations that drive the willingness to enter a fan-team relationship? and (2) how are fandom attitudes related to fandom behaviors?

5.4 Fandom Motivations

Being a fan is being a member of a group. To understand the role of group membership in fandom, the Next-Generation Fandom Survey includes a battery of questions about how individuals interact with groups, how groups offer value, and how an individual's group memberships affect his/her social identity. As the goal is to illustrate the linkage between motivations, attitudes, and behaviors, we do not go into detail on the complete list of survey items or the analysis. Our goal is to illustrate the motivation, attitude, and behavior process in Fig. 5.1 rather than report a comprehensive research study about the motivations for fandom.

The survey items related to group membership desires were used to create segments that reflect the different motivations for belonging to a group. The survey items were about general groups rather than sports fandom. A segmentation analysis based on the responses to the group belongingness and social identity scales suggested four primary types of group membership benefits. The four dimensions and the most relevant survey question are described as follows:

1. We Win: Individuals scoring high on the "We Win" dimension strongly identify with their group's successes and failures. When their group wins (loses), they win (lose). In sports, these fans feel like they are part of the team.

    * "We Win" Key Item: Rate your agreement with the following statement—When my favorite organization succeeds, it feels like a personal success.

2. Reflected Prestige: Individuals scoring high on the "Reflected Prestige" factor benefit from publicly associating with prestigious groups. These are the fans who enjoy the reflected glory of their groups' accomplishments.

    * "Reflected Prestige" Key Survey Item: Rate your agreement with the following statement—The social groups I belong to are an important reflection of who I am.

3. Societal Stability: Individuals scoring high on "Societal Stability" enjoy being members of traditional groups and are worried that societal structures are breaking down. This segment wants their organizations to help maintain cultural norms.

    * "Societal Stability" Key Survey Item: Rate your agreement with the following statement—People's ideas change so much that I wonder if we will ever have anything to depend on.

4. Cancel Culture Enforcement: Individuals scoring high on "Cancel Culture Enforcement" believe that it is important for their groups to identify and sanction bad behavior. This dimension is the flip side to the "Societal Stability" dimension, as the segment believes the power of groups should be used to change cultural norms.

- "Cancel Culture Enforcement" Key Survey Item: Rate your agreement with the following statement—Identifying instances of bad behavior from celebrities is very important.

These dimensions reveal the sources of utility provided by group membership. Two of the dimensions are especially interesting in the context of the group membership benefits discussed in the previous chapter. The "We Win" dimension is highly related to the social identity benefits, as this segment intensely identifies with their groups. The "Reflected Prestige" segment also reflects the notion of receiving a benefit through associating with a group as per the idea of "Basking in Reflected Glory" (Cialdini et al., 1976).

However, the data suggests that these are slightly different motivations. The "We Win" trait is about feeling a very direct and intense connection between themselves and their groups. These people "win" when their team wins. Beyond sports, these people win when their favorite actor wins an Academy Award or their college is ranked highly in academic rankings. The "Reflected Glory" trait is more about an external association. Reflected Prestige occurs when people are associated with prestigious or respected organizations. The "We Win" aspect is more about internal identification, while the "Reflected Prestige" dimension is about external recognition.

To illustrate the importance and usefulness of the group membership motivation data from the Next-Generation Fandom Survey, we will focus on two key fandom motivations: the "We Win" factor and the "Reflected Prestige" factor. Specifically, we will examine the scores on the key items (the specific questions most highly correlated with the constructs).

- The "We Win" Key Item: Rate your agreement with the following statement—When my favorite organization succeeds, it feels like a personal victory.
- "Reflected Prestige" Key Survey Item: Rate your agreement with the following statement—The social groups I belong to are an important reflection of who I am.

Figure 5.5 shows the rate of sports fandom rates for individuals who rate their agreement with the "We Win" and "Reflected Prestige" survey items as a 6 or 7 on a 7-point scale. This figure shows the fandom rates of people who intensely identify with their group's successes (We Win) and who gain utility from publicly associating with prestigious groups (Reflected Prestige). Because we are using data from two different questions to rate the psychological traits, there is an overlap between the "We Win" and "Reflected Prestige" groups since respondents can rate each item highly.

There are two notable results in Fig. 5.5. First, people who score highly on either of the two psychological traits have higher rates of fandom than the general sample (see Fig. 5.3). For example, the overall rate of sports fandom is 40%, but for the "We Win" segment, the rate is 65%. The

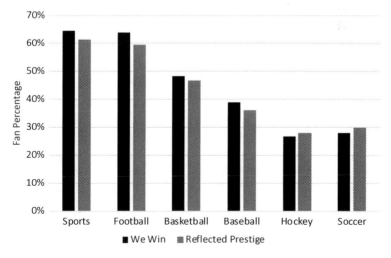

Fig. 5.5 Sports fandom rates versus psychological motivations

implication is that people who identify intensely with their groups are much more likely to be sports fans. This is consistent with the notion that people who are motivated by feeling like part of a successful organization gain utility from sports fandom. Likewise, the people who gain value from "Reflected Prestige" are also significantly more likely to be sports fans. The unsurprising conclusions are that sports fandom is especially appealing to people who want to feel part of a team and like to be associated with prestigious organizations.

A second notable result is that while the "We Win" group has higher fandom rates than the "Reflected Prestige" group for the three most popular US sports (football, basketball, and baseball), the pattern reverses for hockey and soccer. This finding highlights the difference between the two motivations and the nature of fandom for different sports. For the more mainstream sports with larger followings, the "We Win" trait is especially associated with fandom. Perhaps, the "Reflected Prestige" trait is more related to sticking out or being unique. This would be consistent with fandom for a lesser-known sport. The key insight is that different motivations lead to different fandom patterns.

5.5 Fandom Behaviors

The first two stages of the fandom process in Fig. 5.1 are about (1) the motivations that (2) lead to attitudes. The previous section shows the linkage between different motivations and fandom for various sports. The final stage is the link between fandom attitudes and fandom behaviors. Fans are passionate, and they reveal their passion by engaging in a wide range of behaviors such as watching games, buying tickets, collecting memorabilia, following accounts on social media, joining fan clubs, and subscribing to team message boards. Behaviors that publicly identify someone as a fan are especially interesting activities as they are an explicit effort to use fandom to create a social identity. For instance, wearing apparel that features teams' colors and logos is an essential expression of sports fandom. Many fans even symbolically join the team by wearing team jerseys with numbers and player names. Some fans even create custom jerseys that include their own names and chosen numbers. Wearing

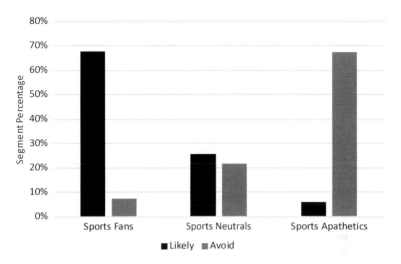

Fig. 5.6 Sports fandom and wearing team apparel

team apparel is also an example of a fan behavior that provides an economic benefit to teams through licensing deals.

Figure 5.6 shows the percentage of sports fans, Apathetics, and Neutrals (fandom ratings of 3 to 5 on the 7-point scale) who rate themselves as likely to wear team apparel and the percentage that avoid wearing team apparel. Sports fans are overwhelmingly likely to wear team apparel, with 67% likely and only 7% avoiding it. The percentages are almost reversed for the Sports Apathetics, with 6% likely and 67% avoiding it. Among the Sports Neutrals, 26% are likely compared to 21% who avoid team apparel.

Figure 5.7 shows the relationship between the "We Win" and "Reflected Prestige" psychological traits and interest in wearing team apparel. The left side of the figure shows the percentage of those who score High (6 or 7 on the 7-point scale) or Low (1 or 2 on the scale) on the We Win key item who are either likely to or avoid wearing team-branded apparel. The right side of the figure shows the results for High and Low scorers on the Reflected Prestige key item.

People who intensely identify with their groups (We Win) and those who receive utility from being associated with prestigious groups (Reflected Prestige) are almost as likely to wear team apparel as sports fans

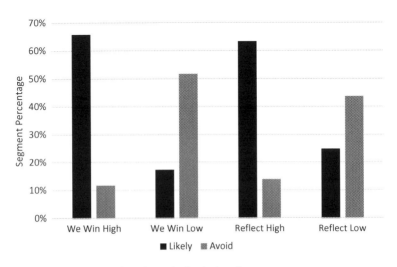

Fig. 5.7 Wearing apparel and psychological traits

with rates of 66% and 63%, respectively. The group membership motivations provide intuitive explanations for the fan behaviors. The We Win segment is part of the team and wants to wear the uniform. The Reflected Prestige segment wants to be publicly associated with the team, and wearing a team's colors and logos directly associates the person with the team.

While the "We Win" and "Reflected Prestige" segments have similar likelihoods to wear team apparel, the individuals who score low on the two key items diverge in terms of avoiding team clothing. The people who rate their agreement with the "We Win" item as a 1 or 2 have a 17% rate of being likely to wear team clothing and a 52% rate of avoiding team clothing. For the "Reflected Prestige" item low scorers, the rates are 25% likely and 44% avoid team clothing. The lower rate of clothing for the low "We Win" segment relative to the low "Reflected Prestige" segment may reflect that people who do not want to identify with groups, do not want to be publicly labeled. The people who do not garner prestige from being associated with groups are less concerned about clothing. A key point of differentiation between the traits may be that "We Win" is about active identification while "Reflected Prestige" is more passive.

The examples of motivations, attitudes, and behaviors from the Next-Generation Fandom Survey illustrate the process of fandom and the value of directly surveying fans. People gain value from belonging to groups, which motivates them to become sports fans. Sports fans then engage in behaviors that reflect their positive feelings toward a team or athlete. In addition to showing the process, the examples are also illustrative of the analysis that are possible, rather than an exhaustive systematic study of fandom motivations, attitudes, and behaviors. For instance, many alternative choices regarding fandom metrics and resulting behaviors could have been made.

5.6 Extensions, Limitations, and Data Integration

The preceding results from the Next-Generation Fandom Survey are intended to demonstrate the use of survey data in fandom analytics. The emphasis is on measuring unobservable motivations and attitudes that fundamentally affect fandom. While many aspects of fandom can be observed, the core of fandom is about feelings and attitudes. Fandom is a relationship, and the strength of the relationship is the strength of the attitude towards the sports entity. The analysis of motivations and attitudes requires direct questioning of fans.

An issue unique to sports fandom surveys is that fandom feelings have both a fairly permanent component and an element that moves based on the day-to-day successes and failure of the fan's team. Measurement of attitudes requires the analyst to make assumptions about the stability of preferences and psychological traits. An attitude towards a team might be a function of whether the team won last night or last season. Sports fandom is often a lifelong passion, but measurements of fandom can vary based on current events. Given that fandom is often extreme and intense, fans may tend to overreact to momentary events like a poor season or the trade of a favorite player.

Fandom survey data also suffers from several common survey data limitations. For example, there may be issues about the direction of causality in relationships between any two survey items. In the preceding material, we make an implicit assumption that fan motivations are fixed psychological traits that influence sports fandom. It is also possible that being a sports fan reinforces different aspects of social identity, and group membership utility may be reinforced through fandom.

Survey responses may also only be correlated with actual behaviors. An individual faced with a question about fandom might choose to answer they are a sports fan because being a fan is something that is common or expected within their communities. However, the person may seldom watch or attend games. There are also standard issues related to surveys and sampling. For instance, relatively few people are interested in answering surveys, so survey samples may be different than non-survey respondents. Survey respondents may tend to be people who are especially interested in the topic of the survey or who are interested in the compensation provided for completing the survey.

These issues are just a partial list of the potential concerns with using survey data. However, the key is that the issues and potential biases are understood and balanced with the unique benefits of survey data. Discussions about survey data should also mention the possibility of integrating primary data from surveys with other types of fan data. For instance, customer transaction and market-level outcome data should be considered in conjunction with surveys and other primary data sources.

Survey data may also be combined with transaction and market-level data, such as television ratings or social media impressions, to provide rich descriptions of the state of fandom. Discrepancies between alternative fandom metrics might motivate additional research and insights. In some circumstances, direct linkage of survey data with transaction data may also be possible. For example, season ticket holders and other ticket purchasers may also be survey respondents for teams. Specifically, season ticket holders may be surveyed about game or season-level satisfaction. Linkage of ticket buyer behaviors such as retention rates, quantities purchased, and ticket prices to survey data can provide insights into the role of fan satisfaction or fans' psychological traits.

5.7 Insights and Connections

Fandom is the product of individual psychological traits and the individual's interactions with sports, media, and other fans. The result of these experiences is deeply felt emotions and connections. Belonging to a fandom is meaningful to how someone thinks about themselves and how they present themselves to the world.

Because fandom involves non-observable attitudes and emotions, fandom analysis needs to be fan-focused and must include direct conversations with fans. Even in an era of big data and sophisticated data science, the survey remains a critical tool for fan analytics. In particular, surveys are the key to understanding the psychological traits that motivate fandom and the attitudinal components of fan-team relationships.

The key insights from this chapter include the following:

* Fandom is a process that begins with psychological motivations related to the value of belonging to groups. These motivations influence the development of fandom attitudes. Fandom attitudes manifest in terms of behaviors like buying tickets, watching games, or wearing apparel.
* Fandom surveys are ideal for collecting unobservable psychological data related to fan attitudes and motivations.
* Understanding differences in motivations may be a useful segmentation approach, as different motivations may result in different types of behaviors.

Consumer traits like loyalty or fandom are challenging for marketers as they are unobservable but drive economically valuable behaviors. However, surveys are imperfect means for assessing these traits as they may suffer from demand effects, extraneous influences, and excessive costs. The issue of any single data type having a mix of benefits and limitations is common in marketing. The solution is to utilize a mix of data types and to be aware of the value and challenges of each data category.

Moving forward in our fandom analytics journey, the next chapter examines the concept and measurement of brand equity in relation to sports fandom. Brand equity is a crucial concept in the marketing world that refers to the economic value a brand produces. Brand equity is related to fandom attitudes because consumer loyalty and willingness to pay is ultimately tied to preference and enthusiasm for a brand (or team). Brand equity is driven by a range of factors such as brand awareness, perceived quality, brand loyalty, and brand associations. These psychological aspects of brand equity play a significant role in influencing consumer behavior and purchase decisions.

Brand equity is intimately related to the measurement of brand attitudes (Keller, 1993). In sports, fandom attitudes reflect the preference and loyalty to a team or athlete and are the primary source of brand equity advantages. The connection between the material in this chapter and the next is that the psychological motivations and attitudes related to fandom are reflected in the marketplace when team and athlete brands create economic value.

References

Blattberg, R. C., & Deighton, J. (1991). Interactive marketing: Exploiting the age of addressability. *Sloan Management Review, 33*(1), 5–15.

Cialdini, R. B., Borden, R. J., Thorne, A., Walker, M. R., Freeman, S., & Sloan, L. R. (1976). Basking in reflected glory: Three (football) field studies. *Journal of Personality and Social Psychology, 34*(3), 366.

Jain, D., & Singh, S. S. (2002). Customer lifetime value research in marketing: A review and future directions. *Journal of Interactive Marketing, 16*(2), 34–46.

Keller, K. L. (1993). Conceptualizing, measuring, and managing customer-based brand equity. *Journal of Marketing, 57*(1), 1–22.

Kumar, V., Leone, R. P., Aaker, D. A., & Day, G. S. (2018). *Marketing research*. John Wiley & Sons.

Lewis, M. (2005). Incorporating strategic consumer behavior into customer valuation. *Journal of Marketing, 69*(4), 230–238.

Lewis, M. (2023). Next generation fandom survey 2023. *Fandomanalytics.com*. Accessed on December 13, 2023 from https://www.fandomanalytics.com/posts/next-generation-fandom-survey-2023

Peppers, D., & Rogers, M. (1993). *The one to one future: Building relationships one customer at a time.* Currency Doubleday.

Weber, S. J., & Cook, T. D. (1972). Subject effects in laboratory research: An examination of subject roles, demand characteristics, and valid inference. *Psychological Bulletin, 77*(4), 273.

6

Fandom Equity

6.1 Economic Value of a Fandom

Fans often have intense, meaningful emotional relationships with their sports teams. Fans care deeply about their favorite teams and often feel like they are a part of the team and experience the team's wins and losses as their own victories and defeats. Fans also often have financial relationships with sports entities; they are willing to devote significant financial resources to attend games and buy team merchandise, and fans also provide an audience that teams and leagues can sell to media and sponsors. The English Premier League (EPL), National Football League (NFL), and National Basketball Association (NBA) are three of the highest revenue sports leagues. In the 2021/2022 season, the EPL generated revenues of £5.5 billion (Buckingham, 2023), the NFL had revenue of $12 billion (Ozanian, 2023) in 2022, while the NBA generated about $10 billion in revenue during the 2021/2022 season (Ozanian & Teitelbaum, 2022).

These leagues can generate massive revenues because they possess massive fandoms. The EPL is headlined by Manchester United, Manchester City, Liverpool, Chelsea, and others. As of November 2023, Manchester

© The Author(s), under exclusive license to Springer Nature Switzerland AG 2024
M. Lewis, *Fandom Analytics*, Business Guides on the Go,
https://doi.org/10.1007/978-3-031-65925-6_6

United had 63.1 million, Manchester City had 49.4 million, Liverpool had 43.6 million, and Chelsea had 41.4 million Instagram followers. The premier brands in the NFL include the New England Patriots with five million, the Dallas Cowboys with 4.7 million, the Pittsburgh Steelers with 3.5 million, and the Green Bay Packers with 2.6 million Instagram followers. The NBA includes the Golden State Warriors, with 32.3 million followers, and the Los Angeles Lakers, with 23.8 million.

The revenues and fandoms of the major sports leagues highlight that these leagues are operated as businesses and that fandom is a monetizable asset. Over time, these teams have developed a form of equity based on the loyalty and passion of their extensive fan communities. More generally, sports fans are consumers, and sports entities may be considered brands. This is a vital insight into the nature of fandom because it clarifies that sports management may employ brand marketing concepts and techniques.

The engagement and interest of fans make fandom an incredibly valuable asset to teams. Fans directly invest substantial time, money, and emotion into their relationships with their favorite sports teams. Fandoms also attract massive sponsorship dollars and media deals to sports organizations. When consumers have significant preferences for and positive attitudes about a brand that results in customer loyalty, decreased price sensitivity, and other positive outcomes, marketers refer to the brand as having high brand equity. The passion for team brands and the resulting behaviors mean that sports organizations possess significant brand equity. Because of the special nature of fandom, we refer to sports organization's brand equity as fandom equity. This chapter discusses the valuation of fandom equity.

6.2 Sports Value Proposition

Sports, like many products, provide value to consumers along multiple dimensions. The core sports product is the game itself, the athletic competition between groups of athletes. However, a fan gets more value from their favorite team they would get from watching talented but unknown athletes engaging in a competition. The additional value largely comes from the aspects of fandom that surround the core sports product. The marketing concept of the value function is helpful for thinking about how fandom provides economic value.

The idea of the value proposition is that products and services consist of a bundle of attributes that benefit a consumer (Payne et al., 2017). The value proposition for Uber would include the availability of getting a ride anytime, the convenience of not having to specify a pickup location, easy cashless payment, and other benefits. The value of using Uber is a combination of these benefits. Uber is generally considered to be a strong brand. It has significant awareness, and its value proposition is well-known. However, while many consumers might enjoy the Uber value proposition, it is unclear if many people would consider themselves Uber fans. Do people describe themselves as Uber users or wear Uber jerseys? We could draw similar parallels with high-profile brands like Apple, Coca-Cola, or Mercedes. Fandom for these brands is possible, but it is far less common than in sports.

Sports and many other cultural organizations provide significant benefits to fans from the community and identity benefits of sports fandom. The sports value proposition includes not just the competition between athletes, but it is the competition between well-known and well-loved teams. The sports product is viewed by fans through the lens of fans' experiences and expectations of their teams. The athletic competition means more because the fan's team is involved and, therefore, so is the fan. Fandom also provides value as a relationship builder that connects families and friends.

The value proposition for sports is a complex multidimensional set of benefits, including the thrilling competitions and the social identity benefits of fandom. Each of these broad categories of benefits could be broken into multiple dimensions. The Penn State fan gets to enjoy watching a winning team but also gets to enjoy the camaraderie of the fandom community. The sports component of a Penn State football game might include getting to see a star quarterback, an exciting running back, and a highly regarded opponent. The fandom aspects might include being in a packed, high-energy stadium, being a group in matching clothes, tailgating in the parking lot, and rehashing the game at a bar with friends.

Conceptually, we can separate the value sports fandom provides to fans into two components. The first component is the quality of the core product. We refer to this aspect as "Performance Value." Performance Value embodies the benefits of generic or unbranded athletic competition. The second component is "Fandom Value." Fandom Value includes the community and identity benefits of being a part of a fan-based group.

The preceding discussion is centered on the value sports provide to fans. However, the separation into a core sports performance component and a social fandom component is useful for defining a sports organization's objective. The organization needs to create a compelling sports product and manage a vibrant fandom. Breaking the user or fan value into components is also helpful for thinking about the value of fandom to a sports organization. From the perspective of the sports organization, the organization's marketplace results can be viewed as a combination of its sports performance (Performance Value) and the value of its brand to fans (Fandom Value) and other factors.

Figure 6.1 is a conceptual equation that defines a sports organization's "Total Value" into three components. In addition to "Performance Value" and "Fandom Value," the equation also includes a component labeled "Marketplace Value." Marketplace Value is included because many sports leagues restrict local competition by allocating exclusive territories to teams. A sports organization's ability to succeed on many marketing metrics is inextricably linked to its local territory, as markets may vary in factors that impact revenue potential, like population and income levels. Markets can also vary in terms of competitive forces, like the number of other leagues or recreational opportunities.

The idea of Fig. 6.1 is that a team's economic success is primarily driven by a combination of (1) the quality of its sports product, (2) the strength of its fandom (brand), and (3) the potential of its local market. The

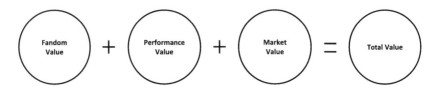

Fig. 6.1 Sports value proposition

strength of the team's brand is the focus of this chapter. Conceptually, the team's brand is the focal point of the team's fandom. The equation in the figure also provides a theoretical basis that can guide empirical measurement of team's fandom equity.

6.3 Fandom Equity

The key concept for analyzing the value of fandom is the idea of brand equity. Fandom fundamentally involves the relationship between a team brand and its fans. Brand equity is the collective economic value of the brand-fan relationships. The economic value of a brand is known as brand equity (Aaker, 1992). A brand's economic value is the incremental value of the branded product relative to an equivalent generic product. In the case of sports, the brand value may be illustrated by considering how much a fan is willing to spend for a game featuring the fan's favorite team playing a rival relative to an athletic competition without the team names, logos, uniforms, and other brand elements.

Brand equity is a foundational concept for marketing practitioners and academics. The American Marketing Association defines brand equity as follows (American Marketing Association, 2023):

* Brand equity is the intangible value a brand holds in the minds of consumers. It represents how well a brand is recognized, perceived, and trusted in the market. A strong brand equity equates to higher customer loyalty and increased market share.

There are many definitions of brand equity, but all relate to the economic value of intangible brand assets. Aaker (1991) provides a detailed description of brand equity that emphasizes a strong brand's key components: brand loyalty, brand awareness, perceived quality, brand associations, and other proprietary brand assets. The definitions of brand equity are useful for explaining the concept and guiding empirical analyses of brand value.

In sports and other entertainment categories, the team or entertainer is the brand in the brand-consumer relationship. As such, the team brand is the focal point for the sports fandom community. The aspects delineated by Aaker are especially relevant in sports. Fan loyalty to a team often dwarfs consumer loyalty to brands. High-equity sports brands have massive awareness in their regions. Manchester United or Real Madrid is known across the globe, while the Los Angeles Lakers and Dallas Cowboys are as well-known as any brand in the United States.

Perceived quality may be less relevant to sports because objective performance measures are readily available. However, perceived quality is still relevant to sports in the form of expectations. Sports fans are often incredibly biased towards their team's chances in any game or upcoming season. In sports, perceived quality might be redefined as expected or perceived future quality.

Brand associations are an essential part of brand equity in sports. Brand associations are consumers' mental connections between a brand and emotions, concepts, experiences, people, and other factors. Because of sports' central role in many people's lives, the range and power of brand associations can be incredibly impactful in sports. Fans' association with teams can be amazingly broad and include memories, family moments, times with friends, exhilarating emotions, civic pride, and more.

Proprietary brand assets include items such as copyrights, trademarks, and patents. In sports, the assets are logos, team colors, mascots, and other items that represent the team brand. These brand assets are again compelling in sports as uniforms, team names, mascots, and logos are the aspects that begin to personify the brand. When fans think about a team, the uniform and logo may be the first thought. These brand assets are often the key elements featured on apparel and merchandise.

The elements of brand equity focus on the non-product or intangible sources of an item' appeal. Brand equity represents the economic value of an offering that is based on intangible brand elements rather than the basic product. For Coca-Cola, brand equity is the brand aspects like the Coke logo, colors, and associations with past experiences and advertising that lead to consumer loyalty or a willingness to pay price premiums relative to a generic cola. In sports, brand equity is critical as a team brand's value is synonymous with its fandom's value. Taking away the brand aspects of a sports product—the team names, uniforms, the league, the traditions, and the fan community—leaves the underlying product almost alien to the branded, fandom-focused sports experience. The brand equity concept is important as it offers guidance for measuring the value of a team's brand or fandom. Given that the value of sports brands may be found in the fan communities or fandoms centered on the team, we subsequently refer to sports-brand equity as "fandom equity."

6.4 Measuring Fandom Equity

Brand equity measurement is challenging because brands are complex, intangible assets whose influence on consumers is usually not easily quantifiable. For instance, it is hard to determine the exact impact of a brand on the consumer's decision-making process since product attributes and brand equity may be inseparable. Additionally, brand equity is influenced by various factors, such as brand awareness, perceived quality, brand loyalty, and brand associations. These factors are difficult to measure accurately, and it is hard to determine the exact contribution of each factor to the overall brand equity. Moreover, brand equity is not a static value; it changes over time due to various firm decisions (e.g., investments in advertising) and external factors (e.g., technical innovations that alter the category).

Marketing researchers have proposed multiple approaches to the empirical measurement of brand equity. These approaches may be based on attitudinal surveys, financial market transactions, or marketplace outcomes. Within each of these categories, there are multiple metrics that may act as proxies for brand equity. For instance, brand preferences and loyalty may be directly assessed via attitudinal surveys. Chapter 5 presented data on the attitude towards various sports. Alternatively, attitudes towards leagues or specific teams could be assessed. Financial market transactions may be useful for measuring brand value when brands are sold. Differences in the sales prices of teams may provide some indication of brand equity if the sales occur in similar markets.

In sports, attitudinal surveys and financial market transactions are challenging. In terms of surveys, the primary issue is that fan surveys are likely to be unduly influenced by teams' current performance. Unlike most product categories, where product quality is stable, in sports, there may be day-to-day swings in preference based on a team's most recent contest. While fandom equity evolves over time, it is unlikely to truly fluctuate meaningfully in the short term. Financial market transactions are less useful for valuing sports brands for several reasons. The most significant is that the number of transactions is fairly small, as teams rarely change ownership. The rarity of financial market transactions also limits generalizability since teams' brands are highly idiosyncratic with unique histories.

Marketplace outcomes are an especially attractive means for measuring brand equity, as metrics like market share and price are determined by consumer preferences. Marketplace metrics are attractive because they are set through countless interactions with the market and consumers. Prices are based on consumer willingness to pay, and market share is based on consumer preferences. For example, price premiums (Aaker, 1996) may reflect differences in perceived value and consumer loyalty. A price premium metric has both positive features and shortcomings. Price premiums directly reflect differences in preference and perceived quality as they reveal the incremental economic sacrifice made for one brand over another. However, a price premium metric may be criticized as lacking a component that reflects the extent of the brand's appeal. A mainstream brand like Coke or McDonald's may charge relatively low prices relative to products marketed as premium soft drinks or fast food. However, Coke and McDonald's are clearly category-leading and extremely valuable brands.

A revenue premium is an especially attractive brand equity measure (Ailawadi et al., 2003). Revenue premiums are useful as they contain information on both willingness to pay and the breadth of consumer demand. Revenue is the product of price and market share, so over (or under) performance on revenue relative to similar products may indicate higher perceived quality, greater awareness, or other factors that drive consumer demand and diminish price sensitivity.

An issue with marketplace outcomes is separating the effects of product versus brand differences on observed price or revenue premiums. For instance, Coke and McDonalds are both examples of brands that have steadily enjoyed marketplace success for many years with products that vary little over time. The lack of variation in quality combined with consistent branding makes it impossible to separate the effects of "performance" and "fan" value for these products. Cola and hamburgers also present challenges since there is no objective measure of quality that can quantify the difference between Coke and Pepsi or McDonald's and Burger King.

A useful property of sports for examining brand equity is that product differences are readily and objectively measured by winning rates. Almost all fandoms will show up when a team is having a great season. Winning is a great driver of fan interest, but winning may vary considerably over time. However, fan preferences are fairly stable, and strong fan bases may consistently turn out even when a team is struggling. Having objective data on team and player quality provides an opportunity to measure the value of team and player brands (Lewis & Yoon, 2018). Objective quality metrics are critical for isolating the fandom component. In the absence of a time-varying and objective measure of quality, it is impossible to separate the effects of team quality from the effects of fandom.

6.5 Measuring Fandom Equity in Major League Baseball

To illustrate the calculation of fandom equity, we use a simplified example from Major League Baseball. Table 6.1 lists MLB teams' market populations, wins, and average home attendance data for the 2019 season. This data set is intentionally limited to illustrate the approach, and 2019 is used as the last full season before COVID-related disruptions. The data includes single measures of market potential, team performance, and consumer demand. Home attendance is selected as the consumer demand outcome. Wins are a measure of performance quality. Population provides a measure of Market Value.

The Total Value equation in Fig. 6.1 says that Total Organizational Value is based on the Market Value, Performance Value, and Fandom Value. The limited data set includes a measure of Total Value (Attendance), Market (Population), and Performance (Wins). The missing element in the formula is Fandom Value. The goal is to determine the impact of this

Table 6.1 Attendance, population, and wins in MLB in 2019

Team name	Home attendance	Population	Wins
Arizona Diamondbacks	26,364	4,574,531	85
Atlanta Braves	32,776	5,710,795	97
Baltimore Orioles	16,347	2,797,407	54
Boston Red Sox	36,106	4,774,321	84
Chicago White Sox	21,442	9,551,031	72
Chicago Cubs	38,208	9,551,031	84
Cincinnati Reds	22,329	2,157,719	75
Cleveland Indians	22,008	2,060,810	93
Colorado Rockies	36,953	2,814,330	71
Detroit Tigers	18,767	4,302,043	47
Houston Astros	35,276	6,656,947	107
Kansas City Royals	18,495	2,087,471	59
LA Angels	37,321	13,340,068	72
LA Dodgers	49,065	13,340,068	106
Miami Marlins	10,016	6,012,331	57
Milwaukee Brewers	36,090	1,575,747	89
Minnesota Twins	28,322	3,524,583	101
NY Yankees	41,827	20,182,305	103
NY Mets	30,531	20,182,305	86
Oakland A's	20,521	4,656,132	97
Philadelphia Phillies	33,671	6,069,875	81
Pittsburgh Pirates	18,412	2,353,045	69
San Diego Padres	29,585	3,299,521	70
Seattle Mariners	22,122	3,733,580	68
San Francisco Giants	33,429	4,656,132	77
St. Louis Cardinals	42,967	2,811,588	91
Tampa Bay Rays	14,734	2,975,225	96
Texas Rangers	26,333	7,102,796	78
Toronto Blue Jays	21,606	6,129,900	67
Washington Nationals	27,898	6,097,684	93

unobservable value of fandom. We refer to this Fandom Value as fandom equity.

The data shows significant variations in outcomes, performance, and market conditions. Average home attendance ranges from about 10,000 per game for the Miami Marlins to over 49,000 for the Los Angeles Dodgers. The metropolitan area population ranges from about 1.5 million for Milwaukee to over 20 million for the New York teams. The Houston Astros led the league with 107 wins, while the Detroit Tigers won only 47 games.

The underlying theory of the Total Value equation is that attendance should be a function of the team's market, performance, and fandom. Equation (6.1) specifies Attendance as a linear function of Population and Wins. Equation (6.1) is formatted as a familiar linear regression equation where the β terms are estimated and ε is an error term.

$$\text{Attendance} = \beta_0 + \beta_{\text{Pop}} * \text{Population} + \beta_{\text{Wins}} * \text{Wins} + \varepsilon \quad (6.1)$$

The equation is designed to create a prediction model that explains the outcome (attendance) in terms of market population and team success. This prediction model does not include the fandom component. The approach can be criticized in several respects. There may be issues such as omitted variables, the linear specification may be inappropriate, and interactions between variables may be relevant (e.g., larger populations may be more responsive to winning). We neglect these types of considerations as our goal is mainly to illustrate the concept of fandom equity measurement. Equation (6.2) shows the estimated equation using the 2019 data. Another possible extension would be to use multiple years of data.

$$\text{Attendance} = 2078 + 0.00057 * \text{Population} + 280.6 * \text{Wins} \quad (6.2)$$

The equation shows that as a population increases by one million people, average per game home attendance grows by 570, and every incremental win is worth 280 attendees. Table 6.2 shows the average home attendance, projected attendance from Eq. (6.2), and how the actual attendance deviates from the forecast. The deviation from the forecast is labeled Over/(Under) performance.

Conceptually, the teams that overperform the forecast have stronger fandoms, while the underperformers have relatively weaker fandoms. The results suggest that teams like the Dodgers, Red Sox, Rockies, and Cardinals have strong fandoms, while the Rays, Athletics, Indians (now Guardians), and Marlins have weaker fandoms. For example, the analysis suggests that the Boston Red Sox's average home attendance is 9811 more fans than an average team playing in a market the size of Boston would

Table 6.2 Actual versus projected attendance in MLB

Team name	Home attendance	Projected attendance	Over/(Under) performance
Arizona Diamondbacks	26,364	26,461	(97)
Atlanta Braves	32,776	30,477	2,299
Baltimore Orioles	16,347	16,749	(402)
Boston Red Sox	36,106	26,295	9,811
Chicago White Sox	21,442	25,652	(4,210)
Chicago Cubs	38,208	29,019	9,189
Cincinnati Reds	22,329	22,277	52
Cleveland Indians	22,008	27,272	(5,264)
Colorado Rockies	36,953	21,529	15,424
Detroit Tigers	18,767	15,643	3,124
Houston Astros	35,276	33,823	1,453
Kansas City Royals	18,495	17,747	748
LA Angels	37,321	27,813	9,508
LA Dodgers	49,065	37,354	11,711
Miami Marlins	10,016	19,424	(9,408)
Milwaukee Brewers	36,090	25,873	10,217
Minnesota Twins	28,322	30,352	(2,030)
NY Yankees	41,827	40,415	1,412
NY Mets	30,531	35,645	(5,114)
Oakland A's	20,521	29,875	(9,354)
Philadelphia Phillies	33,671	26,192	7,479
Pittsburgh Pirates	18,412	20,704	(2,292)
San Diego Padres	29,585	21,525	8,060
Seattle Mariners	22,122	21,211	911
San Francisco Giants	33,429	24,263	9,166
St. Louis Cardinals	42,967	27,140	15,827
Tampa Bay Rays	14,734	28,636	(13,902)
Texas Rangers	26,333	25,939	394
Toronto Blue Jays	21,606	22,298	(692)
Washington Nationals	27,898	29,575	(1,677)

expect. In contrast, the Tampa Bay Rays' per game attendance is 13,902 less than expected. These results have decent face validity even though the model and data are simplified. A key point is that the expectations are developed using a model based on league data. The model shows how fandom works on average in MLB.

6.6 Fandom Equity Alternatives and Limitations

The basic idea of fandom equity analysis is to assess a team's brand performance relative to other teams. A brand's performance can be assessed using various metrics. In the preceding sections, we have briefly mentioned a few marketplace metrics, including price, market share, and revenue. In the MLB example, we used attendance to demonstrate the concept.

These alternative metrics all have benefits and limitations. As noted, a price premium directly represents the added economic value provided by a brand. However, this metric may also be more reflective of value in a small segment than the broader category. Market share premium captures the breadth of a product's appeal, but brands may also achieve market share through low prices rather than brand equity.

There are additional possible metrics that may be beneficial to consider. For instance, social media following and engagement are also correlated with brand equity. Social media following provides a measure of brand awareness and engagement. Importantly, social media fan engagement does not require an economic outlay by fans. In addition, in contrast to other measures like price, attendance, or revenue, the metric is not constrained by stadium sizes or local market factors. A social media following premium may also be a forward-looking metric as social media skews towards younger fans, who may lack the disposable income for regular attendance. Even within the category of social media, the metric may be specialized to emphasize younger fans by examining TikTok following rather than Facebook.

Television ratings and apparel sales are other potential metrics. Television ratings reveal viewing interest but do not require expenditures. The willingness to spend time watching is a key indicator of fandom. However, this measure may be skewed toward casual fandom since no expenditure is required and might be biased toward older fans, who are likelier to have cable television than younger fans.

The best approach to estimating fandom equity is to evaluate a variety of metrics. A revenue premium measure based on home box office revenue is valuable as it examines fans' willingness to attend and spend. The willingness to sacrifice money and time reveals significant fan commitment. However, the revenue premium measure is limited as it is constrained by fixed stadium size and is mostly irrelevant to fandom beyond the local market. Combining a revenue premium metric with a social media premium measure would be a powerful approach as social media performance captures fandom beyond the local market and the casual (and younger) fan.

The discussion of alternative brand equity metrics glosses over a key challenge in the empirical measurement of brand strength. The key challenge in the empirical measurement of brand equity is controlling for product quality. A price, market share, revenue, or social media premium must be evaluated while controlling for product quality. This typically requires an objective and quantified measure of product quality. In most product categories, such a measure does not exist. The issue is especially pronounced in cultural categories. Acting, singing, or comedic talent is impossible to quantify.

In sports, we have objective measures of team quality, but the relationship between fan demand and team quality may not be straightforward. Our example used a simple linear relationship between winning percentage and attendance. This linear assumption may be incorrect as fans may prefer more extreme levels of success. The difference in winning a title versus coming in second may be more impactful than the difference in finishing seventh relative to eighth. A nonlinear specification such as a quadratic term or a step function structure that includes a term for a championship may be more appropriate.

6.7 Insights and Connections

Team and athlete brands are the cornerstones of sports fandom. Fandoms are centered around team brands manned by ever-changing rosters of players, coaches, and executives. Brand equity is critical in most consumer product categories, but brand equity is the dominant asset in sports business. The rosters change, but the fan base roots for whoever wears the uniform. The brand is everything in sports because the brand, team, or player is the consumer's partner in the fan-team (consumer-brand) relationship and the focal point for the fan community.

Given brands' overarching importance in sports, significant attention should be paid to measuring teams' brand assets. There are unique opportunities for measuring brand (fandom) equity in sports and several significant challenges.

- Sports provide an ideal environment for brand equity measurement because product quality is objective and observable.
- A challenge in measuring brand equity in sports is that sports marketplace metrics are frequently imperfect. For example, social media following tends to be downwardly sticky as there is little reason to unfollow a team. In addition, consumer demand metrics such as attendance may be censored by capacity constraints (i.e., we do not know the demand for a team that always sells out tickets).

This chapter leverages earlier material that conceptualized sports organizations as brands that are the collection of shared memories and narratives. Fandom equity analysis is an effort to quantify the value of this body of knowledge and its resulting community. The concept of fandom equity is also related to the material on fan attitudes. Surveys may be used to measure individual attitudes, while the fandom equity empirical analysis uses market-level data.

Moving forward, the notion of the fandom for a team's brand as a valuable economic asset is a core concept that motivates material related to the value of fans and of fandom beyond the organization's specific sport. The next two chapters consider different aspects of the value of fandom. The fandom equity concept focuses on the value of the team brand side of the team-fan relationship. In Chap. 7, the analysis focuses on the fan side of the team-fan relationship and considers fans as economic assets. Chapter 8 considers the value of fandom beyond the core sports category in terms of how fandom may be leveraged to attract sponsorships from brands in non-sports categories.

The notion of fandom equity is also an important conceptualization for the sports analytics side of the organization. While winning is usually the stated goal of sports organizations, the purpose of winning is ultimately to build a large, enthusiastic, and valuable fandom. The connection of the fandom equity concept to sports analytics is critical from an organizational standpoint since winning is what ultimately builds valuable sports fandoms (brands).

References

Aaker, D. A. (1991). *Managing brand equity: Capitalizing on the value of a brand name.* Free Press.

Aaker, D. A. (1992). The value of brand equity. *Journal of Business Strategy, 13*(4), 27–32.

Aaker, D. A. (1996). Measuring brand equity across products and markets. *California Management Review, 38*(3), 102.

Ailawadi, K. L., Lehmann, D. R., & Neslin, S. A. (2003). Revenue premium as an outcome measure of brand equity. *Journal of Marketing, 67*(4), 1–17.

American Marketing Association. (2023). Branding. American Marketing Association. Accessed November 4, 2023, from https://www.ama.org/topics/branding/

Buckingham, P. (2023). Premier league generated. £5.5 billion in 2021-22—More than La Liga and Bundesliga combined. *The Athletic.* Accessed November 7, 2023, from https://theathletic.com/4610513/2023/06/14/premier-league-revenue-football-finance/

Lewis, M., & Yoon, Y. (2018). An empirical examination of the development and impact of star power in Major League Baseball. *Journal of Sports Economics, 19*(2), 155–187.

Ozanian, M. (2023). NFL national revenue was almost 12 billion in 2022. *Forbes.* Accessed November 3, 2023, from https://www.forbes.com/sites/mikeozanian/2023/07/11/nfl-national-revenue-was-almost-12-billion-in-2022/

Ozanian, M., & Teitelbaum, J. (2022). NBA team value 2022: For the first time in two decades, the top spot goes to a franchise that's not the Knicks or Lakers. *Forbes.* Accessed December 13, 2023, from https://www.forbes.com/sites/mikeozanian/2022/10/27/nba-team-values-2022-for-the-first-time-in-two-decades-the-top-spot-goes-to-a-franchise-thats-not-the-knicks-or-lakers/

Payne, A., Frow, P., & Eggert, A. (2017). The customer value proposition: Evolution, development, and application in marketing. *Journal of the Academy of Marketing Science, 45*, 467–489.

7

Fan Lifetime Value

7.1 What is a Fan Worth?

In the year 2000, the average NFL ticket was about $50. If a fan purchased two tickets to each of the team's games, then the fan was worth $100 in revenue for each home game or $800 for the season. If the fan remained a season ticket holder for the next decade and prices stayed constant, the fan would provide $8000 in revenues. If the fan's customer lifetime was extended to 20 years, the revenue contribution would be $16,000, while if the team could upsell the customer to four premium tickets at $100 per seat, the 20-year contribution would be $64,000.

These are noteworthy numbers. If a single customer is worth $64,000 in revenue, there are significant implications for operations and customer service. How much should be spent on service levels, and what should the team be willing to spend to deal with customer complaints? If the customer fails to renew season tickets, how much effort should be spent trying to reacquire the customer? If a fan relationship is worth tens of thousands of dollars, then what are the implications for customer acquisition campaigns?

Our simple example probably also generates all sorts of suggestions and objections. At the top of the list, most sports fans would scoff at the notion that prices would remain constant for two decades. NFL prices have outpaced inflation for many years. The average NFL ticket price in 2019 was slightly more than $104, ranging from about $75 to $150 for an average ticket. The 108% price increase is about double the overall price growth in the United States over the same period. Assuming a constant ticket inflation rate of 4% and a $50 ticket price in 2000, in 20 years, the ticket price will grow to $105 per game, and the customer revenue (again, two tickets per eight-game schedule) is almost $24,000. If we double the ticket price and assume four tickets per game, we start to approach a fan contribution value of almost $100,000 over the two decades.

These simple calculations highlight the economic value of individual fans. The price of tickets, the number of tickets purchased per game, and the length of the ticket-buying relationship all contribute to the long-term value of the individual fan. The calculations are deliberatively elementary to illustrate the point that price, ticket count, and relationship duration multiply to yield substantial revenue contributions.

The calculations might also motivate larger questions about customer economics issues and fandom's power. The example started with an average ticket price in the NFL. However, "average" implies that some teams charge higher and some teams charge lower prices. For instance, the ticket prices may vary significantly across teams within a league. As noted above, the average ticket prices in the NFL ranged from about $75 to $150 per ticket in 2019. The implication is that some teams average fan relationships may be double of other teams. There is also significant variation in retention rates across NFL teams. For example, the league average in the pre-COVID period was around 90% (Meinke, 2022), with the Green Bay Packers having a 99% retention rate and some teams having rates of only about 60% (Ozanian, 2019). Adding retention to the equation quickly leads to even greater disparity in the value of fan relationships.

The range in prices and retention rates suggests that there is considerable variation in the value of fans across teams. There is also significant variation within each team's fan portfolio, as ticket prices can vary by hundreds of dollars within a stadium. The differences in prices and retention rates also highlight the power of fandom since stronger fan-team relationships are likely to lead to diminishing price sensitivity and heightened loyalty (Aaker, 1996).

7.2 Economic Value of Fans

Figure 7.1 specifies the key components of a season ticket buyer's economic value to a team. The figure is built around game ticket purchases. Season ticket holders are also an exemplary example of sports fans as economic assets, as they often generate significant revenues over multiple years. Like many economic assets, the fan relationship needs to be managed if the team wants to maximize the asset value.

The first element of the figure is "ticket prices." Purchasing tickets is the traditional means of generating revenue from fans. An important aspect of ticket prices for customer economics is that within a stadium, there are likely multiple tiers of ticket quality with substantial variance in prices. A premium ticket buyer (i.e., midfield, courtside, etc.) may pay many multiples of a general admission customer's price.

The second element is "buying frequency" which indicates the quantity of purchases. In consumer goods categories, buying frequency is related to usage rate. A loyal soft drink customer might consume several cans daily, while an infrequent buyer might purchase one or two single-serving bottles per month. Sports fans' buying frequency includes two components: the number of games per year and the number of tickets per game. The difference in quantities may be especially significant in a sport like Major League Baseball, where a four-ticket season ticket package (81 games) equals 324 tickets.

Fig. 7.1 Fan Lifetime Value

Knowing the expected prices and quantities is sufficient for calculating the fan's ticket revenue for a season. The NBA fan who buys two tickets for a single game at $20 per ticket is worth $40 in ticket revenue, while the fan who buys two 42-game season ticket packages at $150 per ticket yields $12,600 in revenue. The second fan generates 315 times as much revenue each season.

The third element is the "Fan Lifetime." Some fans may never buy a ticket, while others may purchase for decades. Lengthy fan lifetimes are one of the distinctive elements of sports fandom relative to other fandoms. Considering the potential multi-decade nature of the team-fan relationship is a critical aspect of viewing fans as economic assets. Adopting truly long-term perspectives on fan relationships and marketing strategies may be difficult in an era with frequent managerial turnover and short career tenures. However, if a marketer is tasked with managing the Green Bay Packers or Liverpool F.C. fan base, it is glaringly obvious that many fans will keep their ticket packages for decades. Managing fan relationships that far exceed the manager's expected tenure is an organizational challenge.

Returning to our NBA example, suppose that the expected customer lifetime is ten seasons. Our premium season ticket holder is now worth $126,000 in revenue. Again, there is likely significant variation across a team's fans as some may buy only once or never and others may purchase for decades. An evaluation of the team's customer database would reveal some prospects with zero past revenues and others with hundreds of thousands of dollars of revenue. The simple combination of price, quantity, and lifetime quickly yields an estimate of the fan's long-term value.

The fourth element in Fig. 7.1, "Fan Extras," is included because fans provide value in multiple ways in addition to buying tickets. At the venue, fans purchase concessions and pay for parking in addition to tickets. Outside the stadium, fans can buy merchandise and apparel. However, most critically, fans can be audience members who attract television deals, advertisers, and sponsors.

The "Fan Extras" element is the link from season ticket buyers to the larger portfolio of fans. While season ticket buyers are a vital component of the fan portfolio and may contribute a significant portion of revenues, season ticket buyers may represent a small percentage of fans. A football team selling 60,000 season tickets or a basketball team selling 20,000 tickets may have millions of social media followers and regular TV viewers. Some fans, particularly those out of the local market, may never buy a ticket, but the non-ticket-buying segment of the fan base is still a significant element of a fandom. The millions of fans represent an audience to which an organization can sell access.

7.3 Customer Lifetime Value

Customer lifetime value (CLV) is a primary metric in customer relationship management that represents the economic value a customer brings to a business over the course of their relationship. According to Berger and Nasr (1998), CLV is the total expected contribution attributable to a specific customer over a specified time horizon. CLV is typically calculated by summing the difference between a customer's expected revenues and cost to serve over multiple time periods while adjusting for retention and the time value of money.

CLV is important for organizations to estimate accurately, as it facilitates informed decisions about customer acquisition investments, customer retention, and customer relationship management programs. By understanding the true value of each customer to their business, companies can prioritize the most valuable customers or invest in increasing the value of less valuable customers. The CLV metric helps quantify the value of programs designed to increase customer loyalty, repeat purchases, and referrals. CLV estimates at the segment can also guide investments in customer acquisition programs.

One of the key challenges of estimating CLV is that it can be difficult to predict future customer behavior. However, organizations increasingly possess extensive databases of customer transaction histories that may be used to develop customer acquisition and retention models. For example, organizations may develop models of the relationship between customer acquisition discounts and CLV (Lewis, 2006), or models of the links between price changes and customer retention (Lewis, 2005). Another challenge of estimating CLV is that it can be affected by external factors such as changes in the market, economic conditions, and competition.

Customer lifetime value calculations may range from simple to complex based on the goals of the analysis and the organization's analytics capabilities. Berger and Nasr (1998) provide a review of formulas for calculating CLV that account for myriad factors such as discount rates and inflation. In the most simple terms, customer lifetime value (CLV) can be calculated as the sum of the total revenue generated from a customer over their relationship minus the cost of acquiring and serving that customer. A rudimentary equation for customer lifetime value is given in Eq. (7.1)

$$\text{CLV} = \sum_{t=1}^{N} \text{REV}(t) - \text{CTS}(t) \qquad (7.1)$$

In this equation, CLV stands for customer lifetime value, t indexes time periods, N is the total number of periods, REV(t) is the revenue attributable to the customer in period t, and CTS(t) is the cost to serve a customer in period t. This version of CLV is the sum of the customer's revenue in each period, less the cost to serve the customer in each period. Equation (7.2) adds a retention rate, R, to the calculation. In this specification, retention is constant for each period, so the net percentage of customers retained by period t is R^t.

$$\text{CLV} = \sum_{t=1}^{N} R^t \left(\text{REV}(t) - \text{CTS}(t) \right) \qquad (7.2)$$

Equation (7.2) may be extended to include additional factors, such as a discount rate, to account for the time value of money or inflation. The analysis may also be conducted at different levels, such as for different customer segments. In the context of sports, there are often significant differences in prices paid. Our previous examples have included significant variations in premium versus average prices. However, these examples have likely understated the range in prices which may vary by a factor of fifty within an arena. Different segments may also vary in terms of retention rates and cost to serve a customer. The revenue and cost components could also be extended to include non-ticket aspects of game attendance, like parking fees or concessions.

In Eq. (7.3), the basic CLV equation is rewritten to FLV, for Fan Lifetime Value. This expression, is differentiated from Eq. (7.2) through the inclusion of a term labeled FanExtra(t). The FanExtra(t) term indicates the non-ticket revenue attributable to a fan during season t.

$$\text{FLV} = \sum_{t=1}^{N} R^t \left(\text{REV}(t) - \text{CTS}(t) \right) + \text{FanExtra}(t) \qquad (7.3)$$

The FanExtra component is critical but exceptionally challenging. Customers often have indirect impacts on revenue, such as when a media subscriber has value through advertising. However, in the realm of sports fandom, fans' ancillary and indirect effects may be complex and substantial. Fans may provide value through being a part of an audience through media deals or sponsorships. Incorporating audience value requires significant assumptions related to revenue allocation across customers. Sports fans may also purchase team apparel and collectibles from team-owned and non-team-owned channels. The problem with these purchases is that they are often unobservable.

Fans also have value through community effects. In standard marketing categories, the idea of word of mouth captures the value of consumers recommending a product or service to noncustomers (Berger, 2014). In sports, the role of fans is even more pronounced. Part of the value of being a fan is being a member of a fandom or fan community. Fans help build fan communities that serve to attract and retain additional fans. Victory parades and celebrations across the globe attract hundreds of thousands or millions of fans (Young, 2022). Part of these events' excitement is from the crowd's size and enthusiasm. Fans participating in these events are essentially taking part in a fan acquisition program.

The FanExtra component of FLV is an important aspect of fan valuation but a challenging part that requires frequent assumptions. Much of the extra revenue produced by fans is not directly observable by the team. There are also issues of allocating media rights or sponsorship revenues to individual fans. Because of the complexities of and assumptions required for the "Extra," we drop this component from subsequent equations.

7.4 Fan Retention and Revenue

The basic equations for CLV and FLV in the preceding section include three components: a retention rate, a revenue term, and a cost to serve. In Eqs. (7.1) and (7.2), retention, revenue, and cost are treated as constants. This is a conventional but simplistic approach to customer valuation. In Eq. (7.4), FLV is written with retention, revenue, and cost as functions of variables that are decisions and outcomes of the sports organization. Retention is written as a function of time (t), price (P), and wins (W). Revenue is written as a function of time (t) and price (P).

$$\text{FLV} = \sum_{t=1}^{N} R(t,P,W) * \left(\text{REV}(t,P) - \text{CTS}(t) \right) \quad (7.4)$$

Treating retention and revenue as functions of the organization's pricing policy and sports performance is useful as it explicitly links team decisions and fan behaviors. Season ticket retention is likely driven by the team's pricing decisions and the success of the team. While winning is not fully under the control of the organization, teams' payroll investments are often positively correlated with winning rates (Lewis & Yoon, 20,018; Lewis, 2008).

Treating fan behaviors as functions of organizational decisions and outcomes provides motivation for creating models of retention and winning. For example, fan retention can be modeled using historical data on season ticket renewals. The simplest method for estimating retention would be using the historical average retention rate or a moving average of the recent retention rates. Retention rates may also be modeled using statistical techniques such as linear or logistic regression. These techniques allow for retention to be a function of team decisions and individual fan traits. The added complexity of logistic regression may be warranted since retention rates are bound between zero and one.

Models of retention can conceivably include significant amounts of fan-specific data. Data on winning rates, divisional finish, change in winning rates, number of all-stars, payroll, time as a customer, seating section, pricing, price changes, demographics, distance to the stadium, and many other factors may all influence retention (Lewis, 2005). The inclusion of winning is an important extension for fan valuation as it links team performance to fan behavior. Adding winning to the expression involves some complexity, as future winning is unknown. The analytical challenge is to develop a forecast of winning as a function of payroll investment decisions. This type of linkage is vital as it connects the organization's ultimate goal of building a robust and valuable fandom to its core function of winning games and championships. This is also important as it explicitly connects sports analytics and fandom.

7.5 Fan Base Valuation

Simple Fan Lifetime Value calculations are easy to illustrate, but as models become more complicated, the dimensionality of the equations makes examples cumbersome. The issue is that the calculation has multiple moving pieces: prices may increase over time, retention may decrease with fan tenure, team winning rates may be uncertain, etc. This subsection illustrates several FLV calculations and analysis issues using relatively simple FLV formulas.

FLV projections are a forecast of the expected economic value of an individual fan, and therefore, the calculations should occur at the level of the individual customer. Depending on the data used in the calculations, the level of analysis can range from the average fan to the segment level or to the level of the individual fan. A retention forecast for the population, segment, or individual level will require different levels of data.

For instance, an FLV calculation might use the average retention rate for existing fans. Table 7.1 shows the retention rates and expected revenues for a high retention team (90% retention) relative to a moderate retention team (70% retention). The expected revenue results assume a fixed season ticket price of $10,000, and the analysis uses a five-season time horizon. Notice that the analysis is entirely forward-looking in this example, so the most recent season revenue (year 0) is not included in the FLV estimate.

The calculations indicate that the high retention team has an average 5-year FLV of almost $37,000, while the moderate retention team has an

Table 7.1 Fan Lifetime Value and retention

Year	High retention (90%)	Expected revenue ($10,000/season)	Low retention (70%)	Expected revenue ($10,000/season)
1	90.0%	$9000	70.0%	$7000
2	81.0%	$8100	49.0%	$4900
3	72.9%	$7290	34.3%	$3430
4	65.6%	$6561	24.0%	$2401
5	59.0%	$5905	16.8%	$1681
5-year FLV		$36,856		$19,412

average 5-year FLV of slightly less than $19,500. In this case, a 20% drop in retention rate results in a FLV that is about half of the high-retention team's FLV. Notably, the moderate retention team only retains 16.8% of the original cohort of fans. The low retention team may need to devote additional resources to fan acquisition. For this discussion, we treat revenue as equivalent to profit. The assumption of zero marginal costs to serve a fan is unrealistic, but it simplifies the discussion and does not alter the essential conclusions. We also do not include price increases or a discount factor to account for the time value of money. Again, this simplifies the presentation.

The analysis is straightforward as it only requires the season ticket price and the historical retention rate. The analysis highlights the value of retention and likely motivates questions (and analyses) about the drivers of retention. Why does one team have a retention rate of 90% and the other only 70%? The previous chapter focused on the team brands' side of fandom economics, while the current one examines the fan side. A vital observation is that the team and fans are the two sides of the team-fan relationship. The strength of the team-fan relationship is a product of the complex set of forces that create fandom. The 90% retention team likely has a stronger fan community that is supported by a rich set of stories built through a history of winning.

Rather than comparing teams, the analysis may also be conducted at the segment level for a single team. For instance, a segmentation scheme could be based on ticket price tier. Suppose a team has two ticket tiers: a premium ticket tier with a $10,000 season ticket price and a mid-range tier with a price of $5000 per season. If both segments have an 80% retention rate, then the 5-year FLV for the premium segment is $26,893 compared to $13,446 for the mid-tier segment. However, there is no reason to believe that each segment's retention rate would be the same. Supposing the premium segment has a retention rate of 90%, the premium segment FLV becomes $36,856. If the mid-tier retention rate is 70%, the mid-tier FLV is just $9706. The analysis could also be extended to account for the effects of demographics and other segmentation variables. Perhaps, the retention rate for male premium tier fans is 88%, while the retention rate is 95% for female premium buyers. Incorporating the additional segmentation variable yields an FLV for female premium buyers of $42,982 versus $34,633 for male premium buyers. This type of analysis based on demographics highlights the connection to fan acquisition. The preceding example used a lower retention rate for male fans and yielded a higher value for female fans. However, the missing piece of the fan equity puzzle is the cost of acquiring male and female fans. Perhaps, female premium fans are the most valuable but are exceedingly rare.

The preceding examples highlight the power and potential of FLV analysis. The team can quickly assess the value of different categories of fan relationships. Premium customers from loyal segments are worth several multiples of the FLV of less loyal segments that buy cheaper tickets. The database might also include fans who occasionally buy single tickets that are worth less than a few hundred dollars per season. These FLV estimates might be used to determine retention efforts and to design acquisition experiments. A fan worth tens of thousands of dollars would merit far greater attention than the occasional single-game buyer. The segments could also be profiled in terms of demographics. Perhaps, the most valuable segments are dominated by people who grew up in the market. The team might then tailor acquisition campaigns to emphasize hometown tradition.

The extension to individual-level forecasts of FLV would require more data than the segment-level analysis. Data might include tenure as a buyer, history of ticket buying, age, attendance rate, secondary market sales and purchases, concessions, merchandise, parking pass type, observed demographics, demographics inferred based on address, and other individual data elements. As more data is incorporated, the possibilities for using FLV to target and retain fans increase. Organizations gain the ability to value individual fans precisely and to determine variables for microtargeting efforts.

As a team or firm begins to calculate the value of its fan or customer base, a logical extension is to value the entire fan or customer base. Extending CLV analysis to estimate the value of the firm's entire portfolio of customers is conceptually simple but challenging in practice. In our simple example of 90% versus 70% retention rates in Table 7.1, the 5-year FLVs were $36,856 for the team with 90% season ticket retention and $19,412 for the team with a 70% retention rate. If both teams start with 10,000 season ticket holders, the teams' fan bases will be worth $368 million versus $194 million over the 5-year horizon.

The difference between a 90% and 70% retention rate is probably a function of the organization's fandom (brand) equity and the team's current and expected success. Teams with exceptionally loyal fans may have retention rates of over 90%, regardless of the team's current success. Teams without strong fandoms may see their retention rates closely track winning rates and playoff successes. Retention may also be based on expectations. Tom Brady's decision to join the Tampa Bay Buccaneers resulted in significant demand and increased retention, while his retirement led to price decreases and a spike in cancellations (Kaplan, 2023).

The conversion of FLV to a value of the fan portfolio for the examples of different fan segments is straightforward, as the calculations only require the segment size and the FLV projection for the segment. Calculating the fan portfolio value at the most disaggregated level requires scoring each individual fan and then the summation across the base. However, the summation of existing fan values does not consider future customer acquisition. Blattberg and Deighton (1996) refer to the value of the entire customer portfolio as customer equity. Their conceptualization of customer equity was motivated by a desire to link investments in customer acquisition and retention to overall firm value. The key idea is that investments in acquisition should be based on the long-term value of the customers acquired. This is an interesting notion for sports fandom, as spending to winning a championship may have significantly created fan relationships that last decades.

To value the organization using customer equity-type metrics requires significant assumptions about future customer acquisition. This is also the case in sports. Fan acquisition is a fascinating topic that contains significant challenges. First, fandom acquisition may be a multistage process where people begin as casual fans who follow the team via traditional and social media. Fans may only become season ticket buyers when they reach an age and level of affluence to afford season tickets. Much of this early fandom process may be opaque to teams. Second, evaluating the future prospects of cultural products like sports may be tricky. Similar to how technology trends may alter the future prospects of a product, as the media environment and demographics evolve, the cultural tastes of a society may change.

7.6 Challenges and Extensions

Analyzing a fan base using the customer lifetime value concept is invaluable as it focuses a team's attention on its most important asset, its fans. The fan is the ultimate source of revenue and profits for sports franchises. As such, focusing on the economic value of fans and linking FLV to team performance and marketing actions is a crucial foundation for decision-making. Knowing how winning or price changes operate at the level of the individual fan is enlightening, as the consequences of decisions are revealed by fan outcomes such as retention or ticket tier upgrades. Quantifying the relationship decisions and Fan Lifetime Value is also illuminating as the individual's responses are not obscured by market or league-level noise.

Our examples in this chapter focused on the valuation of season ticket holders. While this is an important fan category, season ticket buyers are just one part of the overall fan portfolio. A team's fan base may include non-season ticket buyers who engage in fan behaviors like buying single-game tickets, watching on television, following on social media, or wearing team apparel. The challenge for non-season ticket buyers is that future revenues are more challenging to measure and predict. In the case of a fan who occasionally buys tickets, a revenue forecasting model is needed to project the expected expenditures in the next season. This model would need to incorporate fan life-cycle changes; rather than predict simple retention, the model would also need a component for predicting changes in ticket buying rates. Incorporating these types of models can greatly increase the complexity of the analysis. For example, suppose there is some probability that the fan becomes a season ticket buyer. This type of fundamental change would likely be correlated with a significant change in retention that would need to be incorporated in a multi-season FLV projection.

Furthermore, fans who do not purchase tickets also have value. Television-watching fans enable teams to negotiate higher local rights fees. Higher television ratings also enable teams to charge higher fees to sponsors for signage that is shown during TV broadcasts. The analysis may be extended to include the value a fan provides as an audience to television or sponsorship exposures. This is a tricky extension as a significant and valuable part of the fandom may never be observed by the team.

Even within the category of season ticket buyers, our analysis is intentionally simplistic. In the 5-year example, we do not consider the possibility that fans alter their behavior over time. In reality, fans may transition from lower-priced seats to more premium seats as they age and income grows. We also did not consider the possibility that a lapsed season ticket buyer could be reacquired (Lewis, 2005). A fuller model of consumer behavior could be used to consider ticket tier, retention, and reacquisition simultaneously. More complete models of the customer life-cycle are possible, but the consequence is that lifetime value calculations quickly become more cumbersome as the analysis becomes probabilistic. For example, an ordered choice model like an ordered logit could be used to model transitions between different seat price tiers. Ordered choice models are an advanced topic, but the basic concept is that these techniques yield probabilities of different outcomes. However, a consequence of an ordered choice model is that the forecasts are probabilities of buying in each tier. This means that the projection for the next season begins with a probability distribution of the fan's ticket quality tier.

Our treatment of Fan Lifetime Value has thus far largely treated the metric as a fixed customer trait. In this conceptualization, FLV is primarily a segmentation variable, and the primary uses are for calibrating segment-level acquisition and retention efforts. Our discussion has also treated the team's marketing policies and payroll investments as fixed. Neither of these assumptions is needed. FLV can also be treated as an objective to be maximized. Treating FLV as an objective is a powerful idea as it acknowledges that the goal of the organization is to maximize the value of its fan base through investments in winning and marketing decisions such as pricing. Treating FLV as a goal may transform how a team thinks about pricing and winning. Rather than setting prices to maximize current season ticket revenue, the menu of ticket prices may be set to maximize the value of fans. Perhaps, some tickets are priced very low to provide an easy point of acquisition, and discounts are offered to re-acquire lapsed season ticket buyers.

Pricing for acquisition or re-acquisition is not a novel idea. The value of thinking about these tactics from an FLV perspective is that a connection is made between managerial decision-making and the value of fan or customer assets. Models developed for retention or ticket package sections may be used to quantify the short-term effects of pricing, promotion, or other marketing decisions. The challenge in viewing FLV as an objective to maximize is that the problem is most appropriately specified as a dynamic optimization problem where managerial decisions like payroll investments and pricing are selected to maximize FLV. Dynamic optimization models would ideally compute the managerial actions that maximize FLV for different customers who vary in terms of tenure as a customer, past prices paid, attendance rates, and all the other factors that drive retention. Lewis (2005) and Khan et al. (2009) provide detailed examples of the use of dynamic optimization to formulate pricing and marketing strategies that maximize CLV for different customer segments. Likewise, including winning rates in an FLV calculation is conceptually a powerful approach to linking athletic performance to fan behaviors.

7.7 Insights and Connections

The value of fandom is related to the value of an organization's fandom assets. The two primary fandom assets are the team's brand and its fan relationships. Fans are the ultimate source of a team's revenues and profits, but fans only spend because of their passion and preference for the team's brand. These two assets are the two sides of the team-fan relationship. Brand (team) and customer (fan) metrics are theoretically equivalent but focused on the opposite sides of the same relationship. Each perspective provides unique benefits and poses challenges.

Focusing on the fan relationship through FLV calculations provides the following benefits:

- A basic equation for Fan Lifetime Value that adds up the financial contribution of ticket-buying fans while considering an average retention rate can be extremely useful for focusing an organization's attention on the economic value of its fan relationships.
- The application of FLV calculations at the individual fan level can provide insights into service recovery or fan reacquisition efforts. Combinations of customer segmentation schemes with FLV estimates can guide fan acquisition investments.
- Enriching the Fan Lifetime Value equation to acknowledge that revenues and retention are a function of team performance and marketing decisions provides an explicit link between team decisions and economic outcomes.
- The preceding linkage of team outcomes to fan value also provides a guide for internal analytics and data collection efforts. Focusing on FLV provides motivation and guidance for creating fan databases that facilitate building revenue and retention models.

Fan Lifetime Value is a valuable metric in terms of decision-making, and the structure of the metric is useful for guiding data collection and customer modeling efforts. Nevertheless, FLV equations and analytics also expose limitations. A fan's economic contributions may be unobservable, and it may be impossible to collect many economically important individual fan behaviors related to social media activity or word-of-mouth activities. Identifying the benefits and limitations of each perspective (brands and customer valuation) highlights the importance of adopting and jointly considering multiple perspectives in fan analytics.

The material related to fandom equity in Chap. 6 is especially relevant to Fan Lifetime Value. A stronger fandom or brand results in significant loyalty and lower price sensitivity. The Fan Lifetime Value equation includes retention rates. This retention rate is the critical linkage between the value of fandom and the importance of winning. The "Fan Extra" component is also a critical, but challenging aspect of fan economics. Fans provide economic value in multiple ways, not just through ticket purchases. Fans provide significant value through their role as audience members. The next chapter focuses on the role of fandom in sponsorship.

Potentially including winning rates in the FLV is an important notion for connecting fandom analytics to sports analytics. The sports analytics function's mission is to improve sports results through better game strategies and player investments. Bringing winning rates or payroll investments into an FLV analysis can change the perspective of an organization by connecting the business and sports objectives.

References

Aaker, D. A. (1996). Measuring brand equity across products and markets. *California Management Review, 38*(3), 102.

Berger, P. D., & Nasr, N. I. (1998). Customer lifetime value: Marketing models and applications. *Journal of Interactive Marketing, 12*(1), 17–30.

Berger, J. (2014). Word of mouth and interpersonal communication: A review and directions for future research. *Journal of Consumer Psychology, 24*(4), 586–607.

Blattberg, R. C., & Deighton, J. (1996). Manage marketing by the customer equity test. *Harvard Business Review, 74*(4), 136–144.

Kaplan, D. (2023). Patriots have NFL's priciest 2023-24 tickets thus far: Buccaneers prices plunge. *The Athletic*. Accessed December 16, 2023, from (2023). https://theathletic.com/4522408/2023/05/16/nfl-average-ticket-prices-2023/

Khan, R., Lewis, M., & Singh, V. (2009). Dynamic customer management and the value of one-to-one marketing. *Marketing Science, 28*(6), 1063–1079.

Lewis, M. (2005). Research note: A dynamic programming approach to customer relationship pricing. *Management Science, 51*(6), 986–994.

Lewis, M. (2006). Customer acquisition promotions and customer asset value. *Journal of Marketing Research, 43*(2), 195–203.

Lewis, M. (2008). Individual team incentives and managing competitive balance in sports leagues: An empirical analysis of Major League Baseball. *Journal of Marketing Research, 45*(5), 535–549.

Lewis, M., & Yoon, Y. (2018). An empirical examination of the development and impact of star power in Major League Baseball. *Journal of Sports Economics, 19*(2), 155–187.

Meinke, K. (2022). The lions had the worst attendance last year. Now their season ticket sales rank among the top ten. *Mlive.com.* Accessed December 14, 2023, from https://www.mlive.com/lions/2022/03/the-lions-ranked-dead-last-in-attendance-last-year-now-their-season-ticket-sales-rank-among-the-top-10.html

Ozanian, M. (2019). The NFL's most and least loyal fans. *Forbes.* Accessed November 2, 2023, from https://www.forbes.com/sites/mikeozanian/2019/07/31/the-nfls-most-and-least-loyal-fans-2019/

Young, R. (2022). Millions of Fans Pack Buenos Aires to Celebrate Argentina's World Cup Win. *yahoo.com.* Accessed November 1, 2023 https://sports.yahoo.com/millions-of-fans-pack-buenos-aires-to-celebrate-argentinas-world-cup-win-210136865.html

8

Sponsorships and Fandom Transference

8.1 Sports Sponsorships

As of fall 2023, The Dallas Cowboys play their games at AT&T stadium, the Los Angeles Lakers play at Crypto.com Arena, and Manchester City FC plays at Etihad Stadium. For a variety of reasons, a telecommunications company, a cryptocurrency exchange, and an airline have all decided to devote millions of dollars or pounds to attach themselves to prominent sports franchises. A look across the NFL also reveals stadium sponsorship deals by automakers (Mercedes), financial services (Lincoln Financial, SoFi), energy (Lucas Oil), consumer products (Gillette), and gambling (Caesars).

The naming of arenas by firms operating in diverse categories highlights something special about sports and sports fandom. Firms in other categories are eager to pay millions to have their brand names associated with sports entities. Throughout the book, we have made repeated references to Formula 1 and Michael Jordan. Formula 1 is an international racing circuit, and Jordan is a retired NBA player, but both are illuminating examples of the power and pervasiveness of sports sponsorships.

Formula 1 is a high-speed racing sport that attracts millions of fans from around the world. With a large and engaged audience, F1 is a natural target for global brands seeking sponsorship opportunities. One of the most prominent sponsorships in F1 is that of Red Bull Racing. The energy drink brand has sponsored the team since 2005, and the partnership has been enormously successful. Red Bull's branding is prominently featured on the team's cars, uniforms, and helmets, and the team has won multiple championships. The Red Bull Racing Car is also adorned with the logos of Oracle (software), Tag Heuer (watches), Mobil (energy), BYBIT (crypto exchange), Hard Rock (hospitality), and other brands.

Another prominent sponsorship in F1 is Mercedes-Benz. The German automaker has been involved in F1 since the 1950s, but the company's Mercedes-AMG Petronas Formula 1 Team sponsorship began in 2010. The Mercedes-AMG Petronas team has also been successful, with the team winning multiple championships during the 2010s. Mercedes sponsorship drives awareness of the Mercedes brand, and the team's success reconfirms Mercedes' status as a performance automaker. In 2023, the Mercedes F1 car also featured logos of Petronas (energy), CrowdStrike (cyber security), Snapdragon (technology), UBS (finance), and other brands.

Michael Jordan is widely considered one of the greatest basketball players of all time, but he may also be the GOAT (greatest of all time) in terms of sponsorship deals. Throughout his career, Jordan has partnered with some of the biggest brands in the world, including McDonalds, Coke, Gatorade, and Hanes. His endorsement deals have been lucrative but also reinforced his status as a cultural icon. Jordan's most high-profile partnership is with Nike. In 1984, Jordan signed a 5-year, $2.5 million deal with the athletic-wear giant. The deal was a gamble for both parties, as Jordan had yet to prove himself as a dominant force in the NBA, and Nike was a relatively new player in the basketball shoe market. However, the collaboration proved to be a massive success. The Air Jordan line of sneakers became a cultural phenomenon, and Jordan's endorsement helped to establish Nike as one of the top athletic-wear brands in the world. Today, the Air Jordan line is still one of the most popular and profitable sneaker lines in the world, and Jordan continues to serve as a brand ambassador for Nike.

NFL stadiums, Michael Jordan, and Red Bull highlight the specialness of sports. Non-sports brands pay millions to associate themselves with NFL franchises, all-star basketball players, and F1 racing teams. The range of brands involved is revealing as sponsoring brands range from luxury automakers to crypto exchanges and mundane consumer products like underwear and hot dogs. Even the example of F1 is interesting. Of the two teams mentioned, Mercedes uses racing to demonstrate technical excellence related to their core product. In contrast, Red Bull uses the excitement of F1 racing to promote its core energy drink product.

8.2 Sports Entities and Sponsoring Brands

Sports arenas feature abundant signage advertising brands; uniforms (and cars) are covered in logos. Teams can have official partnerships across an amazing array of categories. Athletes can serve as endorsers, spokespeople, and brand ambassadors. The intensity and range of sponsorship activity differentiates sports from most categories.

From one perspective, fandom is just an extreme form of customer loyalty. There are consumers who only drink Coca-Cola and others who are willing to wait years to purchase a Tesla. The idea that fandom is just a passionate consumer loyalty is legitimate, but consumer behavior changes in interesting ways as loyalty becomes fandom. It is relatively rare for most brands to have value outside of their standard categories. Coca-Cola is a great brand, but we do not see computer manufacturers or financial services companies pay to be the official computer or bank of Coca-Cola. It is not possible to quantify or precisely define when consumer loyalty becomes fandom, but one of the indicators is that it becomes possible to sell sponsorship rights and monetize the brand in non-related categories.

Sponsorships and brand partnerships are pervasive across sports. The academic literature uses sponsorship as an umbrella term for a firm's financial compensation to targeted entities in exchange for the commercial use of those targets as marketing instruments (Cornwell et al., 2005). The basic idea of a sponsorship is that a firm or brand pays an athlete or team to represent their brand(s). Sponsorships typically target (1) events, (2) organizations, (3) facilities, or 4) individual celebrities. The examples in the previous section are instances of sponsorships targeting organizations (F1 teams), facilities (NFL stadiums), and individuals (Michael Jordan). Event sponsorship is also incredibly prominent. Any viewer of the Olympics (e.g., AirBnB, Toyota, Visa, etc.) or the FIFA World Cup (e.g., Adidas, Coca-Cola, Hyundai-Kia, etc.) is exposed to frequent corporate logos.

The topic of sponsorship can fill an entire book as issues like the selection of sponsors, the design of sponsorships, the structuring of activations, and sponsorship pricing are all rich topics. Our focus is on the relationship between fandom assets and sponsorship activities. Our focus is limited to the psychological processes involved in sponsorships and the challenges in measurement rather than the mechanics of sponsorships.

Figure 8.1 provides a diagram of the workings of sports-brand sponsorships. Sports-brand sponsorships are essentially brand partnerships between a sports entity like a team or athlete and a brand sponsor. These sponsorship patterns (sports entity and brand sponsor) are placed at the left and right of the diagram. Sponsorships work through by a variety of mechanisms related to the team's fandom. The center three circles in the boxed area of the figure are the mechanisms through which sponsorships harness the value of sports' entities fandoms.

The first element of the sports-brand partnership is "Awareness." At a basic level, sports are interesting to other brands because they often attract significant audiences. Tens of thousands of fans may attend games, millions may watch games on television, and social media platforms may reach tens of millions or more. The second element of the partnership is labeled "Associations." Brands seek out sports entities for sponsorships because they want to be connected to the excitement and passion associated with sports teams and athletes. The third element is labeled "Fan Community." Sponsorships have value because teams and athletes have loyal fans that other non-sports brands want to attract. The most successful partnerships are when the sponsoring becomes a part of the fandom subculture.

8 Sponsorships and Fandom Transference

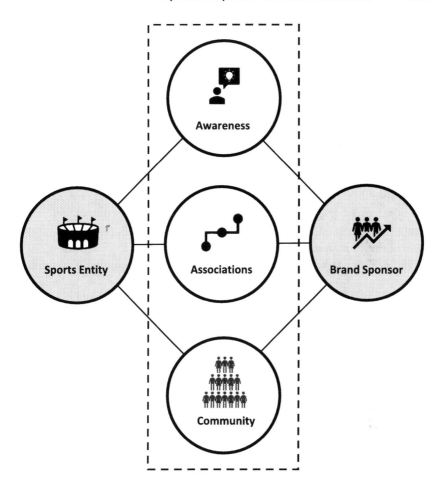

Fig. 8.1 Sports sponsorships routes to influence

The figure does not include directional arrows linking the sports entities and brands. While sponsoring brands are explicitly trying to leverage the fandom of the sports entity, sponsorship partnerships may work in both directions. A stadium naming deal or uniform patch can benefit teams financially, but these deals also affect the team or athlete's brand. Doing a partnership with a brand exposes the team or athlete to how the sponsoring brand is perceived in positive and negative ways.

8.3 Awareness

Sports are integrated into local cultures as sports franchises may have more than a century in a market and are often considered to be an integral part of the local community. The stadium or arena can be a local landmark. Local radio, television, and newspapers cover a team's matches. The players are also local celebrities that are prominently featured in local media. The integration of teams into the local community is so typical that we seldom question why. While people implicitly accept the local sports franchises as part of civic life and local culture, it is a unique position for a profit-oriented business. It is an unusual situation as very few commercial enterprises enjoy the free publicity and attention that is common to major sports franchises.

A consequence of the attention paid to sports franchises is that they provide an opportunity or platform for other brands to reach consumers. Consumers may be drawn to sports entities because they are interested in the game, but they can also be exposed to the teams and athletes simply because of the prominent position and media attention local teams enjoy. For example, consider a stadium naming deal. The value of the deal is largely driven by the number of impressions (views by consumers) created.

In the United States, stadium naming deals have been executed by a wide range of brands, including airlines, automakers, financial services firms, and consumer packaged goods brands. Stadium sponsorships are one of many avenues for reaching consumers, and firms may be choosing to allocate promotion dollars to sports venues versus advertising on cable television, a product placement in a film, working with a social media influencer, or other methods of exposing a brand to consumers. These advertising channels are evaluated based on the number of consumers who are exposed to the brand. The type or segment of consumer is also relevant to the value or cost of advertising.

While the number of consumers watching an advertisement on television is straightforward, sports sponsorships often create more diverse audiences. A stadium naming deal generates impressions with fans attending events. However, the number of impressions per attendee may be complicated. An attendee may see the brand name on the building, and the name of the venue may be included in announcements from the public address system. The brand name may also appear on multiple surfaces in the building. The venue name may appear on physical and digital tickets.

The sponsoring brand may also generate impressions from the physical location of the arena. An arena within the eyesight of a busy interstate may act as a billboard for tens of thousands of commuters daily. Placing a logo on the roof of an arena even displays the brand to airplane passengers. The arena name may also generate impressions through mentions during media coverage. The sponsor's name may be mentioned as a by-product of game coverage by announcers. Venue names will be seen in online searches related to teams or specific games. The Wikipedia pages for major professional teams almost universally include the name and sponsorship details of the team's home venue.

The preceding discussion is meant to be illustrative rather than exhaustive. The key point is that sports franchises occupy a cultural and civic space that attracts attention. Teams can leverage this free attention by selling sponsorship opportunities to interested brands. Teams may also sell in-arena signage, patches on uniforms (or cars in NASCAR or Formula 1), or in-game promotions like character races. For each of these types of sponsorships, part of the value will be based on the count of exposures.

* Awareness is the mechanical part of sponsorships. Sports entities enjoy prominent physical spaces and free media exposure that provides opportunities to expose consumers to sponsoring brands.

8.4 Associations

Sports sponsorships typically involve a non-sports brand paying a sports brand a fee in exchange for using the sports brand in its advertising or having its logo displayed in the sports brand's venue. The hope is that the team's fandom (brand) and fan (customer) equity will benefit the non-sports brand by increasing awareness or transferring some of the team's positive associations to the sponsor. Nike's Air Jordan shoes illustrate the best-case scenario. Michael Jordan adds excitement and credibility to Nike's products and brings his fans to the shoe line.

The second mechanism in Fig. 8.1 for leveraging a sports entity's fandom is labeled as "Associations." A fundamental aspect of sports is that fans often love their teams and have many positive associations. The positive associations with a sports franchise or athlete are intimately related to the stories and narratives. A Formula 1 racing team might have associations of technical excellence, thrilling victories, and off-track glamour. These associations are based on the team's performance and the media coverage of the sport. An NBA team like the Chicago Bulls is associated with a history of championships and Michael Jordan's spectacular playing career.

The potential transfer of desired associations from the sports franchise to the sponsoring brand is a significant part of the logic for sports sponsorships, whether it is a transfer of a general positive feeling or a specific attribute such as excitement or ruggedness (Aaker, 1997). The academic literature has attempted to codify the nature of sports sponsorships by proposing various processes for how sponsorship influences consumers. For example, Porter and Donthu (2008) proposed that sponsorships may create trust through positive attributions of the sponsoring firm's motives. If sports franchises are viewed as a part of the civic culture, then a sponsorship that supports the local team may be viewed as supporting the local community.

Research has also examined the importance of congruency (or fit) between the sponsoring firms and a team because it affects consumer inferences, attitudes, and behavioral intentions (Henderson et al., 2019; Simmons & Becker-Olsen, 2006; Woisetschläger et al., 2017). The Air Jordan sponsorship is a prime example of the importance of congruency. Jordan being a great basketball player is consistent with Air Jordan being a great basketball shoe. The role of congruency is best illustrated using examples of non-congruent partnerships. The Jordan brand is congruent with Nike basketball shoes but would be incongruent with Christian Louboutin high heels.

The celebrity endorsement literature has also emphasized the roles of endorser attractiveness (Kahle & Homer, 1985) and source credibility

(Hovland & Weiss, 1951; Sternthal et al., 1978). Teams and athletes probably enjoy a specific type of attractiveness as athletic excellence is generally aspirational, and sports are viewed as meritocratic. Michael Jordan's success was likely a combination of his bright smile and unparalleled basketball skills.

Sponsorships may provide benefits through a transfer of cultural meaning (McCracken, 1989). This is an important concept for sports sponsorships. Sports play such an integral role in local cultures and social identity that the general transfer of coolness or just an association with the team's or player's cultural meaning is probably the most useful way of thinking about sports sponsorships. Michael Jordan is an expert basketball player with a winning smile, but it is Michael Jordan's larger cultural position that brands wish to be associated with.

However, sponsorship deals are not one-directional relationships. An element of sports sponsorship that merits attention is the transfer of brand perceptions and feelings from the sponsoring brand to the sports entity. In addition to the general issue of congruence, where a non-sports brand may seem to not fit with a sports entity, the more significant issue is when a sponsoring brand becomes controversial.

Nike has been one of the most influential and successful sports sponsors. Nike's Air Jordan partnership is, in some respects, the model for sports-athlete partnerships. However, Nike has not been without controversy. For example, Nike's partnership with Colin Kaepernick has created calls for boycotts by right-wing political figures. Nike's production in and partnerships with China have also created significant controversy. Former NBA player Enes Kanter notably wore shoes adorned with the phrase "modern-day slavery" to protest Nike's relationship with China (Church, 2021). The potential issue for leagues, teams, and athletes is that negative perceptions of a sponsoring brand begin to be associated with the sports organization's brand. Does Michael Jordan or the NBA lose fandom because they become associated with alleged human rights abuses in China?

The story of FTX also highlights the dangers posed by sponsorship relationships. FTX was a cryptocurrency exchange that was founded in 2019 and had grown to more than 1 billion in revenues by 2021. FTX collapsed in November 2022 as a surge of customer withdrawals followed the discovery of improprieties involving the assets held by its affiliated trading firm Alameda Research. The issue for the world of sports was that FTX had significant sponsorship investments, including a stadium naming deal and partnerships with athletes like Tom Brady. In response to the collapse and allegations of illegal activities, the Miami Heat quickly removed the FTX name from their arena (Hur, 2023). Tom Brady found himself the target of lawsuits based on his role as a spokesman for FTX, under the logic that Brady was providing fraudulent financial advice by promoting FTX (Godoy, 2022).

The cases of Nike and FTX illustrate the bidirectional nature of the transference of brand associations. When issues arise that create negative narratives surrounding a sponsor, there is a potential danger that the sports entity will become associated with the negative events. However, while the connection between the sponsor and sports entity makes this a possibility, it appears, in the cases of Nike and FTX, that sponsor scandals often do not impact the fandom equity of sports entities. Fans do not seem to have lost interest in the NBA, and the Miami Heat's reputation does not appear to have been tarnished by the team's relationship with FTX. More research on the topic is needed, but fans do not seem to hold their sports teams and athletes responsible for the scandals of their sponsors.

* Sports entities are attractive for sponsorships because sports tend to possess positive associations such as excitement, achievement, and excellence. Sponsorships are especially powerful if they can transfer a sports entity's brand perceptions to the sponsoring brand.

8.5 Community

The third element of Fig. 8.1 connecting sports entities and sponsoring brands is the fandom community. This point of connection captures the desire of brands to become members of the sports entity's fandom community. Being a part of a fandom community is attractive because fandoms can be extensive. As of December 2023, Manchester United had more than 63.2 million fans on Instagram, Manchester City had 49.6

million, and Chelsea had 41.4 million. As this is a follower count from a single social media site that skews toward Millennials, the true fandoms are likely significantly larger for these clubs. With major sports organizations having fandom communities with tens or hundreds of millions of fans and smaller organizations having thousands of fans, it is advantageous for brands to become members of these communities.

The idea of external brands becoming a part of a fan community is different from the notion of the brand community (Muniz Jr & O'guinn, 2001). In the standard brand community, the brand is the focal point for the community. In sports fandom, the sports organization or athlete is the focal point for the fan community. Sponsorships are increasingly structured to be viewed as partnerships so that the sponsoring brand is part or a member of the fandom community.

Michael Jordan's partnerships with Gatorade and Nike are exemplars of sponsorship campaigns that integrate a brand into a fandom community. Gatorade's 1991 advertising featured Michael Jordan smiling, playing basketball, and drinking Gatorade with background music that included the lyrics "be like Mike." The commercial makes explicit that fans want to aspire to emulate "Mike" in terms of his basketball skills and likable personality. The goal of the ad is also to associate drinking Gatorade with being like Mike. In this way, the advertiser aims to essentially make Gatorade the drink of the Michael Jordan fandom subculture. Jordan's partnership with Nike also highlights the integration of a brand into a fandom community. Air Jordans have become a staple for sneaker collectors and Jordan fans. Nike is the shoe and athletic apparel of Jordan fandom. Wearing Air Jordan's is also "being like Mike."

In the Gatorade and Nike cases, the brands were successful in becoming part of the Jordan fan community. Drinking Gatorade became part of being like Mike and having the latest or coveted pair of Air Jordans granted the fan a level of status in the fandom hierarchy. The Air Jordan line is so successful that it has likely expanded Jordan fandom as new generations of athletes and sneaker collectors are introduced to Michael Jordan through Nike products.

The idea that a brand can become a part of a fandom community is an attempt to leverage a core element of fandom: identification with a team or athlete. In Chap. 5, several psychological traits related to fandom were discussed, including the tendency of fans to intensely identify with sports teams to the degree that they feel as though they win (or lose) when their team wins (or loses). "Being like Mike" is an explicit call to aspire to be like Michael Jordan, drink his preferred sports drinks, and wear his preferred athletic shoes.

- Sports sponsorships can create awareness and transfer associations, but the ultimate success is when the sponsoring product becomes part of the fandom community. If successful, the brand becomes part of the subculture and gains potentially millions of ultra-loyal consumers.

8.6 Analytical Challenges

The analytics of sponsorships is often a challenging endeavor. The challenges often stem from a lack of comprehensive data and clean empirical settings. The sponsorship benefits discussed above, such as exposure of a brand name, the transfer of associations, and the integration into a fandom community, are difficult to measure. These are all effects that are not explicitly measurable from marketplace outcomes. At best, these measures may be assessed via primary research methods such as fan and consumer surveys.

Awareness, associations, and community connections are the mechanisms that lead to successful sponsorships, but the goal of any sponsorship is incremental revenues or profits. The linking of sponsorship activities to revenues and profits is often very difficult. In the next two subsections, two especially challenging aspects of sponsorship evaluation are discussed: (1) data challenges and (2) establishing causality.

8.6.1 Data Challenges

A challenge in evaluating most sponsorships is that there is a lack of a connection between the sponsorship and resulting consumption decisions. This challenge is an issue for both the sponsoring brand and the sports entity. The fundamental issue is that there is often a data gap between the sponsorship and resulting consumer behavior. For example, an airline or automaker sponsoring a team through a stadium naming deal will struggle to connect incremental sales to the sponsorship activities. At the individual customer's level, attributing a purchase or a non-purchase to sponsorship activities may be difficult or impossible.

The challenges of connecting sponsorship activities to individuals are best illustrated by a rare example of a category where it is possible to link sponsorships to consumer behavior. The esports category is an increasingly important part of the global entertainment sector, with revenues projected to be $1.87 billion by 2025 (Gough, 2023). Esports organically grew from video game communities as players sought to compete against one another. As interest in these community gaming tournaments grew, game publishers have created official championships with professional production values and significant prize money. The resulting situation is that the game publishers are the primary sponsors of the esports tournaments. These tournaments are often distributed to viewers via streaming platforms like Twitch.

The unique aspect of sponsored esports tournaments is that it is increasingly possible to link data on exposure to the sponsored tournament to subsequent game engagement: playing and spending. In the purely digital space, the only necessary step is to link the streaming platform username to the gaming username. Jo and Lewis (2024) demonstrate this kind of analysis. The linkage of video game consumption including purchases within the game publishers to viewing activity provides a unique setting for evaluating sponsorships as exposures to the sponsorship and subsequent engagement. The purely digital nature of this category and the sponsored content are unique, at the moment, but this category may be a harbinger of what becomes possible in the future.

8.6.2 Sponsorship Evaluation

In addition to data challenges of linking sponsorship activities to subsequent fan behaviors and spending, sponsorships often create messy data that complicate the identification of the causal effects of sponsorships on fan behaviors. At the level of the individual fan, there is often an issue of self-selection in exposure to a sponsorship (Heckman, 1989). Self-selection is the terminology statistical researchers use to describe situations where subjects "self-select" to receive a treatment. In the case of marketing promotions, self-selection would involve a consumer choosing to be exposed to the promotion. Self-selection is a common occurrence in marketing applications where the goal is to analyze the effect of a specific marketing program because consumers typically choose to participate.

Consider the case of two neighbors. Suppose one neighbor attends a local team's game and is exposed to in-stadium signage for an auto brand. If the fan who attended the game later purchased a car of the advertised brand, we might take this as evidence that the sponsorship worked and at least partially influenced the fan to purchase the car associated with the fan's team. However, such a conclusion might overestimate the impact of the promotion. Fans may be systematically different from non-fans on both observable and unobservable traits. The fan "self-selected" to be exposed to the in-stadium ad by choosing to attend the game. The complexity for the statistical analyst is that the fan is different in terms of both (1) exposure to the in-stadium ad and (2) the trait and experiences of being a fan.

For instance, fans and, in particular, season ticket buyers who are most exposed to sponsorships may have higher incomes. Higher incomes might result in a greater propensity to buy a new car. Unobservable factors may also bias estimates of sponsorship effectiveness. Perhaps, fans who attend games are generally more culturally engaged. This engagement could manifest as a desire to be seen in a new car. In this scenario, the same unobservable underlying trait drives both game attendance and automobile purchases.

At the individual level, the data challenges described above exacerbate the identification of causal effects. In our example of the two neighbors, assuming that somehow data on the auto purchase was linked to season ticket buying, the identification of a causal effect is complicated by omitted variables. Omitted variables might include the fan's demographic data, such as income, the fan's psychological traits, and any information whatsoever about the traits and decisions of the non-attending neighbor.

The analysis of market-level effects is likely the more realistic option when assessing sponsorship effectiveness. When sponsorships begin or if sponsorships have finite durations, then the analysis or effectiveness may be based on a comparison of market results before, during, and after the sponsorship. However, the attribution of changing sales to a promotion may be problematic as other conditions may have changed in the market such as competitor's actions or even general economic conditions. Relatively permanent sponsorships like Michael Jordan's connection to Air Jordan or multi-year stadium naming deals are difficult to evaluate because there is no appropriate data for comparison.

8.7 Insights and Connections

One of the distinguishing features of fandom is that the loyalty to and passion for a sports entity has value beyond the sports category. The key principles related to fandom are related to leveraging the sports property to sell awareness, transfer key associations, and enhance the fandom community.

* Sports are ingrained in popular culture, and therefore, sports properties effectively operate as platforms.
* Sports brands often feature positive associations that can potentially be transferred to sponsors.
* The ideal sponsorships integrate the sponsoring brand into the fandom subculture.

In terms of previous elements of the fandom analytics framework, sports entities have value to non-sports brands because sports fandoms are vibrant subcultures supported by shared stories and strong connections. The shared stories and community and identity benefits that support fandom are what create the ability of sports organizations to monetize associations to their brands.

- The positive associations that a sponsor wants to connect to their brands have their foundation in the stories and narratives associated with sports teams and players.
- Fandoms with stronger communities and identity benefits are potentially the most powerful sponsorship opportunities.

The next element in the fandom analytics framework is to explore the core topic of sports analytics. Building a winning team filled with compelling stars is the vital function that creates the stories that attract and sustain an extraordinary and valuable fandom.

References

Aaker, J. L. (1997). Dimensions of brand personality. *Journal of Marketing Research, 34*(3), 347–356.

Church, B. (2021). Enes Kanter says Nike is "scared to speak against China and wears "modern day slavery" shoes in protest of Uyghur treatment. *CNN*. Accessed January 2, 2024, from https://www.cnn.com/2021/10/26/football/enes-kanter-nike-china-protest-spt-intl/index.html

Cornwell, T. B., Weeks, C. S., & Roy, D. P. (2005). Sponsorship-linked marketing: Opening the black box. *Journal of Advertising, 34*, 21–42.

Godoy, J. (2022). FTX's Bankman-Fried, Tom Brady and other celebrity promoters sued by crypto investors. *Reuters*. Accessed January 2, 2024, from https://www.reuters.com/legal/ftx-founder-bankman-fried-sued-us-court-over-yield-bearing-crypto-accounts-2022-11-16/

Gough, C. (2023). Revenue of the global esports market 2020–2025. *Statista*. Accessed November 2, 2023, from https://www.statista.com/statistics/490522/global-esports-market-revenue/

Heckman, J. J. (1989). Causal inference and nonrandom samples. *Journal of Educational Statistics, 14*(2), 159–168.

Henderson, C. M., Mazodier, M., & Sundar, A. (2019). The color of support: The effect of sponsor–team visual congruence on sponsorship performance. *Journal of Marketing, 83*(3), 50–71.

Hovland, C. I., & Weiss, W. (1951). The influence of source credibility on communication effectiveness. *Public Opinion Quarterly, 15*(4), 635–650.

Hur, K. (2023). NBA's Miami Heat sheds FTX from its arena's name. *CNN*. Accessed January 2, 2024, from https://www.cnn.com/2023/04/04/business/ftx-arena-kaseya/index.html

Jo, W., & Lewis, M. (2024). "Sponsored product-based competition and customer engagement: A study of an Esports competition in the video game industry free content, consumer learning, and voluntary transactions: The effect of Esports viewership on customer expenditures". Working paper.

Kahle, L. R., & Homer, P. M. (1985). Physical attractiveness of the celebrity endorser: A social adaptation perspective. *Journal of Consumer Research, 11*(4), 954–961.

McCracken, G. (1989). Who is the celebrity endorser? Cultural foundations of the endorsement process. *Journal of Consumer Research, 16*(3), 310–321.

Muniz, A. M., Jr., & O'guinn, T. C. (2001). Brand community. *Journal of Consumer Research, 27*(4), 412–432.

Porter, C. E., & Donthu, N. (2008). Cultivating trust and harvesting value in virtual communities. *Management Science, 54*(1), 113–128.

Simmons, C. J., & Becker-Olsen, K. L. (2006). Achieving marketing objectives through social sponsorships. *Journal of Marketing, 70*(4), 154–169.

Sternthal, B., Dholakia, R., & Leavitt, C. (1978). The persuasive effect of source credibility: Tests of cognitive response. *Journal of Consumer Research, 4*(4), 252–260.

Woisetschläger, D. M., Backhaus, C., & Cornwell, T. B. (2017). Inferring corporate motives: How deal characteristics shape sponsorship perceptions. *Journal of Marketing, 81*(5), 121–141.

9

Sports Analytics: Player Evaluations and Game Decisions

9.1 Sports Analytics

Until now, our treatment of fandom analytics has focused on fandom's marketing and consumer aspects. How the stories of sports become the foundation for communities is built around team brands, and how these team brands can be monetized through fan relationships, media rights, and sponsorship deals. Throughout this discussion, we have repeatedly alluded to the importance of winning. The role of winning brings us to the core of fandom analytics: sports analytics. For this topic, we begin with the sport that has been the cradle of modern sports analytics.

For over a century, baseball enthusiasts have been collecting data on various aspects of the game. The availability of substantial amounts of data at the pitch-by-pitch level has allowed baseball to develop a tradition of statistics and analysis. Fans and professionals alike have been fascinated by statistics such as batting average, earned run average, and on-base percentage that quantify player performance. Over time, the collection and analysis of baseball statistics has become increasingly sophisticated, with new metrics being constantly developed and refined. The structure of baseball, where the outcome of every pitch is easily tracked, and the historical interest in the sport have created a rich data environment that has led baseball to be the most data-driven of the major sports. A key aspect of baseball is that outcomes are often quantifiable, allowing decisions to be based on expected probabilities.

Bill James is recognized as the most significant figure in baseball analytics. In the 1970s, James, a baseball writer and statistician, introduced the concept of sabermetrics. Sabermetrics is a statistical approach to baseball that seeks to quantify player performance and value in new and innovative ways. Baseball has long had simple summary statistics, such as batting averages, that provide a measure of each player's rate of hitting safely or earned run average (ERA). James proposed new metrics, such as on-base percentage (OBP) and slugging percentage (SLG), which have since become staples in baseball analytics. These metrics look beyond traditional statistics like batting average and home runs, providing a more comprehensive view of a player's performance. Analytics have since become a crucial tool for teams looking to make informed decisions on player selection, game strategies, and tactics.

Michael Lewis's book Moneyball (Lewis, 2004) popularized sports analytics with the public. *Moneyball* tells the story of how the Oakland Athletics baseball team used data and statistics to build a winning team while operating under financial constraints. The book highlights the innovative approach of general manager Billy Beane, who relied on statistical analysis to identify undervalued players and build a team that could compete with teams with substantially higher payrolls.

Moneyball includes stories of players that illustrate the power and challenges of analytics. Kevin Youkilis is nicknamed the "Greek God of Walks" and becomes an example of the value of on-base percentage (OBP). The insight is that a walk is often just as good as a single, so identifying advanced statistics that include walks can provide a competitive advantage. Scott Kazmir is used as an example of the downside of uncertainty. Kazmir was drafted by the New York Mets as a high school senior. The cautionary insight is that the data available on high school pitchers is insufficient to predict major league success.

A foundational element of baseball analytics is Baseball's Pythagorean Theorem. Baseball's Pythagorean formula is a formula for predicting a

9 Sports Analytics: Player Evaluations and Game Decisions

team's win-loss record based on the runs scored and allowed. The equation is presented in Eq. (9.1).

$$\text{WinPercent} = \frac{\left(\text{Runs Scored}^2\right)}{\left(\text{RunsScored}^2 + \text{Runs Allowed}^2\right)} \quad (9.1)$$

The formula says that a team's winning percentage can be predicted from the relatively simple relationship of runs scored squared divided by the sum of runs scored squared and runs allowed squared. The Pythagorean formula is the starting point for much of baseball analytics as it establishes a relationship between scoring and winning. The Pythagorean formula provides valuable insights into a team's strengths and weaknesses, and it can be a useful tool for making informed decisions about trades, roster moves, and other strategic decisions.

Today, every major league baseball team has a dedicated analytics department, with teams investing heavily in technology and data analysis tools. Teams use data to analyze player performance, identify potential recruits, and develop game strategies. With the advent of new technology like AI and machine learning, baseball analytics is likely to become even more sophisticated and accurate in the future.

While baseball is the leader, sports analytics have become essential to almost all major sports. For example, in soccer, tracking data such as player position, speed, and distance covered has helped coaches and analysts to identify areas where players need to improve. Advanced metrics such as expected goals (xG) and expected assists (xA) are also used to measure player performance and predict future outcomes. With the help of analytics, teams can now make more informed decisions on player recruitment, tactics, and training.

In recent years, basketball analytics has revolutionized the sport, with teams using data to identify strategies to improve team performance. Metrics such as player efficiency rating (PER) and true shooting percentage (TS%) are used to measure player performance. Perhaps, the greatest impact of analytics in basketball has been in shot selection (Ballantine, 2021). Data and analytics have led to a shift towards more three-point shots as data allows for the calculation of the expected value of different types of shots. Analytics allow coaches to make more informed decisions on player rotation, shot selection, and game strategy.

9.2 Sports Analytics and Fandom

Fandom is often a defining personality trait that motivates fans to devote hundreds of hours and thousands of dollars to following a team. The foundations for this devotion are the narratives surrounding the team's past, present, and future. A glorious past, a dominating present, and a hopeful future are the building blocks for a vibrant fan base. Glorious, dominating, and hopeful are all adjectives that would describe a winning team. The powerful relationship between winning and fandom implies that the key to creating an engaged and resilient fandom is to be successful on the field, pitch, or court.

Winning creates fandom, and analytics is increasingly a key to winning.

Figure 9.1 shows a diagram of the relationship between sports decisions and fandom. The figure is reminiscent of the Fandom Analytics Framework presented in Chap. 2 in that "Sports Strategy and Decision" is at the core of the diagram. Figure 9.1 is centered on the consequences of analytics (decisions) and the mechanisms through which sports decisions impact fandom.

The outer elements of Fig. 9.1 are labeled, from the left and moving clockwise, player acquisition, winning, fan acquisition, and fandom (brand) equity. The idea of the figure is that player acquisition is the primary driver of winning and that winning leads to near-term fan acquisition, which is the foundation for fandom (brand) equity. Fandom equity is connected to player acquisition by the logic that players may be attracted to teams with more substantial fandoms. Teams with more fandom equity may be appealing because they can enhance a player's ability to attract sponsorships and grow the player's brand.

The diagram is limited to the key mechanisms, as it could also be argued that sports strategy determines the style of play, which might influence fandom. However, the overwhelmingly critical relationship between sports decisions and fandom is in terms of winning.

9 Sports Analytics: Player Evaluations and Game Decisions

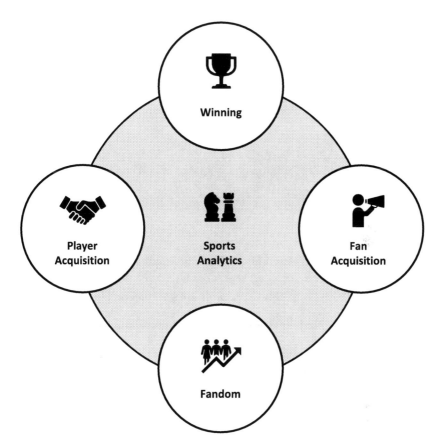

Fig. 9.1 Sports analytics and fandom

The figure includes direct connections between sports decisions and the player acquisition and winning elements. This structure reflects that sports decisions directly affect roster composition and winning rates. The conceptual model is that player acquisition decisions are based on analysis of the player market. The analysis may involve complex statistical models or be based on heuristics and subjective assessments of executives. Sports decisions may affect winning through two paths. First, there is an obvious connection between player quality and team quality. Second, there is also a growing use of analytics to support in-game decision-making.

The topic of sports analytics is big enough to merit one or more stand-alone books. These books could be structured in multiple ways. The coverage could be sports-specific or could be focused on empirical methods. In a single chapter, our goal is to provide a conceptual foundation for thinking about how sports analytics fits into the Fandom Analytics Framework rather than providing a comprehensive overview of sports analytics techniques.

Given this goal, we structure the discussion about sports analytics into two broad categories: player (people) analytics and game (strategy) analytics. Player analytics focuses on the evaluation of personnel or human capital and could fall into the general category of people analytics. Game analytics focuses on decisions related to in-game strategies and tactics.

There is overlap between these two categories, as a team's roster will impact the efficacy of different tactics. For example, a basketball team composed of skilled shooters will be more effective running plays to generate three-point shots than a team built around bigger, powerful players who specialize in rebounding and inside scoring.

9.3 Player (People) Analytics

Almost all organizations are driven by the effectiveness of their talent. People analytics, also known as human resources analytics, is about the use of data analysis to make improved personnel decisions (Leonardi & Contractor, 2018). The relationship between human talent and outcomes is especially pronounced in sports. A famous quote in American college football is: "It's the Jimmys and Joes, not the X's and O's." This quote has been stated in different ways and attributed to multiple coaches (e.g., Barry Switzer, Jimmy Johnson, and others). Despite the fuzzy origins of this quote, the meaning is clear. Talent identification and acquisition have more to do with success than a coach's strategies.

Sports is an interesting setting for people analytics. Sports have more performance data and objective outcomes than many occupations. However, sports also have issues due to the multidimensionality of player activities and disagreements about the subjective importance of these activities. Given that there are often many metrics and multiple player

9 Sports Analytics: Player Evaluations and Game Decisions

positions in different sports, there are endless possible sports analytics projects. Nonetheless, the common theme across almost all player analytics is in determining performance metrics and forecasting performance. Whether the issue is selecting a player in a draft, signing a free agent, or making a trade, the overarching mission of analytics is to provide a quantifiable comparison of different alternative players and projections of the player into the future. As such, the core topics in this section are (1) performance metrics and (2) performance forecasting. A third subsection is included to consider the role of performance metrics in the identification of undervalued players.

9.3.1 Performance Metrics

Sports are filled with statistics. Soccer has goals, assists, tackles, headers, and shots taken. Basketball has points scored, rebounds, assists, and steals. Baseball has batting average and runs batted in (RBIs) for hitters and earned run average and strikeouts for pitchers. These statistics are performance metrics that reveal the productivity or output of players. However, while each of these statistics has value, fans and sports professionals are quick to point out their shortcomings. For example, batting average is a measure of a batter's skill in making contact and successfully getting on base. While getting on base is necessary for scoring runs, batting average is an incomplete measure of a batter's performance. The batting average metric neglects the value of extra-base hits and bases-on-balls (walks).

This incompleteness gets to the heart of the challenges inherent to creating sports performance metrics: players perform multiple tasks and have multiple goals. Baseball hitters want to get on base but also need to move themselves and other runners around the base path to score runs. There are also multiple ways to reach base as base-on-balls (walks) and being hit by a pitch and allow the batter to advance to first base.

Much of the activity in sports analytics revolves around building improved performance metrics that contain more complete measures of a player's contribution. For instance, On-base Plus Slugging (OPS) is a popular metric used in baseball analytics to measure a player's overall offensive performance. The metric combines a player's on-base percentage (OBP) and slugging percentage (SLG) to provide a more comprehensive view of a hitter's effectiveness. The OPS formula is given in Eq. (9.2).

$$OPS = OBP + SLG \qquad (9.2)$$

On-base percentage is calculated as the sum of the player's hits, times hit by pitches, and walks divided by the sum of the player's at-bats, hit by pitch, walks, and sacrifice flies. Slugging percentage is the total number of bases from hits divided by at bats. In this formula, a single counts as one base, a double as two bases, a triple as three bases, and a home run as four bases.

OPS provides advantages relative to batting average as OPS offers a more complete measure of a player's offensive value by including additional data on how frequently a player reaches base and the value of extra-base hits. While there is no direct connection between OPS and the Pythagorean formula's relationship between runs scored and winning percentage, OPS is directly related to a player's contribution to a team's runs scored. A critical point is that OPS provides a single number that can be used to compare players across different positions. Alternatively, the analysts might need to compare multiple metrics like batting average, RBIs, and home runs to compare the offensive output of two players.

However, OPS can also be criticized. The statistic is constructed as the simple sum of on-base percentage (OBP) and slugging (SLG). While OBP is relatively simple to compute, it does involve additional steps relative to a simpler statistic like batting average. OPS is also less interpretable than batting average, which is a simple percentage. A batting average that is 50 percentage points higher means that the hitter gets one additional hit every 20 at bats. An OPS that is 20 points higher has no simple interpretation.

Furthermore, OBP also contains an enormously questionable implicit assumption that OBP and SLG are of equal value to a player's offensive production. This assumption of equal weights is arbitrary and undoubtedly incorrect. The weighting of individual components to create an advanced statistic is a critical aspect of performance metric creation, but weights are almost always based on judgment rather than data. OPS is

9 Sports Analytics: Player Evaluations and Game Decisions

also entirely focused on a player's offensive performance and does not include a player's defensive abilities or liabilities. A more nuanced critic could also complain that the statistic should consider a player's position in a batting order since a player with a stronger batter following might receive different types of pitches than a player followed by a weaker batter.

While baseball has been the center of sports analytics, almost all sports have created performance metrics that attempt to summarize multiple elements of player performance into a summary statistic. For instance, the NFL passer rating statistic measures a quarterback's overall passing performance. It considers four key passing statistics: completion percentage, yards per attempt, touchdown percentage, and interception percentage. These statistics are combined into a single rating that ranges from 0 to 158.3. The range of the statistic is arbitrary as it has no clear relationship with anything resembling the outcome of an NFL game.

The NFL passer rating statistic involves multiple components and is listed in Eq. (9.3). The first component involves completion percentage, which is computed as completions (Comp) divided by pass attempts (ATT). The second component is yards per passing attempt (Yards/ATT). The third component is touchdowns per pass attempt (TD/ATT). The fourth component is interceptions per pass attempt (INT/ATT). The four components are combined into a single value using Eq. (9.3).

$$\text{PassRating} = \left(\frac{\left(\frac{\text{Comp}}{\text{ATT}} - .3\right)*.5 + \left(\frac{\text{Yards}}{\text{ATT}} - 3\right)*.25 + \left(\frac{\text{TD}}{\text{ATT}}\right)*20 + 2.375 - \left(\frac{\text{INT}}{\text{ATT}}*25\right)}{6} \right) *100 \quad (9.3)$$

The first component, completion percentage, captures the accuracy of the passer. The second component, yards per attempt, represents the importance of aggressively moving the ball downfield. The third component, TDs per attempt, accounts for the quarterback's "clutch" ability to complete passes that result in scores. The fourth component, interceptions per attempt, is an adjustment for the negative impact of turnovers. Collectively, the stat combines accuracy, aggressiveness, scoring, and mistakes into a single number.

Equation (9.3) is also notable in terms of the machinations through which the four components are combined. For instance, the completion percentage element is adjusted by subtracting 0.3, and the result is multiplied by 0.5. The other elements are also transformed as they enter the equation. The transformations lack an obvious logic, and the weighting of the components seems arbitrary. The passer rating statistic may also be criticized for being incomplete as the statistic does not control for factors like quarterback scrambling, sacks taken, or receiver performance, such as dropped passes.

The NFL passer rating, like OPS, summarizes a complex athletic position into a single metric that can be used to compare players. The key points from the discussion of the OPS and passer rating statistics include the following:

1. Performance metrics should begin from the premise that player performance is multidimensional.
2. The selection of weights to combine different aspects of player performance often involves arbitrary assumptions.
3. Advanced performance metrics typically involve more data and calculations and are frequently less interpretable. The added complexity of a performance metric should be balanced with the added insights.
4. The goal of performance metrics is to create a single number that can be used to compare players. However, almost all performance metrics can be critiqued as being incomplete.

OPS and the NFL passer rating are performance metrics that combine multiple pieces of information to create an improved summary measure. These metrics have existed for decades and were created in eras that lacked fast computers and easy access to play-by-play data. As statistical software and data have become more available, performance analytics have significantly advanced.

Wins Above Replacement (WAR) is representative of the next generation of advanced analytics. WAR is a baseball statistic that measures a player's overall value to their team in comparison to a replacement-level player (Baumer et al., 2015). It considers a player's offensive and defensive contributions, as well as their position, and calculates how many wins that player is worth to their team above what a replacement player would provide. This statistic has become increasingly popular in recent years as teams use it to make informed decisions on player contracts, trades, and free agency signings. By comparing players across different positions and teams using a single metric, WAR provides a valuable tool for evaluating player performance and value.

Conceptually, WAR is motivated by the idea that underlies Baseball's Pythagorean formula (Eq. 9.1). Baseball players perform multiple defensive and offensive tasks, and these actions create runs for their team or reduce the opposition's scoring. A home run directly adds a run to the player's team, while better fielding (fewer errors, throwing out runners, etc.) incrementally reduces the opponent's runs. A player's net impact on scoring can be translated to wins using the Pythagorean formula. A comparison to the impact of an average or replacement player's impact on wins allows the analyst to measure the Wins Above Replacement.

Measures like WAR and other modern metrics like John Hollinger's player efficiency rating (PER) or ESPN's Quarterback Rating (QBR) are conceptual advancements from previous statistics like the passer rating or On-base Plus Slugging (OPS) as they attempt to capture the true contribution of a player rather than rely on measures that are correlated with overall contribution. However, the richness of these statistics comes with a significant cost as these measures require detailed data and cannot be calculated via a simple formula like OPS or even the more cumbersome NFL passer rating.

9.3.2 Performance Forecasting

Performance metrics provide a convenient means to compare players. A single number like the NFL passer rating may be used to compare quarterbacks with different skill sets, like a quarterback with a powerful arm who is good at throwing deep passes with a quarterback with a lesser range but better accuracy. A metric like WAR may be used to compare baseball players who play different positions by looking at how a defensively oriented short-stop contributes relative to a slugging right fielder. However, these performance metrics are backward-looking, reflecting what the athlete has done in previous seasons. Sports analytics almost always requires a projection of what a player will do in the future. These projections may assume recent past results are a decent estimate of future performance, or a formal forecasting method may be employed.

Forecasting is a vast discipline that employs a multitude of methods. Furthermore, the range of methods is currently expanding as machine learning techniques evolve and reach mainstream practitioners. Rather than discuss different forecasting methods, our intent is to discuss several challenges in performance forecasting that are especially relevant to sports. For the most part, standard statistical models such as linear regression are suitable for forecasting future performance. Linear regression and similar techniques are useful tools for forecasting as they allow the analyst to incorporate explanatory variables such as past performance and to include factors such as player age that change over time.

The starting point for forecasting is selecting the preferred performance metric. Standard regression analysis might be used to predict the next year's results for a metric like points scored (or runs or goals) or an advanced metric like OPS or QBR. The performance metric might be categorical for positions that do not score, such as whether the player becomes a starter or is selected for an all-star game. In these cases, more advanced analytics, such as discrete choice models like an ordered logit, may be appropriate.

The most notable player performance forecasting challenges are related to player life-cycles and transitions. For instance, an amateur draft is a common entry point for talent in American sports leagues. These drafts have historically emphasized collegiate athletes for leagues like the NBA and NFL, while for MLB, high school athletes have also been a primary target. The NBA draft now also includes a significant number of international players.

Projecting the performance of collegiate, high school, or European players as rookies in an American professional league is especially challenging because the level of competition is changing. The issue is that the data available on past performance is not generated playing against professional-level competition. Similar issues exist in international soccer as soccer talent is sourced from the entire globe. Forecasting the performance of a South American player going to MLS or an MLS player moving to the EPL or Bundesliga is difficult as there is relatively limited data on past transitions between specific leagues.

There are no fundamental rules regarding the best way to forecast athletic performance. The data available is different across leagues and player positions. The best guidance is to acknowledge the limitations of forecasting and to emphasize organizational commitment. Given the challenges in forecasting, the most successful organizations will be those that commit to constantly refining models and data.

9.3.3 Undervalued Players

The novel *Moneyball*'s (Lewis, 2004) key message was not primarily about finding better performance metrics or projecting athletic performance into the future. The primary insight was the importance of finding players who are systematically undervalued in the salary market. The Oakland Athletics were a team operating in a small and less affluent market which meant the team faced significant payroll constraints relative to teams in larger markets. As a team with less financial resources, the A's were unable to compete for high-profile, high-priced free agents. The A's needed to find inefficiencies in the salary market to remain competitive.

A paraphrased version of the *Moneyball* story is that baseball salary markets did not appropriately value players who were able to reach base through walks. The narrative was that teams offered salaries based more on well-known measures like batting average rather than the lesser-known statistic of on-base percentage. There is a logic to this type of inefficiency as batting average is a more familiar and celebrated metric. A player who leads the league in batting average, home runs, and runs-batted-in achieves Baseball's Triple Crown. Baseball fans generally know who led the league in batting average but would not know the on-base percentage or base-on-balls leaders. If this heightened attention results in premiums for higher batting averages rather than on-base percentage, then a team can achieve the same production at a lower cost by acquiring players who specialize in walks.

Identifying salary market inefficiencies requires models that use performance metrics to predict (1) team performance and (2) player salaries. This is a challenging proposition as it entails developing models of performance metrics that are clearly related to team success. In our OPS and the NFL passer statistic examples, these metrics logically capture much of the offensive output of baseball players and quarterbacks, respectively. However, these stats are not directly linked to winning. Organizations must decide if they want to analytically link established stats to outcomes such as scoring or winning or if the performance metrics are sufficient measures of contribution to team success. This is an additional issue for creating performance metrics. The suitability of a metric is driven by how it is used in decision-making.

Let us suppose that we are interested in identifying inefficiencies in the quarterback salary market. A rudimentary approach might involve the following three steps.

Step 1:
The first step would be to develop a model that predicts team success in terms of quarterback performance. A potential model might look at the relationship between the team's winning percentage and the components of the passer statistic (Eq. 9.3): completion percentage, yards per attempt, TDs per attempt, and interceptions per attempt. A regression of winning percentage versus the four quarterback data points is only one possible model. Alternative measures of team performance, such as point differential, might be an option for the team performance metric. The statistical model might also include control variables, such as the team's defensive metrics. The output of the model would provide data on which aspects of QB performance are most related to team success.

Step 2:
The second step would involve developing a model of quarterback salaries. This model would also include the QB performance metrics and other control variables such as quarterback age or draft position. These variables would be used as explanatory measures in a model that explains QB salaries. The output of the model would reveal how the salary market

works in terms of what attributes or skills drive market demand. The explanatory variables must be consistent with those used in the team performance model.

Step 3:
The third step involves a comparison of the performance and salary markets. The goal would be to identify disparities between the two models. Hypothetically, we might find that interception rate is strongly (negatively) related to team performance but marginally or insignificantly related to salaries. Perhaps, the salary market is overwhelmingly driven by TD rate, and interceptions are forgiven by General Managers, but games are decided by mistakes (interceptions). The vital theme of *Moneyball* (Lewis, 2004) was that on-base percentage was more valuable to OPS than to the salary market.

The above discussion of NFL quarterbacks is hypothetical and meant to be illustrative of the potential issues. There are multiple challenges in the actual identification of market inefficiencies. The preceding example of an NFL quarterback is distinctive as the quarterback position enormously impacts outcomes. The linkage of a defensive back or offensive lineman's performance to game outcomes is far more tenuous.

The critical point is that the identification of undervalued players requires models of both game outcomes and salary markets. Modeling game outcomes based on individual performance metrics is likely to result in limited model explanatory power and fit (low R Square). Conceptually, the identification of market inefficiencies is straightforward but, in practice, extremely challenging.

9.4 Game (Strategy and Tactics) Analytics

Sports analytics also have significant applications to in-game decision-making. Maybe Jimmy and Joe are more important than game tactics, but making the right substitutions or calling a better play can also impact game outcomes. As data has become more available, it has become increasingly possible to quantify the value of many in-game decisions.

The insight that facilitates the analysis of tactics is that games can be viewed as a sequence of decisions as coaches make substitutions and adjust strategies. Coaching decisions are especially obvious in sports like baseball or football, with explicit pauses between game actions. Every offensive play in American football begins with decisions about the players of the field, the formation, and the play called. A basketball coach might use a time-out to instruct his team to attempt a three-point shot or to intentionally foul.

The impact of coaching decisions is most easily illustrated in baseball for two reasons. First, baseball has a discrete structure with a clear separation between each pitch. This discrete structure allows the analyst to characterize and evaluate the result of each pitcher-hitter interaction. We can observe if a pitch is a strike or a ball or if an at-bat resulted in a hit, walk, or out. Second, baseball has a relatively easy structure to link scoring to a pitcher-batter outcome.

Baseball's discrete structure lends itself to analysis because each at-bat changes the state of a game. In this discussion, the "state" of the game relates to how a specific game may be described. Baseball has a relatively clean structure, but almost all sports games can be described through a few variables. In baseball, each at-bat results in changes to the number of outs or the positions of runners on base. The number of outs either increments or stays the same, and base runners either advance or do not. Suppose a batter comes to the plate with one out and a runner on first base. The description of one out and a player on first is a parsimonious description of the state of the game. If the runner strikes out, there is still a runner at first, but now two out. If the batter hits a single, perhaps the game shifts to runners on first and second with still only one out. These different states of the game are of different value to the offensive team. The offense prefers the game in runners on the first and second base with one out because this is a more valuable state than a runner on the first with two outs. Baseball includes a record of data that makes it possible to value these different states.

In terms of analysis techniques, the most applicable class of models for in-game decisions are Markovian models. Markovian models are a type of mathematical model used to analyze systems that change over time. These models are designed to predict the future states of a system based on its current state and the probabilities of transitioning to different states. Markovian models are particularly useful in situations where a system's behavior is influenced by random and unpredictable events (Ross, 2014). While the terminology may be unfamiliar, the basic concept of a Markov process is straightforward. For example, a common textbook example of a Markov process might be a table of probabilities related to whether it will be sunny or rainy tomorrow based on the weather today. The important idea is that the "system" evolves probabilistically based on its current state.

A Markov Decision Process (MDP) is a mathematical framework used in decision-making processes where outcomes are partly random and partly under the control of a decision-maker (Puterman, 2014). An MDP is a mathematical model that represents decision-making problems as a set of states and actions, with probabilities assigned to each state transition and associated rewards or costs. The model is based on a Markov chain, a sequence of events where the probability of each event depends only on the state of the previous event. MDPs are commonly used in artificial intelligence, operations research, and economics to model dynamic decision-making problems and develop optimal policies.

A classic example of a Markovian Decision Process in baseball is when a team has a runner on first base with no outs, and the manager must decide whether to have the batter attempt a sacrifice bunt or hit away. Sacrifice bunting involves having the batter intentionally hit the ball softly to allow the runner to advance to second base. Hitting away, on the other hand, allows the batter to swing for any type of hit. Analytics allows this binary decision (bunt or hit) to be based on the state of the game at the time of the at-bat and the expected state of the game for each of the two options: (1) bunt or (2) swing away.

The pertinent information for evaluating the choice between bunting or swinging away is the run expectancy table. Table 9.1 provides an example of a run expectancy table. The table is designed to present the expected runs an offensive team will produce in the remainder of an inning based on the state of a game. The "state of the game" is described using two variables: base runners and outs. The rows of the table show the base

Table 9.1 Run expectancy

Base runners\outs	0	1	2
---	0.476	0.254	0.097
1--	0.865	0.508	0.205
-2-	1.073	0.667	0.308
--3	1.272	0.974	0.377
12-	1.435	0.902	0.440
1-3	1.753	1.147	0.500
-23	2.005	1.390	0.548
123	2.367	1.508	0.767

runners' positions. The first row is listed as —. The dashes indicate that there is not a runner on any of the three bases. The second row is listed as 1--. This indicates a runner on first base and no runners on second and third. The final row of the table is 123, indicating that there are runners on first, second, and third bases. The columns of the table show the number of outs in the current inning.

The table entries are the expected number of runs a team will score from that point forward in an inning. For example, the cell value for row — and column 0 is 0.476. This indicates that the expected runs for a team beginning an inning with no base runners and zero outs is 0.476 runs. If the first batter makes it to first base with zero outs, the expected runs for the team grow to 0.865 runs. If the first batter makes an out, the team's expected scoring in the inning drops to 0.254. The numbers are calculated based on the average scoring by teams with games in the specified state.

A sacrifice bunt decision might begin with the game being in a "base runners" state of 1-- and an "outs" state of 0. The analysis could also be done with a starting state of 1 out. The goal of the sacrifice bunt is for the batter to bunt the ball to move the runner to second base while sacrificing (making an out) himself. The baseball manager's decision is based on comparing the expected value of the two options: swinging away or bunting.

In the starting state, the expected value for the team is 0.865 runs (the value in outs column 0 and base runners row 1--). If the sacrifice bunt is successful, the game shifts to state -2- (a runner on second base) and 1 out. The expected scoring from this state forward is 0.667 runs. A comparison of the swinging away expected value (0.865 runs) and the sacrifice bunt expected runs (0.667) suggests that the sacrifice bunt is usually the wrong decision.

In practice, the decision is more complex than the preceding description. We have assumed that sacrifice bunts are always perfectly executed. There is also some probability that a sacrifice bunt results in runners safe at first and second with zero outs. If this is the result, the expected runs for the team jump to 1.435. There is also the possibility that the bunt attempt results in both runners being out. This scenario drops the expected runs to 0.097. Our analysis could also be viewed as simplistic as we do not consider the skill of the batter as a hitter or bunter. Defining a game using only two state variables is clearly a simplification. The question for the analysts is whether adding factors is worth the incremental effort.

The basic structure demonstrated in the sacrifice bunt decision is like many binary decisions across various sports. In American football, the decision to punt or run an offensive play on fourth down should be based on the expected consequences of each decision given the "state of the game." In this case, the state of the game might be defined by where the ball is on the field, the number of yards needed to obtain a first down, and the time left in the half. Basketball teams often are faced with the binary decision of whether to foul at the end of the game. This decision should be based on time remaining and expectations of making free throws. In hockey and soccer, the decision to pull the goalie near the end of the game also has a binary decision (pull or not) and a Markovian transition structure (the probabilities for how the state of the game changes probabilistically).

9.5 Cognitive Biases and Sports Decisions

Analytics has always been at the heart of sports management and fandom. What has changed is the nature of the analysis. Experts may have made sports decisions in past generations using a lifetime of experience playing, coaching, and watching their preferred sport. These executives were supported by a staff of coaches and scouts who also brought years of experience. The "analysis" methodologies may not have utilized statistics and spreadsheets, but analysis still took place.

The history of sports is a record of experts making decisions. Coaches and GMs learn from previous coaches and, through their actions, influence the next generation of players, coaches, and executives; over time, experts making decisions lead to heuristics and rules of thumb like the Parcells' Rules for drafting quarterbacks or the practice of the lefty-righty switches in baseball. Embedded in these types of heuristics is the accumulated knowledge of one or more experts.

The Parcells' rules for drafting quarterbacks are the heuristics former coach Bill Parcells used to screen potential collegiate quarterbacks (Leon, 2010). The rules include criteria related to the player's mental and physical toughness, intelligence, work ethic, demonstrated success, and accuracy. The specific rules include the following:

- Be a 3-year starter.
- Be a senior in college.
- Graduate from college.
- Start 30 games.
- Win 23 games.
- Post a 2–1 touchdown-to-interception ratio.
- Complete at least 60% of passes thrown.

The rules can be used to support decision-making by using them as screening criteria. Players who fail to meet the criteria may be eliminated from the pool or be subject to further evaluation. The rules also have a structure that suggests the creation of variables where satisfying the criterion sets the variable to one and zero otherwise. If this step is performed, the Parcells rules may be used to generate seven binary variables. The rules may then be used as explanatory variables in the analysis of quarterback performance.

In baseball, lefty-righty switches refer to the strategy of substituting a left-handed pitcher for a right-handed pitcher or vice versa. This is done to gain an advantage against the opposing team's lineup, based on the

9 Sports Analytics: Player Evaluations and Game Decisions

belief that there is a meaningful difference in their performance against left-handed or right-handed pitchers. The conventional wisdom is that matchups that have the same-handed pitchers and batters favor the pitcher, while opposite-handed matchups favor the batter. The advisability of such a switch may be evaluated similarly to the sacrifice bunt analysis described above.

Heuristics like the Parcells' Rules, lefty-righty switches, and other heuristics are the product of experience. Experience represents a form of data collection and summarization that occurs naturally and informally at the individual level. As heuristics become accepted and employed by multiple managers or sports executives, almost informal testing occurs, and heuristics represent the "wisdom of the crowd" (Surowiecki, 2005). As data becomes more available, it also becomes feasible to formalize and quantify these types of rules of thumb. Heuristics often contain significant information as they are the product of deep experience and sports expertise. However, heuristics can also lead to suboptimal decision-making because the decision rules are the product of humans and have embedded cognitive biases.

Cognitive biases are systematic errors in thinking that can influence people's decision-making processes. These biases can affect how individuals perceive information, evaluate evidence, and make judgments. Understanding cognitive biases is a critical aspect of sports analytics. Reliance on rules of thumb or heuristics can facilitate decision-making but also lead to suboptimal decisions. The analytics function can improve decisions and outcomes by understanding biases and the factors that influence decision-making.

The academic literature has identified a significant number of cognitive biases. Understanding the range of possible biases is an important skill for sports executives. There is a natural tendency for individuals to rely on experience and rules of thumb as expertise develops. What also needs to be acknowledged is that biases may develop in parallel to expertise because the people's experience and results are idiosyncratic. Even experts with great depth of experience are making inferences based on relatively small sample sizes. Given this reality, an important but appreciated analytics function should be identifying potential cognitive biases.

For example, one cognitive bias applicable to sports is the sunk cost fallacy that leads people to continue investing in an activity or decision based on the resources they have already sunk into it rather than on its current and future value. In other words, people tend to focus on the costs they have already incurred and feel that they must continue to invest in the activity or decision, even if it no longer makes sense to do so. This can lead to inferior decisions and missed opportunities. It is important to recognize the sunk cost fallacy and to make decisions based on the current and future value of an activity or decision rather than on the already invested resources. Using NBA data, Staw and Hoang (1995) illustrated a sports-related application of the sunk cost fallacy. Staw and Hoang hypothesized that General Managers would be biased toward higher-picked players because of the sunk costs of investing in higher draft picks. The conjecture is that decision-makers will show biases in retention and playing time towards players drafted with higher picks than players with similar performance metrics. Staw and Hoang found that teams played higher-picked players more and kept these players longer.

The availability and negativity biases are other cognitive biases that often impact sports decision-making. The availability bias is a cognitive bias that occurs when people make judgments based on the most readily available information (Tversky & Kahneman, 1973). This can lead to overestimating the likelihood of certain events because they are more memorable. In sports, the availability bias might lead decision-makers to select players from schools or regions that have produced recent successful rookies. The availability bias suggests that decision-makers end up making biased decisions because they do not adequately evaluate enough information or overly weigh more recent or more publicized information. The negativity bias is a cognitive bias that causes people to be more sensitive to negative experiences and emotions than positive ones (Rozin & Royzman, 2001). This can lead to a greater focus on negative events and information than positive data. The negativity bias might lead sports executives to overweight negative information relative to positive data. Perhaps, an off-field infraction or injury leads to a greater negative reaction than the positive benefits of an athlete exhibiting exemplary character or an outstanding physical performance.

The sunk cost fallacy, availability, and negativity bias examples highlight the interplay between analytics and decision biases. The availability and negativity biases are possible flaws in decision-making. The negativity bias may or may not exist for certain decision-makers. An important role of analytics is to check for potential biases.

9.6 Insights and Connections

This chapter provides an overview of two key sports analytics themes. The discussion is structured around the analysis of players and in-game tactics. The primary insights from this discussion include the following:

* Sports are sufficiently complex that performance metrics that summarize multiple dimensions are needed to facilitate player comparisons. Performance metrics need to balance the inclusion of additional information with ease of calculation and interpretability.
* Performance metrics are needed as inputs for player forecasting and analyses of salary market inefficiencies.
* In-game analytics often utilize Markovian frameworks that quantify the expected values of options to make tactical decisions.
* Human experts' analyses are prone to suffer from cognitive biases. A prime benefit of statistical analysis is that it may be used to identify human decision-maker's biases.

The connections between sports analytics and the other aspects of the Fandom Analytics Framework are mostly straightforward. Better roster and game strategy decisions lead to winning which creates the stories that provide the foundation for fandom communities. The gap between sports analytics and fandom analytics is that sports analytics are focused on improving winning rates rather than fandom levels. The lack of a direct connection to fandom may seem to be a non-issue, especially to sports purists. However, the reason why a team needs to win is ultimately to develop a valuable fandom. This is a nuanced point as winning is the key driver of fandom, but organizations can benefit from explicitly understanding the core mission of a sports franchise.

Existing research has tended to relate winning to current attendance (Kim et al., 2019). The issue with analyzing the relationship between winning and attendance is that fandom is more complex than attendance. To fully understand the causal impact of winning on fandom, it is necessary to examine how different levels (championships versus regular season winning percentages) and patterns of winning (sequences of success versus periods of failure) affect the key fandom assets: team brands (fandom equity) and fan relationships (fan lifetime value).

Winning leads to fandom, but it may be challenging to crack the code of the relationship between winning and fandom. Teams do not need to win in every season and fans may even be enthusiastic about rebuilding processes. The relationship between winning and fandom is unlikely to be linear, and the occasional amazing season may have more impact than being consistently above average. The impact of winning may also degrade over time, like a stock of advertising. The effects of winning may also be heterogeneous across markets. The payoff from winning a championship in a larger market with competitive teams in other sports may be different than a small market team winning a title. The relationship between patterns of winning is a massively under-researched topic.

The complexity in analyzing the long-term effects of winning on fandom is that sample sizes quickly become very small (e.g., most leagues generate 30 or so data points each season). The ideal approach to understanding the impact of winning on fandom is to exploit granular, fan-level data as described in the chapter on Fan Lifetime Value. Fan relationships produce amazingly detailed data histories. Teams can potentially measure a variety of metrics such as renewal rates, prices paid, attendance rates, reselling activity, merchandise purchases, and other measures that are correlated with fan relationship strength.

The field of sports analytics also contains lessons for other cultural categories. The possibilities provided by sports analytics should be illuminating for other marketers since the link between quality and fan interest is so pronounced in sports. The general lesson of building brands by improving products should not be lost on other cultural institutions and consumer marketers. We return to the topic of fandom beyond sports in Chap. 12.

References

Ballantine, P. (2021). How has analytics changed shot selection? Accessed January 6, 2024, from https://usustatesman.com/column-how-has-analytics-changed-shot-selection/

Baumer, B. S., Jensen, S. T., & Matthews, G. J. (2015). openWAR: An open source system for evaluating overall player performance in major league baseball. *Journal of Quantitative Analysis in Sports, 11*(2), 69–84.

Kim, Y., Magnusen, M., Kim, M., & Lee, H. W. (2019). Meta-analytic review of sport consumption: Factors affecting attendance to sporting events. *Sport Marketing Quarterly, 28*(3), 117–134.

Leon, D. (2010). The tuna formula: how to choose a quarterback the right way! *The Bleacher Report*. Accessed December 21, 2023, from https://bleacherreport.com/articles/382371-the-tuna-formula-how-to-chose-a-quarterback-the-right-way

Leonardi, P., & Contractor, N. (2018). Better people analytics. *Harvard Business Review, 96*(6), 70–81.

Lewis, M. (2004). *Moneyball: The art of winning an unfair game*. WW Norton & Company.

Puterman, M. L. (2014). *Markov decision processes: Discrete stochastic dynamic programming*. Wiley.

Ross, S. (2014). *Introduction to probability models*. Academic press.

Rozin, P., & Royzman, E. B. (2001). Negativity bias, negativity dominance, and contagion. *Personality and Social Psychology Review, 5*(4), 296–320.

Staw, B. M., & Hoang, H. (1995). Sunk costs in the NBA: Why draft order affects playing time and survival in professional basketball. *Administrative Science Quarterly, 40*, 474–494.

Surowiecki, J. (2005). *The wisdom of crowds*. Anchor.

Tversky, A., & Kahneman, D. (1973). Availability: A heuristic for judging frequency and probability. *Cognitive Psychology, 5*(2), 207–232.

10

Sports Analytics: Leagues, Teams, Players, and Fans

10.1 Winners and Losers

As of 2024, Manchester City is the dominant EPL team, having won five of the last six league titles (Grez, 2023). In Formula 1, two teams have dominated in the recent past. Mercedes won eight consecutive Formula 1 Constructor's Championships from 2014 to 2021, while Red Bull won from 2010 to 2013, 2022, and 2023. Tom Brady and the New England Patriots won six Super Bowls from 2002 to 2019. Michael Jordan's Chicago Bulls of the 1990s won NBA championships in six of 8 years. These types of teams and athletes most easily come to mind when fans think of sports. The championships are the shared moments and stories that support robust fandoms.

These dominant sports performances also result in the key figures transcending sports and becoming celebrities. Highly successful teams and athletes are featured in the media and discussed in public and private discourse. Manchester City was featured in the Apple TV program Ted Lasso (Lawrence et al., 2020–2023). The Mercedes and Red Bull racing teams and their key drivers Lewis Hamilton and Max Verstappen are central figures in Netflix's *Drive to Survive* (Gay-Rees & Martin, 2019-present).

Michael Jordan's exploits have garnered worldwide attention since the 1990s and continued through properties like *The Last Dance* documentary (Hehir, 2020) through the 2020s. Tom Brady's Super Bowl championships were often watched by more than 100 million Americans, and his marriage and divorce have made him a celebrity outside of sports.

But what about the teams that do not win?

As of 2024, the Haas Racing team had never won an individual race since its founding in 2016 and its best Constructor's Cup finish was a fifth-place finish in 2018. Norwich City FC has been relegated from the EPL six times. As of 2024, a dozen NFL, ten NBA, and five MLB teams have never won a championship. How do these teams develop or maintain a fandom? And what are the consequences for the leagues when some teams are chronically uncompetitive?

An important observation is that Manchester City, Mercedes Racing, Red Bull Racing, the Patriots, and the Bulls do not operate independently. Manchester City belongs to the EPL. The Mercedes AMG Petronas and Red Bull Racing Teams belong to Formula 1. The New England Patriots belong to the NFL. The Chicago Bulls are an NBA franchise. The EPL, Formula 1, the NFL, and the NBA are all different leagues with different rules for how teams compete. Yet, they all share some similarities as they are in the business of selling competition, and their product is the joint production of winners and losers.

It is often invisible to fans, but each league's rules play a critical role in determining which teams win and the overall level of competitiveness. The talents of Lewis Hamilton, Max Verstappen, and Michael Jordan are readily apparent, but how did they end up with Mercedes, Red Bull, and the Chicago Bulls? The lack of a spending cap in Formula 1 allowed the big-budget Mercedes team to dominate for years and the financially well-resourced Red Bull team to sign Verstappen. The rules for the NBA draft allowed a poorly performing Chicago Bulls team to acquire Michael Jordan.

Teams can use analytics to select players and tactics that maximize their fandom. However, leagues are made up of collections of teams, each trying to win championships and build fandoms. Leagues have different incentives, as the goal is to maximize the shared fandom of the collective teams. This chapter discusses the relationship between league structure and overall fandom. This discussion is focused on how organizational structures and competitive rules create incentives for teams and athletes that impact a league's ability to acquire and retain fans.

10.2 League Organization

The previous chapter focused on the application of analytical techniques to improve team performance. The logic for creating models and analytics to improve player selection and in-game outcomes is that winning creates the stories that are the foundation for a team's fandom. Player selection and in-game analytics are about designing teams that create content that attracts fans. In this chapter, we shift attention to how the design of a league impacts a league's and its member teams' fandoms.

Leagues and sports organizations typically negotiate sets of rules that govern the economic incentives of competition. Formula 1's rules and regulations regarding mechanical specifications and budgets are determined through its FIA governing body. Major professional US leagues periodically negotiate Collective Bargaining Agreements (CBAs) between teams and players. These CBAs primarily focus on the rules that impact the allocation of revenues between teams and players. However, since almost everything from playoff structure to free agency rules influences player workload and compensation, almost all fan-visible aspects of league structure are relevant to CBAs.

Figure 10.1 shows a simplified process through which league rules affect fans. The left side of the diagram represents the negotiations between the key stakeholders in a sports league. These negotiations often occur between player organizations and representatives of team owners. Negotiations may be complicated and may also occur within player and

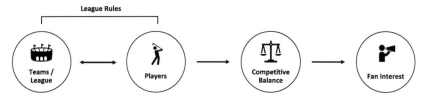

Fig. 10.1   League rules and fan interest process

ownership groups. There may be internal negotiations within these groups as different types of players (veterans versus rookies) and owners (big market versus small market) face different incentives. Negotiated rules related to league operations may create economic incentives for teams to invest, or not invest, in payroll and for players to change or stay with teams. Understanding the consequences of player and team incentives created through league rules is the primary goal of this chapter.

As teams and players make decisions that optimize their payoffs, downstream effects may impact fandom. The bar above the Teams/Leagues and Players icons in Fig. 10.1 is labeled "League Rules." These rules or agreements are the result of negotiations between the primary stakeholders and may govern issues like the amounts that can be spent on players (or cars in F1), rules for player movement like drafts and free agency, and the sharing of revenues across clubs.

The next part of the diagram is labeled "Competitive Balance." Competitive balance is the term for the level of competitiveness across a league. Competitiveness is essential to a sports league, as sports are fundamentally about fair contests between worthy adversaries. However, while the games themselves require an even playing field for competitors, economic realities often lead to systematic advantages between clubs. In particular, teams with greater financial resources may be able to outspend their competitive rivals consistently. When economic realities create systematic differences in team quality, there is the potential for leagues to become chronically unbalanced, with some teams that are consistent winners and other clubs that regularly struggle.

The final element of Fig. 10.1 is "Fan Interest." The level of competitiveness within a league is commonly believed to impact fan enjoyment. Sports will always have a unique competitive structure as individual teams can maximize their returns by consistently winning, but dominance by one or a few teams may erode overall fandom if chronically unsuccessful teams become unviable for lack of fans.

The purpose of this chapter is to analyze the economic incentives and likely consequences of different types of league rules and structures. Our goal is to conjecture about how resulting behaviors by players and teams will impact leagues' fan appeal. An essential point about most league negotiations is that while several key stakeholders are included, the fan is never explicitly represented. Fan interest may be partially represented by teams and leagues interested in maintaining the value of their brands (fandom equity), but fan interest can often be lost in negotiations focused on maximizing and splitting current revenues.

10.3 Competitive Balance

The "uncertainty of outcome hypothesis" (Rottenberg, 1956) conjectures that fans prefer competitive contests with uncertain outcomes. The idea is that fans prefer for games to be even or competitive matchups. The logic is that sports are exciting because the outcomes are unknown, and matchups between equals should be more suspenseful. A common metric for assessing competitive balance levels is a sports league's standard deviation or dispersion of winning percentages (Doria & Nalebuff, 2021). This metric is minimized when a league reaches perfect parity, defined as all teams winning half their games. The metric increases with more disparity in winning rates. The dispersion of winning rates is an intuitive measure of competitive balance because the number grows as the league becomes less balanced. However, in practice, assessing competitive balance, generally, and the dispersion metric, in particular, involves several complexities.

The first issue with the dispersion of winning rates as a measure of competitive balance is that there is no obvious ideal point. In the classic sports entertainment rivalry between the Harlem Globetrotters and Washington Generals, the Globetrotters are estimated to have lost only between three and six times in more than 16,000 contests (Whitley, 2015). While the Globetrotter-Generals rivalry lacks drama in terms of game outcomes, the rivalry endured and sold tickets for decades. While the Globetrotters-Generals rivalry is better characterized as occurring in sports entertainment rather than sports, in traditional sports, fans may also become less interested when teams are too evenly matched. A league with all teams winning half their games might be perceived as lacking greatness and being composed of mediocre teams.

The second issue is whether the dispersion of winning rates is a sufficient measure of competitive balance. Perhaps, winning percentage dispersion mainly captures regular season balance, while fans are primarily interested in championships. The Hirfindahl-Hirschman Index (HHI) has been proposed as a metric for championships or other measures of success (Owen et al., 2007). Hirfindahl-Hirschman indexes are commonly accepted measures of industry concentration and may be used to assess an industry's competitiveness. The basic calculations of the index involve summing up the squared "shares" of the industry participants. Suppose an industry has two participants. In case A, one firm has a 90% market share, while the other has 10%. In case B, both firms have 50% shares. In case A, the HHI is computed as $0.9 \times 0.9 + 0.1 \times 0.1 = 0.82$. In case B, the HHI is computed as $0.5 \times 0.5 + 0.5 \times 0.5 = 0.5$. The lower HHI indicates less concentration and, therefore, more balance. The example is given in terms of market share, but the translation to championships is direct.

For sports, a league with a lower HHI would indicate that more teams win championships, while a higher HHI indicates that relatively few teams dominate championships. For example, in the last ten seasons of F1 ending in 2023, Red Bull won 30% of the titles, and Mercedes won 70%. The HHI for F1 over the last decade is $0.7 \times 0.7 + 0.3 \times 0.3 = 0.58$. If ten separate teams had each won a single championship, the HHI would be $(0.1 \times 0.1) \times 10 = 1$. Again, an issue with HHI is that there is no obvious ideal level of concentration (of championships). Whether it is better for championships to be evenly distributed across teams or if some concentration is preferred by fans is an unanswered empirical question.

Sports economists have devoted significant attention to studying competitive balance levels (Fort & Maxcy, 2003), but no consensus on optimal balance has emerged. The fundamental issue is that summary measures of competitive balance exclude the richness of the sports stories or drama that leads sports to be a special category. Intuitively, we know that fans need to have both positive associations from the past and hope for the future. Since positive memories of the past usually come from past victories and hope for the future is about impending winning, measures of balance are relevant to the long-term health of fan bases across the league. However, single or multiple summary statistics are unlikely to be sufficiently rich descriptions to capture the nuances of the competitive environment.

For instance, many leagues have historically dominant teams. Manchester City and Manchester United in the EPL, the Los Angeles Lakers in the NBA, the New York Yankees in MLB, Alabama collegiate football, and Duke in collegiate basketball are some of the most storied teams in their leagues. Fans may prefer a league where the dominant team wins titles at an above-average rate and where there is a mix of good and bad teams rather than parity. Furthermore, while teams that lose consistently are unlikely to create the wealth of stories and narratives of iconic teams, even consistent losers can generate fan-building narratives from the occasional special season.

The impact of competitive balance on fan interest is probably unquantifiable. Fandom is about the stories and narratives that fans associate with their teams. Other teams feature in these tales and each season is a story. A dominant team can play the role of the imposing villain in a team's underdog story. Batman needs the Joker, and David needs Goliath. Sometimes, it is not just winning; it is who you beat. American collegiate sports have a tradition of fans rushing the court or field when teams upset a dominant team like Duke or Alabama. Nondominant teams have supported this tradition as something that creates fandom unity and a great visual (Li, 2024). The complexity and importance of narratives within sports competitions means that competitive balance is something to be monitored and understood but not something that can be optimized. The best way to view competitive balance levels is as a contributor to the stories of each team's fandom.

10.4 Interventions

Competitive balance undoubtedly matters, but in a complex manner. Fans need to have hope, but sports also benefit from having the ingredients of a great dramatic story, like courageous underdogs, unbeatable villains, and seemingly insurmountable challenges. If hope drives fan interest, a policy that creates more balance may be beneficial. However, if drama is more critical, a league might favor policies that result in less balance.

There are many aspects of league design that may affect fandom, such as length of season, playoff structure, the number and location of teams, or rules like three-point shots in basketball or pitch clocks in baseball. Our focus in this section is limited to rules that affect the economic decisions of players and teams. This section discusses how (1) amateur drafts, (2) free agency, (3) salary caps, (4) revenue sharing, and (5) relegation influence competition between teams. Our approach is to provide a conceptual discussion of how each intervention may alter competitive balance by changing the economic incentives of teams and players. These incentives are critical to fandom because teams' decisions about payrolls and how aggressively they compete have direct consequences for the sports product presented to fans.

10.4.1 Amateur Drafts

One of the first policies that any sports league requires are rules that govern player acquisition. The primary entry point for players in American professional sports is amateur drafts (Massey & Thaler, 2013). These drafts include multiple design elements, such as the rules for entry into the draft, the number of rounds, and, critically, the rules that establish the draft order for the league's teams. Drafts are challenging enterprises for teams as they are asked to evaluate talent from a different league, but effective drafting is the key to building a competitive team in major American sports.

Typically, drafts are reverse-ordered based on team performance, where the team with the worst record in the previous season selects first from the draft-eligible prospects, and the champion selects last. A draft structured in reverse order of finish is a mechanism for competitive balance. Reverse order drafts are explicitly designed to manage competitive balance, as the worst team can select the most promising new talent.

Reverse-order amateur drafts, however, can create perverse incentives for teams to lose games intentionally (Lenten, 2016). This is a problem since a foundational principle of competitive sports is that teams should strive to win every game. Not attempting to win a game or match is a violation of the implicit contract between fans and teams, as the fan is purchasing a ticket to a competitive contest. However, the reverse-order draft creates incentives for teams to make decisions that violate this implied agreement.

On the surface, the goal of the reverse-order draft is to equalize talent across a league. However, suppose a team is out of playoff contention but not in last place in the league. Also, suppose that the upcoming amateur draft features a single player who is viewed as a certain future Superstar. The marginal value for a non-playoff team in winning additional games is fairly low. For instance, there is little upside for an NBA team that has won twenty games through the first eighty games of a season to strive to win the last two contests. However, the marginal value to building fandom of acquiring a future Superstar may be enormous. Trying to win a few extra games in a meaningless season may or may not encourage a few more ticket purchases, but acquiring a player like Michael Jordan or LeBron James can enormously impact a team's fandom equity.

The practice of intentionally losing games to improve draft position is known as "tanking." Tanking can be economically optimal as losing games in the short run may maximize a team's long-run utility function. The problem for leagues is that teams failing to compete can damage the perceptions of the league and create disgruntled fans. The economic conflict is that the long-run utility functions of teams and the league are not aligned. The team can benefit from intentionally losing, while this practice may damage the league's reputation for honest competition.

The NBA draft has evolved over time to try and guard against teams tanking to improve draft position. Interventions like shifting from a deterministic rule whereby the worst record gets the first pick to a lottery system where the non-playoff qualifiers have weighted chances to acquire top picks have all been attempted. However, tanking is still a prevalent occurrence.

The issue of unexpected consequences of reverse order drafts is best illustrated by the case of the Philadelphia 76ers and "The Process." "The Process" refers to the rebuilding strategy employed by the Philadelphia 76ers from 2013 to 2019. The strategy involved losing games to secure high draft picks and build a young, talented roster. The process was controversial and drew criticism from some fans and analysts, but it ultimately resulted in the 76ers becoming a competitive team in the NBA

(Rappaport, 2017). The process seems to have had minimal long-term consequences for 76ers fandom.

10.4.2 Free Agency

The other major channel for acquiring athletic talent is free agency, where players are allowed to shop their services across all teams. Leagues have long restricted player movement in various forms. Free agency has a history as a contentious issue between players and leagues. The genesis of the modern free agency system was the case of Curt Flood. Curt Flood was a Major League Baseball player who challenged the reserve clause, which allowed teams to restrict player movement. Flood refused to honor a trade following the 1969 season, and his challenge ultimately led to the establishment of free agency in professional sports (Barra, 2011).

The basic premise of free agency is that players get to sell their services to the highest bidder. However, pure free agency does not exist in sports, as leagues typically negotiate rules related to player movement. For instance, leagues may specify rules for rookie contracts that allow teams to have rights to players for a specified number of years and often have options that can extend the team's control. Often, there are also rules about compensation when a team loses a free agent. While player movement opportunities are something players covet, player movement creates challenges for teams to build consistent winners and develop fandom. Fandom equity is created through winning and featuring star players. Free agency complicates player retention, especially of superstars.

The main argument against free agency is essentially an argument in favor of competitive balance. Major League Baseball has traditionally had less revenue sharing and restrictions on payrolls than other leagues. A consequence of no or limited restrictions on payroll spending and significant differences in market potential is that teams in larger and more affluent markets may enjoy greater economic returns from winning. According to the 2020 US Census, the New York metropolitan area included over 20 million people, while the Milwaukee metro area had only about 1.5 million. The massive difference in market potential means that the New York teams will have larger local media deals and likely greater pricing power. The returns to winning will also be skewed towards the larger market as the natural fanbase is larger. Neglecting out-of-market fandom, every championship in Milwaukee grows the fandom of potentially 1.5 million fan assets, while a New York title possibly grows the value of 20 million fan assets. A one percent growth in in-market fandom in Milwaukee yields about 15,000 fans, while New York gains 200,000 fans.

The key point is that the value of winning may vary across markets, so different clubs may obtain different values from the same player. The incremental utility gained by a larger market can result in a greater willingness to pay free agents. Free agency without payroll constraints is therefore likely to result in a concentration of talent at teams with bigger revenue bases.

Free agency can also operate against competitive balance through players' off-field economic incentives. In addition to wishing to maximize salaries from teams, players may also select markets to optimize off-field earnings. Players may prefer markets with larger populations or media opportunities to grow their endorsements and build their brands. In sum, teams in larger markets may have greater incentives to sign free agents, and free agents may have incentive structures that lead to signing with larger markets. These team and player incentives can reinforce each other and diminish competitive balance.

10.4.3 Salary Caps

The preceding discussion of free agency and the financial advantages of larger markets leads to the topic of salary caps (Fort & Quirk, 1995). Salary caps are rules that dictate the amounts that can be spent on payroll and individual players. Given the vast differences in the economic potential of markets, the idea of a salary cap is an obvious remedy to competitive imbalances, as a cap limits the ability of organizations in more lucrative territories to outspend rivals. The salary cap is conceptually the most direct competitive balance intervention as it makes all organizations equal in terms of investments in players.

In practice, salary caps involve multiple decisions that can impact the efficacy of caps in maintaining balance. If salary caps are set relatively high, then less lucrative markets may still spend less than teams with greater fandom equity. Salary caps also come in different forms and can operate at the level of individual players and the total payroll. Salary caps may be hard caps with strict limits to spending or soft caps that allow teams to exceed a cap but also pay a penalty or luxury tax to other league members.

A salary floor that enforces a minimum spending level is also possible. One possible approach to team management is to use a strategy that shifts between trying to win and building for the future (e.g., tanking). For example, a small market team might observe that a roster can be built economically by using younger players who are not yet eligible for free agency. The small market team might pursue a minimal salary policy that yields uncompetitive teams and premium draft picks. The team might repeat the process as the high draft picks reach free agency by trading away stars to again lower the payroll and acquire another wave of picks. Conceptually, the salary floor is an anti-tanking policy. Salary floors may be especially attractive to players' bargaining representatives as they force teams to engage in a reasonable level of spending. Salary floors are an interesting intervention in terms of fandom, as minimum payroll constraints are consistent with the idea that teams are forced to maintain some minimum level of competitiveness. The empirical question is whether a minimum level of competitiveness is meaningful to fans.

While salary caps help maintain competitive balance, they can also have unintended or adverse effects on fandom. For instance, the teams with the greatest fandoms are also the teams that have had the most success in terms of championships. These championships have often come over relatively short periods, and fans can speak about sports dynasties where a core group of players won multiple championships during a brief period. Salary caps can unintentionally force teams to dismantle championship teams prematurely because they cannot match players' free agency offers while remaining under the salary cap. Losing fan favorites and key performers from championship teams is a surefire anti-fandom strategy.

10.4.4 Revenue Sharing

Revenue sharing is an intervention designed to level the economic playing field between big and small market franchises (Késenne, 2000). In general, revenue sharing aims to reduce or eliminate advantages from market differences by pooling some portion of league revenues. Revenue sharing is especially relevant in leagues that allocate territories to clubs. The allocation of territories creates inequities as markets differ in terms of population, income levels, and competitive environments. Structural inequities between teams are problematic because teams comprising a league are competitors and partners. When the NFL grows in prominence, all the teams benefit. When MLB loses appeal, all the teams suffer eventually.

The challenge in implementing revenue sharing is that the practice can also be viewed as a subsidy from successful teams to unsuccessful teams. Implementing a system where some competitors subsidize their competition will inevitably lead to resistance. In sports without traditions of revenue sharing, the idea of contributing profits to other teams seems suboptimal for teams with more fandom assets. For fandom equity-rich teams, revenue sharing is a direct cost that reduces profits and resources that could be invested in payroll.

Revenue sharing may be viewed as a necessary equalizer for teams that lack fandom assets, such as newer clubs or teams in smaller markets. If all teams are equal partners in a league and the league's goal is to maximize fandom across a nation or region, then structural revenue disparities from market differences are not consistent with the league's mission. For these clubs, revenue sharing may be viewed as a cost or tax assessed to teams that are assigned more lucrative territories.

Revenue-sharing policy decisions have significant implications for competitive balance. The NFL has long used a policy where teams evenly split the league's national media revenues. This type of even split has led to significant parity in the NFL and allowed small-market teams like the Green Bay Packers and the Pittsburgh Steelers to remain among the league's elite brands.

The nature of team and league revenues also influences the willingness of leagues and teams to embrace revenue sharing. Willingness to share revenues may vary based on the percentage of revenues from local versus league-level sources. Typically, sports organizations collect revenue from multiple sources. There can be local revenues, such as box office revenues and local media deals, and league-level revenues from deals with national media. Revenues from local versus national media may be viewed very differently by clubs since national deals are explicitly related to the overall league's appeal, and local deals are team specific.

A comparison of the NFL and MLB illustrates the issue of local versus national fandom. According to data from espn.com, the total attendance for MLB in 2023 was 70,747,361, while the attendance for the NFL in 2022 was 18,818,804. In contrast, in 2022, the World Series final game drew a television audience of 12.87 million viewers (Adler, 2022), while the 2022 Super Bowl drew 112 million viewers (Young, 2022). While these viewership numbers are not direct proxies for revenues, the reversal in audience size across the leagues for home attendance versus championship viewing highlights that the NFL is more oriented towards national audiences while baseball emphasizes local fandom. Leagues with local fandom are likely to meet more resistance to revenue sharing than leagues with more of a national following. National television deals are more logically evenly split between teams, while teams likely feel entitled to retain revenues from ticket sales and local media that are explicitly the result of the teams efforts. It is also reasonable to speculate that the NFL's revenue-sharing practice has enabled the league to become more national, while MLB's lack of revenue sharing may lead to more insular decisions that have limited the sport's national appeal.

In contrast, other leagues have adopted more complex formulas that base revenue sharing on teams' local revenues. Lewis (2007, 2008) examined the role of revenue sharing on teams' payroll investment decisions. Lewis's starting assumption is that teams attempt to optimize fandom equity by maximizing two sources of revenue: home box office and revenue-sharing transfer payments. For small market teams, the finding is that revenue sharing creates an incentive to lower payrolls because the incremental revenue-sharing payments exceed the revenue lost from losing a greater percentage of games. When a revenue-sharing plan is based on the deficiencies in local revenues, teams will be able to maximize revenue by setting payroll at a level that maximizes the sum of fan revenues and league subsidies. In other words, revenue sharing can be dangerous to competitive balance if transfer payments reduce incentives to win.

10.4.5 Relegation

Relegation is a process used in many sports leagues around the world. It involves poorly performing teams being moved from a higher division league to a lower one based on their performance. Relegation adds an element of excitement and pressure to a league as teams must compete to avoid being relegated. The opposite side to relegation is promotion. Promotion involves successful lower-division teams being promoted or advanced to an upper division.

Relegation provides a strong incentive to remain competitive. The bottom teams in leagues with relegation have incredibly strong incentives to remain competitive, as incremental losses can result in dropping to a league with lower fan appeal and media revenues. Similarly, relegation-promotion leagues also increase the incentive for lower-division teams to compete in order to reach more prominent divisions.

As with all interventions, there are design decisions related to each specific implementation of a relegation policy. For example, relegated teams may receive parachute payments, such as a share of the upper division's media rights. These parachute payments can ease the pressures on payrolls as the team adjusts to a lower revenue base. However, parachute payments can also create competitive imbalances in the new league.

The fundamental issue with relegation is that clubs are built to compete in their current leagues based on current circumstances and future expectations. In a league with relegation, a club with a smaller fandom may find itself starved for resources relative to the high fandom equity teams. The lower fandom equity teams may also be less willing to invest because of the higher probability of relegation. The uncertainty introduced by relegation is a factor that can change teams' investment decisions.

Relegation-promotion systems may also limit the ability of lower-level teams and leagues to build fandom. A team that regularly transitions between divisions may struggle to create rivalries and may build a history of back-and-forth transitions, from winning lower-division seasons to losing upper-division campaigns. Just as a championship creates stories that build fandoms, relegation may create narratives that deter fandom.

Analysis of the impact of relegation on competitive balance levels in the EPL suggests that relegation has led to less balance over time (Plumley et al., 2018). The challenge in relegation systems is the disruption to rosters and club economics. Promoted teams may have a payroll and roster that is near the bottom of its new higher-level competition. Promoted teams are also likely to have much less valuable fandom assets in terms of brands and existing fans, while teams consistently at the top of the league develop stronger brands and revenue streams. Relegation may lead to segments of powerful teams that do not experience relegation and other less successful teams that operate with fewer resources and face disruptions via relegation.

While relegation has complicated effects at the team level, its effects on overall league fandom outcomes are also complex. In US sports leagues, high-equity teams occasionally have poor results. For example, during the 2021–2022 NFL season, both New York NFL teams, the Giants and Jets, finished with 4–13 records. These results placed the two teams located in the largest market among the bottom five teams. The notion that a relegation system could remove the teams located in the New York market would seem strange to American sports fans. Removing the New York teams would also possibly have negative consequences for the overall league. Rivalries would be disrupted, and media rights revenues would come under pressure.

Relegation highlights an important aspect of many competitive balance interventions. These interventions can interact with each other and with team characteristics. In the case of relegation, the brand (fandom) advantages of more established teams may cause a policy designed to increase balance to skew competition towards higher fandom equity brands. For relegation to enhance competitive balance levels, it may be necessary also to include significant revenue sharing and salary caps to equalize resources and expenditures.

10.5 Analysis Issues

Our discussion of leagues', teams', and players' incentives and competitive balance interventions has emphasized logical arguments for how different policies may lead to unanticipated effects on competition. The discussion has focused on logical arguments because quantifying the effects of these different policies is often extremely difficult. Data samples are small (30 teams per year generate 30 data points), and there is usually a lack of counterfactual data. We have no data on how NFL fandom would have evolved without revenue sharing.

Lewis (2008) provides an example of a data-based approach to examining the consequences of a revenue-sharing policy change. Lewis' analysis examined the change in baseball teams' payroll decisions following the implementation of additional revenue sharing. However, this study requires a complex dynamic analysis of the impact of a revenue-sharing policy change on intangible fandom assets. In general, analytics need to be more accessible to be truly impactful. The analysis also assumed that the only change in the MLB environment was the change in revenue sharing. In a sports world that is rapidly changing due to technological and demographic trends, an assumption of a static environment is tenuous.

More generally, our discussion has frequently highlighted the differential impact of competitive balance interventions on teams in varying market sizes and with different fandom equity levels. Statistical analysis of these heterogeneous effects is likely to be difficult for a variety of reasons, including the relative lack of data on team reactions (given the size of most leagues) and the dimensionality of different programs. Analysis challenges are also complicated by the interactions that occur between interventions.

The most realistic approach to analytics of league policies is a detailed examination of how proposed policies change the economic incentives of different members of the sports ecosystem. Qualitative analysis of economic incentives should then be followed with simple analytics that look at metrics related to team decisions and fan reactions. What happens to payrolls when revenue sharing is implemented? How does payroll allocation between younger and older players change when rookie contracts and free agency rules are changed? How do long-term and short-term fandom metrics react when league rules change? This may be a less satisfying approach for most analysts, but given the data limitations and empirical challenges, it is the best path.

10.6 Insights and Connections

Sports contests are explicitly intended to be fair competitions. For sports to have meaning, the athletic competition cannot be biased to one side or the other. The goals are the same size for each soccer team, basketball hoops are ten feet high, football teams get four downs to gain ten yards, and baseball teams get three outs each inning. Scandals involving teams or referees being caught cheating can be extremely damaging. Part of the reason sports create compelling narratives is that the competitions are meritocratic, meaning that the drama is real.

However, while the games are fair, economic factors frequently make for uneven competition. The New York Yankees pitchers throw from the same mound as their opponents, but their payroll might be four times as high as some opponents (Spotrac, 2023). The games are fair, but the competition frequently is not. To mitigate competitive imbalances, leagues have employed various interventions. Revenues may be shared. Struggling teams may have greater access to new talent. Constraints may be placed on bigger market teams' spending. The way leagues are organized and operated has an impact on fandom. The impact can operate at the league level or favor the fandom development in different markets relative to others.

There are two key fandom analytics principles useful for evaluating competitive balance interventions. First, the emphasis should be on the diverse economic incentives of teams and players. Second, competitive balance should be viewed not just as a factor that influences attendance but as a factor that influences the creation of team stories and narratives that underlie fandom.

The material in this chapter is especially related to previous issues related to fandom equity and market resources (Chap. 6). Organizations with greater resources create potential issues because they often can outspend rivals. The challenge of implementing league rules that restrict competition is that these rules implicitly limit a league's iconic teams from building fandom equity. Salary caps create a type of fairness, but they also limit the ability of organizations to build and maintain the types of dynastic championship teams that create powerful fandom.

The analysis of how a league's rules create incentives that influence teams' decisions and competitive balance levels is the final element of the fandom analytics framework. The next portion of the book is focused on the implications of how fandom works more generally and where fandom is likely to evolve over the next few years. The final two chapters extend the discussion to consider how fandom works beyond sports and what the future of fandom looks like.

References

Adler, D. (2022). 2022 World Series tops all primetime TV for 7th straight year. *MLB.com*. Accessed December 21, 2023, from https://www.mlb.com/news/2022-world-series-tv-ratings-and-viewership

Barra, A. (2011). How Curt Flood changed baseball and killed his career in the process. *The Atlantic*. Accessed on December 21, 2023, from https://www.theatlantic.com/entertainment/archive/2011/07/how-curt-flood-changed-baseball-and-killed-his-career-in-the-process/241783/

Doria, M., & Nalebuff, B. (2021). Measuring competitive balance in sports. *Journal of Quantitative Analysis in Sports, 17*(1), 29–46.

Fort, R., & Maxcy, J. (2003). Competitive balance in sports leagues: An introduction. *Journal of Sports Economics, 4*(2), 154–160.

Fort, R., & Quirk, J. (1995). Cross-subsidization, incentives, and outcomes in professional team sports leagues. *Journal of Economic Literature, 33*(3), 1265–1299.

Gay-Rees, J., & Martin, P. (Producers). (2019-present). Formula 1: Drive to survive [TV Series]. *Netflix*. https://www.netflix.com/

Grez, M. (2023). How Manchester City won the premier league once again. *CNN.com*. Accessed December 2, 2023, from https://www.cnn.com/2023/05/21/football/how-manchester-city-won-the-premier-league-once-again-spt-intl/index.html

Hehir, J. (Director). (2020). The last dance [Documentary series]. *ESPN Films*.

Késenne, S. (2000). Revenue sharing and competitive balance in professional team sports. *Journal of Sports Economics, 1*(1), 56–65.

Lawrence, B., Sudeikis, J., Hun, B., Kelly, J., Ingold, J., & Wrubel, B. [Executive Producers]. (2020–2023). Ted Lasso [TV Series]. Ruby's Tuna Inc.; Doozer; Universal Television; Warner Bros. Television Studios.

Lenten, L. J. (2016). Mitigation of perverse incentives in professional sports leagues with reverse-order drafts. *Review of Industrial Organization, 49*(1), 25–41.

Lewis, M. (2008). Individual team incentives and managing competitive balance in sports leagues: An empirical analysis of Major League Baseball. *Journal of Marketing Research, 45*(5), 535–549.

Lewis, M. (2007). Baseball's losing formula. *New York Times*. Accessed November 7, 2023, from https://www.nytimes.com/2007/11/03/opinion/03lewis.html

Li, D. (2024). Storm brewing in college basketball: Should fans be banned from rushing floor? Accessed March 1, 2024, from https://www.nbcnews.com/news/sports/storm-brewing-college-basketball-fans-banned-rushing-floor-rcna140697

Massey, C., & Thaler, R. H. (2013). The loser's curse: Decision making and market efficiency in the National Football League draft. *Management Science, 59*(7), 1479–1495.

Owen, P. D., Ryan, M., & Weatherston, C. R. (2007). Measuring competitive balance in professional team sports using the Herfindahl-Hirschman index. *Review of Industrial Organization, 31*, 289–302.

Plumley, D., Ramchandani, G., & Wilson, R. (2018). Mind the gap: An analysis of competitive balance in the English football league system. *International Journal of Sport Management and Marketing, 18*(5), 357–375.

Rappaport, M. (2017). The definitive history of 'trust the process.' *Bleacher Report*. Accessed November 2, 2023, from https://bleacherreport.com/articles/2729018-the-definitive-history-of-trust-the-process

Rottenberg, S. (1956). The baseball players' labor market. *Journal of Political Economy, 64*(3), 242–258.

Spotrac. (2023). MLB team payroll tracker. *Spotrac.com*. Accessed December 5, 2023, from https://www.spotrac.com/mlb/payroll/2023/

Whitley, D. (2015). Globetrotters lose by eliminating the generals. *SFGate.* Accessed December 21, 2023, from https://www.sfgate.com/sports/article/Globetrotters-lose-by-eliminating-the-Generals-6446622.php

Young, J. (2022). Super Bowl 2022 attracted more than 112 million viewers, but failed to toprecord. *CNBC.com.* Accessed on December 21, 2023, from https://www.cnbc.com/2022/02/15/super-bowl-2022-ratings-.html

11

Fandom Beyond Sports

11.1 The Swifties

Sports fandom has been our primary focus in this manuscript, but fandom is much broader than sports. Sports fandom is important and fascinating and worthy of deep exploration. Exploring sports fandom also provides a foundation for understanding fandom beyond sports. The starting point for generalizing fandom analytics is acknowledging that sports have several idiosyncrasies that differentiate it from other cultural categories. Thinking about how sports fandom is similar and different to other types of fandoms is useful for analyzing sports fandom and for extending the fandom analytics message to other categories.

In 2023 America, perhaps the most notable fandom on display has been Taylor Swift fans, also known as Swifties. Swift fandom merits discussion for multiple reasons. Swift's fandom is passionately loyal, economically valuable, and culturally impactful. Swift fandom bears similarities to sports fandom, but it also exhibits important differences. Like sports fans, Swifties spend big money to attend, dress in costume, and travel for their idol. Swift's *Eras* tour has demonstrated the scale of Swift's fandom, generating over five billion dollars in economic impact

(Kopstein & Espada, 2023). Concert attendees are estimated to have spent an average of $1279, including $384 on travel and lodging, $159 on merchandise, and $234 on outfits for the concert (Bhattarai et al., 2023).

Swifties exhibit loyalty that rivals the most passionate sports fandoms. Swifties have a reputation for being extremely protective of Taylor. Swift's music references past relationships and breakups, and fans consistently take her side. They aggressively defend her on social media and attack anyone who dares to criticize her with an onslaught of tweets and comments defending her honor. The Swifties' loyalty is best exemplified by their reaction to Swift's public feud with producer Scooter Braun. In response to a dispute over the rights to her first six albums, Swift used her social platforms to ask fans to reach out to Braun's celebrity clients to apply pressure on Braun (Donnellan, 2023). The feud culminated with Swift rerecording her first six albums. Swift's rerecorded versions enjoyed spectacular success despite being recordings of music that was often a decade old (McIntyre, 2023). Swifties' ability to function as a cohesive group has even extended to the legal system. In response to a chaotic environment at the beginning of ticket sales for the *Eras* tour and frustration with fees, a group of Swift fans launched a lawsuit against Ticketmaster (Korn et al., 2023).

Swifties are also known for their ability to decipher Taylor's cryptic messages and clues. When she releases hints about new music or upcoming projects, fans spend hours dissecting every word and image. These investigations lead to significant social media activity across the Swiftie community. For fans, understanding Taylor's plans and meanings requires obtaining a significant knowledge base about Taylor's music and personal life. Swifties are also known for creating content demonstrating their knowledge of Swift's activities and proposing theories about her meanings. The Swiftie fandom community provides an opportunity to demonstrate exceptional levels of knowledge, insight, and loyalty.

Another common behavior among Swifties is making significant efforts to attend concerts. Fans will travel across the country or overseas to see her perform and camp out for hours or even days to get the best seats possible. Many fans attend multiple shows on the same tour. Another Swiftie behavior is collecting every piece of merchandise available. From t-shirts to phone cases, fans want to own every piece of memorabilia. They also love wearing their merchandise as a badge of honor and a testament to their dedication.

Taylor Swift fandom bears substantial similarities with sports fandom. Like sports fandom, there is a community of fans. This fandom community is as protective of Taylor Swift as New York Yankees or Liverpool FC fans are of their teams. Fans are willing to purchase all sorts of Taylor merchandise and clothing and even dress in costume for games. These behaviors are reminiscent of the jerseys and face painting seen at sporting events. Fans invest time and effort into becoming Taylor Swift experts. A Taylor Swift fan's expertise of lyrics and backstories is equivalent to a sports fan's knowledge about his team's past achievements, heroic players, and future prospects.

Nevertheless, there are also dimensions where Swift fandom differs from sports fandom. For example, sports fandom is often driven by familial relationships and geography. Sports fandom is frequently transmitted from parent or grandparent, and sports often become a source of shared family experiences. It is unlikely that most Taylor Swift fandom was passed from mother to daughter. Sports fandom is also often location specific. Growing up in New York or Liverpool is highly correlated with becoming a Yankee or Liverpool FC fan. In contrast, Taylor Swift fandom is less influenced by geography, with Swifties hailing from all over the United States and worldwide.

Taylor Swift is the biggest story of fandom in 2023, but Swifties are just one example of a fandom. Star Trek fans, known as Trekkies, are often considered the genesis of modern fandom (McArdle, 2016). Again, there are similarities between Trekkies and sports fans. Trekkie fandom is built around the stories and characters of the Star Trek universe. Trekkies are known to dress in Star Trek uniforms, travel to conventions, collect memorabilia, and become experts on Star Trek trivia. Swift is a singer, and Star Trek was originally a science fiction-based television show, but many of the traits of fandom exist whether the category is sport, music, or science fiction.

Fandom also exists in categories beyond sports and entertainment. Sports, music, and science fiction are cultural products, and anytime a category becomes culturally relevant, fandom may develop. The phrase "culturally" relevant is critical as it implies that fandom can arise in many disparate categories. Politicians like Donald Trump and Barack Obama have fans. Museums, symphony orchestras, and ballets have fans. A soft drink like Coca-Cola or a car company like Tesla can develop fans. CEOs and tycoons can have fans. While fandom is common in sports and much less common in something like consumer products, fandom is something for all organizations to aspire to.

11.2 Fandom Dimensions: The WILD Categorization Scheme

This chapter focuses on creating a methodology for characterizing fandom in different categories. Stepping out of the realm of sports to consider Taylor Swift fandom is a valuable exercise. One cannot help but observe the similarities and differences between Swift fandom and sports fandom. In terms of passion, Taylor Swift's fandom compares to the most intense fandoms. Argentina's World Cup Victory brought out an estimated crowd of five million in Buenos Aires—a crowd so dense that the victory parade was canceled (AP, 2022) while Taylor Swift's Argentinian fandom is so intense that fans camped in tents for 5 months to secure front row seats for her concert (Sharf, 2023). Discussing extreme instances of fandom is useful because the behaviors and emotions that make fandom distinctive are especially pronounced. The extraordinary passion of sports fans and Swifties illustrates a commonality across fandom in different categories.

However, Taylor Swift fandom is distinct from sports fandom on several key dimensions. While Swift has an extensive and long musical career, with her first album released in 2006, her longevity does not compare to sports franchises. The relative lack of longevity means that Swift fandom has little to do with family traditions and has not been passed from grandparents or parents to children.

Considering non-sports fandom like Taylor Swift fandom may motivate additional questions and insights about sports and can start us down the path to thinking about how fandom varies across different types of cultural products. For example, the preceding point that Swift fandom is

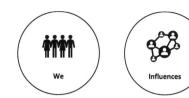

Fig. 11.1 WILD fandom categorization scheme

unlikely to have been passed from older to younger generations might motivate more general questions about why intergenerational fandom occurs in some categories and not others. Understanding the how and why of intergenerational fandom might help sports organizations refine their marketing efforts and might suggest new approaches in non-sports categories.

The comparison between generational fandom transmission between Taylor Swift and sports fandom is one possible dimension that may be considered. The primary objective of this chapter is to develop a system for categorizing fandom along four important dimensions. Figure 11.1 is a simple visual that displays these dimensions. The first dimension is "We" (win/lose). A vital aspect of fandom is how closely fans identify with a cultural entity. The second dimension is "Influences." Fandoms vary significantly in terms of what influences people to become fans. The third dimension is "Life-cycle." Sometimes, fandom can be a lifelong passion with distinct stages, and sometimes it can be momentary. The fourth dimension is "Display." Display is related to the propensity for fandom to be public. The WILD acronym is constructed to be memorable and to contain a relatively small number of categories for describing fandom. The WILD fandom classification system aims to capture category differences efficiently rather than exhaustively.

11.3 W: We Win

The idea of fans being one with their teams or idols is a core aspect of fandom since being intensely connected with a fandom group suggests that being a fan is often part of an individual's social identity (Tajfel &

Turner, 2004). The tradition of the 12th Man in American football may be the height of fans being a part of a team. American football teams have 11 men on the field during game action, but teams often refer to an additional non-playing member of the team, the 12th Man.

Texas A&M University has long featured the 12th Man concept to honor its supporters. The 12th Man narrative dates to 1922 when a team member, E. King Gill, who was assisting in the press box and not in uniform, donned a uniform mid-game to bolster the team's depleted reserves (Lomax, 2016). Texas A&M trademarked the "12th Man" term in 1990 and now receives royalties from other teams like the Seattle Seahawks that use the 12th Man terminology.

The 12th Man concept shows the powerful connection between sports fans and their teams, as many fans feel as though they are almost team members. There is perhaps no more committed fan than the supporter who views his team's successes and failures as his own. When their team wins a championship, they might use the phrase "We Won." When the team loses because of a referee's call, the same fan might say, "We were robbed by the officials." Fandoms are groups or subcultures, and the decision to be affiliated with a fandom group is often driven by social identity benefits as fans define themselves in terms of their cultural passions. Fans who identify with a team to the degree that the team's wins and losses are the fan's wins and losses are the epitome of "We" fans.

"We" fandom is incredibly common in sports and varies in relevance across other categories. Her fans' reactions to Swift's conflict with Scooter Braun suggest that they view her protectively. This suggests at least some element of collective identity. On the other hand, it seems less likely that you would hear a Swiftie say things like "We Won" to celebrate Taylor Swift winning a Grammy. Though, if any artist's fans would express this feeling, it would probably be Swift's.

Fans of movies, television, or standup comedians are less likely than sports fans to personalize a favorite film's, show's, or performer's successes as their own. However, fans of politicians are very likely to view an electoral victory or defeat as personal. The We (win/lose) dimension of fandom may be assessed quantitatively using survey data or conceptually using expert judgment. The following types of questions may be used to assess the "We Win" trait:

* Do fans feel like winners (losers) when their fandom entity wins (loses)?
* Do fans talk about their fandom entity's achievement as their own?
* Are fans protective of their fandom entity?

11.4   I: Influences

The factors that influence the formation and development of fandom vary substantially across categories. Social media has heightened interest in the topic of influencer marketing, but the role of influence is relevant in all consumer categories. Advertising, friends, reviews, and social media personalities may all influence consumers to try products or to become loyal customers. In our context, influence relates to the factors that instigate and reinforce fandom.

Traditionally, sports fandom has been facilitated by a rich set of influences. Many of these influences have been tied to geographic and community factors, as sports teams are often viewed as members of the community and enjoy widespread support and substantial media coverage. A young person coming of age in a community with significant sports might be exposed to the local teams by family members and local media. Emerging fandom might be reinforced by peers at school and further media coverage.

Entertainment and other cultural categories may have different types of influencers. Popular music probably enjoys little support from older family members or from local media. In past generations, local radio and MTV might have been the primary introducers of musical content. In the 2020s, social media sites like TikTok or recommendation engines on music distribution services may be the primary influencers. The movie industry is a fascinating example for considering fandom influences. For a new piece of intellectual property, influence has traditionally been purchased through advertising or having stars do press and talk shows. However, family and peer influences may influence and support fandom for an established brand like Star Wars or the Marvel Cinematic Universe. Social media is also a critical influence platform for movies as film stars like The Rock can reach hundreds of millions of potential film viewers.

The issue of fandom influencers is related to the role of fandom in culture. In some cases, fandom is continually reinforced by community and media influences. In these cases, fandom can play a unifying cultural role as community members may become fans to be fully functioning community members. If the local community vigorously supports the local soccer team, community influences can create a cycle where each new generation supports the team. If music fandom is more concentrated by age, then local influences will matter less, but social media forces may be more relevant.

Identifying the potential influencers that drive fandom for a category or specific cultural entity can be instructive for the entity's marketing professionals. In our example of movies, the point was made that established characters and fantasy universes may benefit from family and community influences. In contrast, a new franchise may need to purchase initial exposure. The film production company may therefore focus on established characters with built-in audiences or leverage stars with massive followings when launching a new character.

The role of influence can also vary within the sports category. For instance, a new or "expansion" sports league suffers from the same issue of lacking local community influencers. Football is the dominant American sport, but there seems to be little room for a secondary football league (Kaplan & Shea, 2022). These leagues begin without a foundation of stories and no local fan community. Without an established fandom, these leagues must try to influence new fans through advertising and promotions. However, advertising and promotion do not have track records as effective influencers for sports products. New sports leagues might benefit from thinking beyond sports about fan acquisition in categories that also lack local and family-based influencers.

The following questions may be used to assess the "Influence" dimension of a fandom:

- Do family members facilitate fandom?
- Do peer influences create or support fandom?
- Does local media support fandom?
- Does national and international media support fandom?
- Do social media algorithms support fandom?
- Can advertising create initial fandom in a category?

11.5 L: Life-Cycle

The notion of product and customer life-cycles is widespread in marketing (Terzi et al. 2010). Product life-cycle models often include stages such as introduction, growth, maturity, and decline. There are more variations in customer life-cycle frameworks, but frameworks usually feature stages like awareness, consideration, trial, retention, advocacy, and reacquisition (Gupta et al., 2006). In fandom and cultural categories, product and customer life-cycles are both of critical importance. Product and customer life-cycles may also interact in important ways.

The critical observation is that cultural entities differ in their periods of relevance. Some are enduring, essentially permanent parts of the larger culture, while others may be more fleeting. The oldest English soccer clubs date back to the 1860s (Macfarlane, 2022), and several American baseball teams and the precursor to MLB were also formed in the post-Civil War era (Hill, 2020).

Current major professional and collegiate sports teams may evolve, shift locations, change names, and grow or shrink in relevance, but these entities have indefinite lifespans. In contrast, a pop music star or movie may be relevant for a mere moment. Again, there can be variation within a category. The music world uses the term "One-Hit Wonder" (Greene, 2011) to signify an artist who had a single popular song, but there are also musical artists who enjoy decade-long careers. Furthermore, other musical entities, such as a symphony orchestra, may have unlimited lifespans. The length of a cultural entity's life-cycle is very relevant to its approach to fandom. An enduring entity like a baseball team or symphony orchestra can adopt a long-term perspective on fandom management and engage in brand building or develop customer management capabilities. An entity with a finite life-cycle such as a pop musician or individual athlete should emphasize promotion and revenue maximization.

The preceding comment about developing a customer management system highlights the interplay between the cultural entity's life-cycle and the fan life-cycle. Fans' life-cycles or periods of interest vary substantially across cultural products. Sports fandom has been extremely long-lasting with fandom for a given team lasting entire lifetimes. However, some forms of entertainment or content seem destined to be more temporary. Music and fashion seem to have shorter life-cycles, partly because these types of content are something that consumers use to define themselves for short periods. As in the case of the product life-cycle, the ideal approach to fandom management changes as customer life-cycles vary in length. With pop music or fashion, the organization should strive to maximize immediate awareness and revenues. For a category with a multi-decade fan life-cycle, fan management should adopt a longer-term perspective. For instance, a sport organization might offer deeply discounted ticket packages to families or youth groups because acquiring a 10-year-old fan might be acquiring a fan for the next 80 years.

A critical aspect of fandom is the length of the potential product life-cycle. The standard managerial guidance is that marketing strategies should be based on the product life-cycle stage such as a new product should emphasize advertising to build awareness while a product in decline should limit investment in R&D. However, in cultural categories the life-cycle stage may be difficult to observe. Major professional sports seem to be perpetually in the realm of growth and maturity. However, it could be argued that a sport like baseball might be facing decline. A complicating factor in assessing a cultural entity's life-cycle is that external factors like demographics and technology changes may drive decline rather than something intrinsic to the entity.

Fandom and fan life-cycles may be assessed through the following questions:

- What is the expected life-cycle of the cultural entity?
- To what degree is the cultural entity tied to an individual performer?
- Is the cultural entity an enduring institution?
- Is fandom concentrated in a certain age range?
- Is fandom influenced by temporary fashion trends?

11.6 Display

You may remember our earlier example of soccer fans taking displays to the ultimate level with the tifo. A soccer tifo is a large banner or flag display created by supporters of a team. It is often used to create a visual spectacle and show support for the team during a match. Tifos are so beloved and spectacular that it has become a competitive endeavor where fandoms outdo each other (Bridger, 2015). Dortmund's yellow wall is particularly known for its efforts with tifos ranging from visual masterpieces like a smokey special effect of the team initial, thanks to past players, and spelling out powerful but standard fan themes like "Dortmund until I die" (90 Min, 2019).

The fourth dimension of the classification scheme is "Display." Display relates to fans' enthusiasm for publicly revealing their fandom. Sports is especially known for public displays, as fans regularly wear team colors and logos when attending games. Sports fans may even engage in face painting or waving everything from foam tomahawks during Atlanta Braves baseball games to yellow towels during Pittsburgh Steelers football games. Displays are a form of "basking in reflected glory" (Cialdini, 1976).

The level of display varies across and within categories. There is likely less apparel associated with musical acts than sports teams, but Taylor Swift fans curated outfits for her shows and concert t-shirts have long been a staple of fandom. Taylor Swift fans creating their own customer outfits that represent their favorite Taylor Swift era is a fascinating action relative to Penn State fans all dressing in a single color for a "White Out" game. Appreciating the Swifties' display might require substantial knowledge about Taylor swift's music while the Penn State display is easily interpretable. The Swift display seems more about creating an impression with the Swift fandom, while the Penn State display is about signaling community membership.

Political fandom is an interesting case for display. Occasionally, a politician reaches a level of fandom that inspires fandom-oriented clothing like Donald Trump's Maga hats or Bernie Sanders Bernie Bros t-shirts (Stephens, 2020). However, political fan clothing reveals an important category difference. Clothing that expresses political fandom may be inflammatory and can cause confrontations. This is an important observation as it reveals the power of political fandom and highlights the role of anti-fandom (Gross, 2020). While our emphasis has been on the positive feelings of fandom, anti-fandom or feelings of antipathy towards a sports team, entertainer, or politician is also an important cultural phenomenon. Expressing political, or any, fandom via clothing reveals the fans passion for the cultural entity, but in certain categories (politics) and environments (European soccer), passions are so high that identifying as a fan can invite conflict.

The display of memorabilia is another important market of fandom. Memorabilia reflects a desire to accumulate objects and an interest in exhibition. The desire to accumulate suggests that the objects have emotional meaning and the willingness to exhibit shows pride in being identified as a fan or supporter.

Another aspect of "Display" is the tendency of fans to display their knowledge of the cultural entity. Sports fans often possess a wealth of information about their teams' past achievements, current roster, and future prospects. Music fans may be able to sing along with their favorite artist's songs and may know the meanings behind every lyric, and movie fans can recite sequences of dialog. Displaying knowledge can be a means to establish the fan's position in the fandom community's hierarchy. Interestingly, the importance of knowledge display also varies across categories. Many political supporters have little knowledge of policy positions, and fans of universities may not be able to name a single faculty member or administrator.

Assessment of the propensity and character of fan displays may be performed via the following items:

- Do fans wear the entity's colors and logos during events?
- Do fans wear the entity's colors and logos outside of events?
- Do fans decorate their homes with the merchandise that features the entity?
- Do the fans engage in shared performances and chants within and outside the arena?
- Do fans proudly demonstrate their knowledge about the cultural entity?

11.7 WILD System

The WILD categorization scheme provides a convenient and efficient framework to compare fandom across and within categories systematically. The framework can be used to profile a fandom in general terms or as the basis for a more quantitative comparison.

With few exceptions, sports tend to be the gold standard for sports fandom, and comparisons with sports may be instructive for other cultural institutions. For example, an entertainment company might compare the fandom for a movie franchise with fandom for professional football. Football fandom (US Football or International Football) is probably far more likely to have fans who feel like they win or lose with their teams (W Dimension). The football fans' influences (I Dimension) may include family relationships, local media, civic traditions, peer/friend effects, and other community-based factors, while the film franchise might predominately acquire fans from advertising campaigns. The sports fan life-cycle (L Dimension) might last for the fan's entire lifetime, while the movie fandom might exist for a summer. In terms of Display (D Dimension), sports fandom might inspire frequent public displays of clothing and private displays of memorabilia. The movie fandom might inspire an occasional t-shirt or collectible poster.

The result of the preceding exercise might be motivation to attempt to grow fandom along different dimensions or to accept limitations. A sports franchise with limited fandom might explicitly focus on developing a 12th man-like tradition (We), intergenerational fandom (Influences), or creating traditions of shared clothing (Display). A cultural institution like a university might attempt to leverage lessons from sports. Emphasizing cohesion might inspire alumni to identify more closely with the school (We), while aggressively recruiting the children of alumni might create an intergenerational influence (Influence).

11.7.1 The Extra Dimension

The WILD framework is intended to be efficient rather than exhaustive. Fandom is multidimensional, and it is a challenge to create a simple classification system, especially one that spells a word associated with fans. However, memorability is a positive feature.

One feature that is not included but is critical to analyzing fandom is the roles of hate and anti-fandom. Fandom is about passion that leads to intense engagement and deep feelings of affection and attachment toward a team, celebrity, or institution. In other words, fans love their teams. The opposite of fandom can be almost as powerful, just in the opposite direction. An unspoken aspect of fandom is the role of rivalries and hated opponents. Anti-fandom is a little different than rivalry but is also rooted in fans' tendency to associate with cultural entities closely. Anti-fans are the people who build social identity through opposition to or dislike of a cultural product. Taylor Swift and the Dallas Cowboys have massive fandoms, but they each have anti-fans (Goldsztajn, 2024) who define themselves as Taylor or Cowboy haters.

The existence of hated rivals is an important part of fandom. In sports, rivalries are common and add to the intensity of fandom. FC Barcelona and Real Madrid in La Liga, the Lakers and Celtics in the NBA, the Bears and Packers in the NFL, and Ohio State and Michigan in the NCAA are examples of intense rivalry that characterize fandom for each of the clubs involved. Teams without hated rivals are never the top brands or fandoms in any league. In politics, the hated rival is the main opposition party. In the United States, hatred of the opposition party can be as motivating as enthusiasm for the favored party. While entertainment categories may have anti-fans, these categories may tend to lack rivalries. The lack of competition means that Taylor Swift does not have a natural rivalry with Beyonce or BTS. Rivalry might be another dimension worth exploring for brands trying to create fandom-level passion.

11.7.2 Comparisons and Generalizations

The WILD framework provides a means for the structured comparison of fandoms. Our discussion has included generalizations about fandom in different categories, such as how sports fandom is often a lifelong obsession while pop musician fandom is often fleeting. When creating comparisons of fandom across categories, the critical word in this sentence is "often." Occasionally, a musical artist might have a decades-long career (e.g., Dolly Parton, Cher, Elton John). A movie might come and go over a summer or might become the foundation for sequels released over generations (e.g., Star Wars).

The problem with category comparisons is that there is significant variation in fandom within categories. Sports are known for public displays, but the degree of display varies considerably. The tifos of Borussia Dortmund, the White Out games of Penn State, or the cheese head hats of the Green Bay Packers are at one extreme, while many teams aspire to these levels. Taylor Swift inspires so much passion that her fans curate outfits to attend her concerts, and Donald Trump has millions of supporters wearing red "Make America Great Again" hats. Most entertainers and politicians can only wish for so much passion.

11.7.3 Industry Structure

Industry structure can also influence fandom. For example, the structure of international soccer has an impact on the development of local soccer fandom in the United States. The American Professional Soccer League, the MLS, operates on a smaller scale and with smaller budgets than major European soccer leagues. A consequence of MLS's relative status is that top players frequently move on to higher-ranked and higher-paying leagues. Some estimates put the ratio of EPL salaries to MLS salaries in the range of about 10 to 1.

The minor league status of MLS may change the dynamics of soccer fandom relative to other sports properties. For instance, the importance of long-term star players may be reduced in soccer relative to other leagues as MLS teams may sell star players to teams in top European leagues. A consequence of this is that MLS fandom needs to be more team-focused than star-focused. Until the league's economics change, the MLS cannot develop and retain stars like Michael Jordan or Tom Brady. Stars like Lionel Messi and Pele (North American Soccer League) may participate in American pro soccer, but they are unlikely to have long-term careers with US teams. This is an important insight as it implies that elite players will seldom be primarily associated with MLS teams.

The result is that MLS fandom needs to rest on a different foundation than other American sports. MLS must develop stories and fan traditions that are not dependent on being the best soccer product in the world. This is an unusual and challenging position for an American sports league, as the other major pro leagues are all sold as the best in the world.

Politics is a category where outcomes largely depend on political communities and candidates' ability to inspire engagement. However, while being able to create passionate fandom would seem ideal for a candidate, the consequences of fandom may be different in politics because of the zero-sum nature of elections. Whereas fandom is the crucial differentiator in sports, anti-fandom can play a decisive role in politics. Political fandom has power as it leads voters to higher levels of engagement, such as more donations, volunteering, and public displays of logos on clothing and car bumpers. However, political fandom may not be decisive in political consequences because anti-fandom can influence votes.

While a team or musician can fill an arena if they have sufficient fans regardless of anti-fandom, anti-fandom can derail a political candidate. For example, if a team or musician has several hundred thousand fans in a city and a 50,000-seat arena, the team or musician should be able to fill the stands and charge robust ticket prices. Even if the team or musician has many more anti-fans of haters, the existing fandom is sufficient to sell out the arena. In most categories, anti-fandom is mostly a fascinating cultural outcome that does not impact economic success. However, in the realm of politics, anti-fandom or hate can be a motivating factor that can swing elections. Donald Trump enjoyed spectacular fandom within Republican circles in 2020, but he also was hated by Democrats and progressives. So even if Joe Biden did not inspire passion, the Trump anti-fandom provided the fuel needed by the Biden campaign.

11.8 Insights and Connections

The WILD fandom categorization scheme provides a means for systematically describing fandom. The acronym's first letter, W (We), is related to the intensity of the connection between fans and the object of fandom. The second letter, I, represents the influences that inspire and induce fandom. The third element, L, represents differences in the fandom life-cycle. The final letter, D, is included to capture differences in how fans display their fandom.

* The WILD categorization scheme provides a framework for characterizing and comparing fandom in different categories.

The categorization scheme is intended to provide a framework that facilitates the description and differentiation of fandom across categories. Sports tend to have powerful fandom across each dimension. For example, in terms of the first dimension of the categorization scheme, sports fans often feel like members of the team, whereas in entertainment, the intensity of connection is less. These types of differences have implications for fandom analysis. While measuring the intensity of identification with a team may be useful for fandom, measuring identification with a film franchise or television show may be less diagnostic.

* Category differences in fandom provide insights into how fandom insights and marketing benchmarks can be leveraged across industries.

Category differences may also be relevant to marketing analytics. One aspect of the life-cycle dimension is the expected fandom life-cycle. In sports, fan life-cycles can extend over entire lifetimes. Meanwhile, a pop musician may have a relatively short period of relevance. An FLV analysis in sports may benefit from considering a far longer time period than a similar analysis for a pop music fan.

* Category fandom differences may necessitate different approaches to marketing analytics.

The WILD categorization system also provides multiple touchpoints that connect the book. One of our earliest examples was the Penn State "White Out" games. The "White Out" game is a public display of a fandom community. It is an important starting point for fandom analytics to observe that the shared act of display is a foundational aspect of sports fandom. Recognizing the crucial nature of this trait also provides a basis for thinking about fandom beyond sports by considering the prevalence and nature of display in other categories.

The WILD framework also provides a structure for qualitatively benchmarking fandom. The material in Chapters 5, 6, and 7 was focused on the quantitative assessment of fan attitudes, fandom (brand) equity, and fan lifetime value. These concepts require fan surveys, market outcomes, or customer transaction-level data. This data may be expensive or unobtainable. The WILD framework may be used to compare fandoms versus peer and aspirational competitors quickly without collecting data on market outcomes or fan attitudes.

References

90 Min. (2019). Borussia Dortmund: 8 of the best yellow wall displays. *90 min. com*. Accessed November 24, 2023, from https://www.90min.com/posts/6457840-borussia-dortmund-8-of-the-best-yellow-wall-displays

AP (2022). Argentina soccer team abandons World Cup victory parade amid swarms of people. *USA Today*. Accessed August 8, 2024 from https://www.usatoday.com/story/sports/soccer/worldcup/2022/12/20/argentina-world-cup-2022-victory-parade-abandoned/10932807002/

Bhattarai, A., Lerman, R., & Sabens, E. (2023). The economy (Taylor's version). *The Washington Post*. Accessed November 2, 2023, from https://www.washingtonpost.com/business/2023/10/13/taylor-swift-eras-tour-money-jobs/

Bridgen, J. (2015). Top ten greatest Tifos in footballing history. *BEsoccer.com*. Accessed November 22, 2023, from https://www.besoccer.com/new/top-ten-greatest-tifos-in-footballing-history

Cialdini, R. B., Borden, R. J., Thorne, A., Walker, M. R., Freeman, S., & Sloan, L. R. (1976). Basking in reflected glory: Three (football) field studies. *Journal of Personality and Social Psychology, 34*(3), 366.

Donnellan, S. (2023). A complete timeline of Taylor Swift and Scooter Brauns Feud. *People Magazine*. Accessed November 2, 2023, from https://www.usmagazine.com/celebrity-news/news/taylor-swift-and-scooter-brauns-feud-a-complete-timeline/

Goldsztajn, I. (2024). Charles Barkley say football fans criticizing Taylor swift are either 'a loser or a jackass'. *Marie Claire*. Accessed February 2, 2024, from https://www.marieclaire.com/celebrity/charles-barkley-taylor-swift-football-fans-loser-jackass/

Greene, A. (2011). Rolling stone readers pick the top 10 one-hit wonders of all time. *Rolling Stone.* Accessed November 5, 2023, from https://www.rollingstone.com/music/music-lists/rolling-stone-readers-pick-the-top-10-one-hit-wonders-of-all-time-14391/3-norman-greenbaum-spirit-in-the-sky-16706/

Gross, E. (2020). Trump Calls for Goodyear Boycott over Ban on MAGA Hats. *Forbes.* Accessed November 6, 2023, from https://www.forbes.com/sites/elanagross/2020/08/19/trump-calls-for-goodyear-boycott-over-ban-on-maga-hats/

Gupta, S., Hanssens, D., Hardie, B., Kahn, W., Kumar, V., Lin, N., et al. (2006). Modeling customer lifetime value. *Journal of Service Research, 9*(2), 139–155.

Hill, D. (2020). MLB history: First professional baseball league founded. *Foxsports.com.* Accessed November 5, 2023, from https://www.foxsports.com/stories/mlb/mlb-history-first-professional-baseball-league-founded

Kaplan, D., & Shea, B. (2022). USFL survives year 1, looks ahead to second season, expansion, team sales. *The Athletic.* Accessed on November 6, 2023, from https://theathletic.com/3402390/2022/07/06/usfl-fox-sports-birmingham-stallions/

Kopstein, J., & Espada, M. (2023). The staggering economic impact of Taylor Swift's Eras Tour. *Time Magazine.* Accessed December 2, 2023, from https://time.com/6307420/taylor-swift-eras-tour-money-economy/

Korn, J., Maruf, R., & Bernal, C. (2023). Taylor swift fans take Ticketmaster to court over Eras tour ticketing chaos. *CNN.* Accessed November 2, 2023 from https://www.cnn.com/2023/03/27/media/taylor-swift-ticketmaster-court/index.html

Lomax, J. (2016). The 12th man tradition. *Texas Monthly.* Accessed November 5, 2023, from https://www.texasmonthly.com/the-daily-post/12th-man-tradition/

Macfarlane, A. (2022). Oldest English football clubs: A look at the founder teams, History of Soccer.info. Accessed November 5, 2023, from https://historyofsoccer.info/oldest-english-football-clubs

McArdle, M. (2016). This is how Star Trek invented modern fandom. *GQ Magazine.* Accessed on December 30, 2023, from https://www.gq.com/story/this-is-how-star-trek-invented-fandom

McIntyre, H. (2023). Taylor Swift's re-recorded albums are huge successes–But they were a real. *Forbes Magazine.* Accessed November 2, 2023, from https://www.forbes.com/sites/hughmcintyre/2023/07/27/taylor-swifts-re-recorded-albums-are-huge-successesbut-they-were-a-real-risk/

Sharf, Z. (2023). Taylor Swift Fans in Argentina have camped out in tents for five months in order to be front row at the Eras Tour. *Variety*. Accessed November 11, 2023, from https://variety.com/2023/music/news/taylor-swift-fans-argentina-camping-out-eras-tour-1235778141/

Stephens, B. (2020). Bernie's angry bros. *New York Times*. Accessed November 6, 2023, from https://www.nytimes.com/2020/01/31/opinion/sanders-bernie-bros.html

Tajfel, H., & Turner, J. C. (2004). The social identity theory of intergroup behavior. In *Political psychology* (pp. 276–293). Psychology Press.

Terzi, S., Bouras, A., Dutta, D., Garetti, M., & Kiritsis, D. (2010). Product lifecycle management–from its history to its new role. *International Journal of Product Lifecycle Management, 4*(4), 360–389.

12

The Future of Fandom and Fandom Analytics

12.1 Evolving Sports Fandom

Sports fandom has changed over time and continues to evolve. Some sports have grown to have massive global appeal, while other sports have faded from the limelight. The first FIFA World Cup in 1930 drew 590,000 attendees, while the 2022 World Cup Final drew over 1.5 billion viewers (Summerscales, 2023). The first Super Bowl had about 25 million viewers in the US market, while the Super Bowls of the 2020s generated around 100 million viewers (Super Bowl television ratings, 2023). In contrast, Major League Baseball's 1978 World Series had a 56 rating share and over 44 million viewers, but only a 12 share and less than ten million viewers in 2020 (World Series television ratings, 2023). The sports market has grown both in the United States and internationally, but preferences have also shifted.

The sports world of the 2020s is a rapidly changing space. In just the first few years of the 2020s, fans have witnessed remarkable changes in a variety of sports. Examples from boxing, golf, and American collegiate sports illustrate the remarkable changes occurring in the sports industry and sports fandom. We have not mentioned boxing through the first 11 chapters, but boxing is a sport with a rich heritage and fascinating current circumstances. A century ago, boxing, horse racing, and baseball were the three major US sports (Hauser, 2009). In the recent era, boxing has struggled to maintain a broad fan base with pointed challenges among younger demographics. However, a significant amount of attention paid to boxing in the 2020s has been centered on stars with substantial appeal within Generation Z. Jake and Logan Paul rose to fame as social media celebrities but found mainstream success as boxers. In his third fight, Jake Paul's match against retired MMA fighter Ben Askren generated 1.5 million pay-per-view (PPV) buys, tying it for the twelfth most purchased boxing event (Binoy, 2022) of all time. Logan Paul's fight with Floyd Mayweather generated $50 million in revenues on over one million buys (Zucker, 2021). Notably, Logan entered the fight with a 0–1 record as a professional compared to Mayweather's record of 50–0. The Pauls' PPV events often include other social media stars, celebrity announcers, and popular musical acts. The Pauls' impact on boxing is primarily a function of new technology, driven by their ability to manipulate social media rather than through athletic prowess.

* Social media is changing who controls access to audiences.

Another notable feature of boxing is that while its popularity has waned with the public, it has significant strength with the Hispanic segment. Hispanic boxers like Roberto Duran, Oscar De LaHoya, and Julio Cesar Chavez Jr. have been some of the most commercially successful boxers over the last 40 years (Matthews, 2017). Even in an era dominated by the Paul brothers' sports entertainment version of boxing, the most reliable PPV draw has been the Mexican fighter Canelo Alvarez (Raghuwanshi, 2023). The popularity of boxing in the Hispanic community is especially important to the sport, given the rapid growth of the Hispanic segment in the US market.

* Changing demographics are influencing the experiences and preferences of audiences.

Golf fandom has largely been centered on the American-based PGA tour and American star golfers like Arnold Plamer, Jack Nicklaus, and Tiger Woods. LIV Golf is an effort to create a global golf tour. LIV's strategy has focused on signing established PGA stars such as Bryson DeChambeau and Phil Mickelson and developing a significant contingent of international venues in locations including Spain, England, Singapore, and Saudi Arabia. The two organizations seemed to be on the path to a merger in 2023 (Draper, 2023). Part of the logic of LIV Golf is that it can target a global rather than a US sports audience. The competition between LIV and the PGA is interesting as it is a competition between a well-funded, internationally oriented organization and a legacy organization with established brand equity and iconic tournaments. LIV Golf also quickly became a source of controversy as it was funded by the Sovereign Wealth Fund of Saudi Arabia. LIV is interesting as the organization has been accused of being an effort to use the positive associations with sports to "sportswash" the Saudi's global image (Pells, 2023).

* Technology is creating the possibility of global rather than local or national audiences.
* Similar to how sports partnerships have been used to build non-sports brands, the positive associations of sports are increasingly used to burnish political reputations.

American collegiate sports developed as student extracurriculars and grew into tradition rich sports programs with passionate fan support and storied rivalries. College sports have also long had a tradition of amateurism that has led to a strange set of economics involving significant revenues for schools but minimal compensation for athletes. However, the last decade has witnessed the collapse of historic conferences and the advent of Name, Image, and Likeness (NIL) marketing rights for amateur athletes (Lewis, 2021).

College sports has had a long tradition of regional conferences that have recently come under pressure. For instance, the Big Ten Conference was made up of large research-oriented Midwestern Universities but, as of 2025, will have expanded to include East Coast schools like Maryland and Rutgers and West Coast schools like USC and Oregon. In particular, the Big Ten and SEC (Southeastern Conference) expansions represent a shift in power away from the traditional conferences to a small number of high-profile and powerful team and league brands. While the major sports schools seem to be moving towards just a few elite conferences, collegiate sports have also seen a shift towards athlete empowerment with the adoption of NIL rights for athletes. Previously, uncompensated amateur collegiate athletes are now able to leverage their fame and social media presence to earn millions. While conference realignment and NIL might seem to be distinct trends, both are driven by the ability of sports entities to monetize their fandoms.

* As athletes and organizations develop fandom (brand) equity, the result is greater empowerment at the athlete and team levels.

The future of sports fandom is uncertain, but the forces shaping fandom are identifiable. Barring unforeseen shocks like a disruptive technology or social upheaval, we can make some educated suppositions about how sports fandom is likely to evolve over the next few years. Several of the themes in the boxing, golf, and collegiate athletics examples above are likely to continue to drive the evolution of sports fandom over the next few years.

However, there is a critical point that needs to be made. The evolution of fandom is not a naturally occurring process. The preceding examples of the Paul brothers, LIV Golf, and collegiate sports may be enabled by technological and demographic trends, but they are all implemented by people and organizations driven by profit and influence-oriented objectives. The roles of marketing and fandom-oriented organizations are also critical to how sports and other forms of fandom will evolve. Fandom is now actively managed, and marketing activity seems destined to increase given the immense potential of the global and national sports markets.

12.2   Current Trends Impacting Fandom

This chapter aims to project the near-term future of sports fandom from the perspective of 2024. This discussion is largely centered around the US marketplace. While the US sports marketplace is fading as the dominant

12 The Future of Fandom and Fandom Analytics

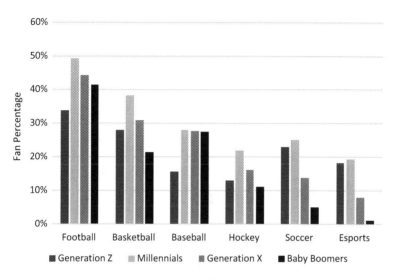

Fig. 12.1 US sports fandom by generation in 2023

market, the US market is a useful context as more data is available and marketing is more sophisticated. Generally, US market trends are being or will be soon felt in other markets. As a starting point for how sports fandom is changing, examining how fandom is changing across generations is useful. Figure 12.1 shows US fandom rates across demographic cohorts from the Next-Generation Fandom Survey of 2023 (Lewis, 2023). The bars show the percentage of each generational cohort that rated their fandom for the sports of football, basketball, baseball, hockey, and soccer at a level of six or seven on a seven-point scale. The figure also includes fandom for esports. In general, fandom is lowest in the Generation Z and Baby Boomer segments. The issues driving diminished Baby Boomer fandom are fascinating and important, but the prospects of major professional leagues and the sports industry are much more intertwined with the fandom of Generation Z.

A quick read of the data suggests that major sports like football, basketball, baseball, and hockey will face challenging futures. The fandom rates in Generation Z are often ten percentage points lower than in the Millennial group. In contrast, soccer and esports seem to have growing rates of fandom. These disparate trends suggest the need to systematically

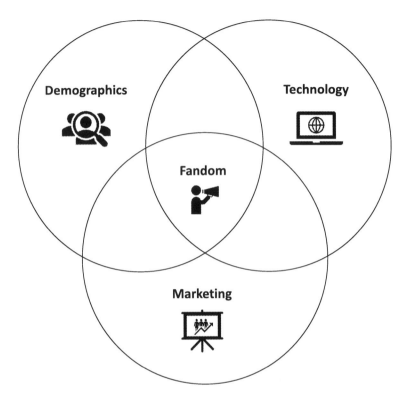

Fig. 12.2 Fandom evolution forces

investigate why Gen Z sports fandom patterns are diverging from previous generations.

Figure 12.2 provides an organizing framework for structuring this discussion about how fandom is likely to evolve. The figure is constructed as a Venn diagram, with the three circles being Technology, Demographics, and Marketing. These circles identify the factors that drive the evolution of sports fandom. Demographic factors affect the fandom stories and traditions within a community. Technology influences how current content is distributed and consumed. Marketing involves different sports organizations' strategies and tactics to grow and manage fandom. These three components, (1) the fandom embedded in populations, (2) the technological environment through which sports are distributed, and (3) the efforts of sports organizations, are the key factors driving the future of fandom.

The inclusion of marketing as a force driving the evolution of sports fandom raises an additional issue. Marketing is an organizational activity. For instance, the targeting of PGA athletes or the location of tournaments is a decision made internally by LIV Golf. The marketing decisions made by organizations are interesting on two levels. First, the decisions have a direct influence on how fandom changes. The Paul brothers, LIV Golf, and the Big Ten are making decisions that will shape boxing, golf, and college football fandom. Second, these decisions have million or billion-dollar consequences. In a previous era, sports leagues, teams, and athletes were largely dependent on the media to reach the fans. Now, there are increasing opportunities for sports organizations to directly reach consumers and monetize their fandom assets. As such, there is also value in reconsidering how sports organizations should be structured to meet the challenges and opportunities of the evolving nature of fandom.

12.3 Demographics

Fandom plays a critical role in defining a society, as fandom reflects the cultural passions of the population. This is a vital observation because it implies that fandom is rooted in a population. The Chicago populace of the 1990s was consistently exposed to the exploits of Michael Jordan and the Bulls. The Argentinians of 2022 were at the center of the soccer universe and Lionel Messi was the biggest star. The Chicagoans of the 1990s and the Argentinians of the 2020s play vital roles in transmitting fandom to the next generation through their shared stories about Jordan in Chicago and Messi in Buenos Aires.

The people who witness the championships and outstanding performances are the people who initially learn the stories of the teams and players. The local or national community has traditionally been the audience exposed to the content that forms the knowledge base for a sports fandom. The people in the team's geographic region are the many people who share the experiences and memories about the team. These are the people who largely make up the team's fandom community. The implication is that sports fandom may be affected by changes in demographics and population patterns. When the people change, fandom changes. The character and intensity of fandom may change, and future fandom transmitted across generations likely declines.

The importance of fandom transmission through family relationships and within communities means that demographic changes may have a substantial impact on fandom. In 1970, the United States had a population of approximately 203 million people with a median age of 28.1 years old, and the largest age group was between 15 and 24 years old. The majority of the population are identified as White, comprising 83.1%, while African Americans made up 11.1%, Hispanic Americans made up 4.4%, and Asian Americans and Native Americans each accounted for less than 1% of the population (all statistics from the US Census Bureau). As of July 1, 2020, the United States had a population of approximately 331 million people, with a median age of 38.5 years old. The population was 76.3% White, while African Americans made up 12.4%, Hispanic Americans made up 18.5%, and Asian Americans accounted for 5.9% of the population.

Immigration is the primary driver of demographic changes in the US population. According to PEW Research, the number of immigrants in the United States grew from 9.7 million in 1970 to 44.7 million in 2018. This growth means that the foreign-born population was less than 5% of the total in 1970 but 12.5% in 2018. PEW also reports that 49.3% of immigrants were classified as White in 1980 versus 17.7% in 2018 (Budiman et al., 2020). The percentage of immigrants has continued to increase, reaching 15% in 2023 (Camarota & Zeigler, 2023).

The structure of families has also changed over time. The number of children living in two-parent homes has dropped from 85% in 1968 to 70% in 2012, according to the Census Bureau's Current Population Survey (Hernez & Washington, 2021). As the trend away from two-parent families is also a trend towards children living with only mothers, there is a significant trend away from fathers in homes.

These demographic trends all suggest less familial transmission of sports fandom for the traditional major American sports of football, baseball, basketball, and hockey. Immigrants will often lack exposure to American sports leagues and may have preexisting fan loyalties. A Mexican immigrant living in Chicago may be devoted to the Mexican National Soccer Team while having minimal interest in the local NFL team. The immigrant did not grow up with American football and may or may not be interested in investing the effort to learn about the game and team. It is also an open question as to whether the Mexican immigrant will be a fan of the local Chicago MLS team. If fandom is a lifetime passion, then it can be difficult to acquire fans with preexisting fandoms.

The changes in household structure also have consequences for fandom. Sports consumers have traditionally been male, and sports fandom has usually and primarily been transmitted from fathers to sons. Sports fandom remains lower for females of all generations (see Chap. 5). The reduction of two-parent homes decreases the probability that sports become a foundational point of connection between fathers and sons (and daughters).

There are other societal trends that may influence fandom in less direct ways. For example, the American population has become significantly less religious over the past 50 years. Pew Research (2022) reports that the percentage of the American population who are unaffiliated with a religious organization rose from 5% in 1972 to 29% in 2022. While the relationship between religious faith and sports fandom is indirect, there is a correlation. Data from the Next-Generation Fandom Survey revealed a statistically significant correlation of 0.24 between respondents' sports fandom and degree of religiousness (Lewis, 2023). While this correlation is not particularly high, it reveals a linkage between traditional cultural groups and sports fandom. As society becomes less homogeneous and cultural fragmentation occurs, there may be indirect effects on sports fandom. As the overall culture becomes less cohesive, sports culture may also become less cohesive.

The positive correlation between religiosity and sports fandom may seem surprising as there is little to connect sports and faith. However, religion and sports are both examples of traditional American culture. Sports fandom has multiple components, including interest in the specific sport and a desire to be included in the community. This second aspect is related to an interest in engaging in mainstream culture. Religiosity and sports fandom are both partially driven by a desire to engage with the broader culture. We can expect greater cultural fragmentation as society becomes more diverse along demographic and cultural dimensions. This general cultural fragmentation will likely lead to a decrease in engagement with sports.

Current demographic trends suggest a challenging future for many sports organizations. Within the US market, the demographic segments that have supported mainstream sports are shrinking in relative terms. Fewer two-parent families may also be weakening the generational transmission of fan stories and traditions. In contrast, mass immigration does seem to offer promise for soccer fandom. However, it is unclear whether Mexican and other immigrants whose fandom is for their home countries' national teams will become fans of American soccer teams.

The critical insight from the preceding discussion of demographic trends is that demographic change creates issues beyond simply repositioning products to appeal to different racial and ethnic segments. Changing demographics creates generational issues. Sports fandom is often a product of a childhood spent among fans. Immigrants often lack that early exposure and indoctrination. More fatherless homes also potentially weaken the familial fan acquisition channel. These conclusions suggest an additional aspect of fandom analytics. Our focus has been mainly on individual-level factors that effect fandom. The preceding highlights that macro-level analyses are also relevant to fandom.

* Current demographic trends will likely reduce or change the character of traditional American sports fandom. Games like baseball may face challenges, while soccer may experience a more welcoming environment.

12.4 Technology

The example of the Paul brothers being able to leverage their social media followings to become sports or "sports entertainment" stars highlights how a changing technology and communication landscape is impacting fandom. Sports consumption has long been enabled by technology. Newspapers allowed the fans to keep up with their teams without attending games. Radio made it possible to consume games from hundreds of miles away in real time. Television provided nationwide coverage and a visual element that fostered fan-player relationships. The Internet and social media now allow instantaneous updates and direct player-fan interactions.

History suggests that technology has been a primary driver of changes in sports consumption and sports fandom. The essential technological trends that have altered consumers' relationship with sports and other entertainment products have been related to people's ability to be connected to sources of information, the speed of content distribution, and the growth of social media. Given that these trends are all based on improvements in communication technologies like smartphones and high-speed wireless networks, many current consumption trends are likely to continue over the next few years.

Current information and communication technology trends suggest continuing increases in the availability and accessibility of content. This trend towards ever-increasing accessibility and a growing array of options has implications for several aspects of fandom. The following three issues are particularly relevant to how technology will continue to affect fandom and fan-athlete relationships:

1. The communal aspects of sports consumption.
2. The effects of technology on attention spans.
3. The development of alternative platforms.

There are other aspects of technology that also impact fandom. For example, sports gambling is growing rapidly and is viewed as both a future revenue stream and a tool for increasing engagement. Artificial intelligence (AI) is also frequently discussed as a future tool for managing marketing relationships, such as fan relationships. We discuss these aspects of technology in the section on marketing because these developments, while driven by technology, are actively managed by leagues and organizations.

12.4.1 Communal Consumption

The technological developments that have supported the growth of the sports industry have, until recently, all supported the communal consumption of sports. In the 1920s, the daily newspaper may have been the primary distributor of sports information. In the 1950s, the radio may have become the primary source for sports content. In the 1970s, broadcast television became the central source, while cable TV dominated the 1990s and 2000s. These technologies all fostered communal consumption. The daily newspaper could be shared across the breakfast table, while the radio and television might have been the central entertainment device in the home.

The development of smartphones and tablets has changed the dynamics of content viewing. There is no longer a need for a family to gather around a single central television, as each family member has a device that can access content. The lack of communal consumption has diminished the role of family in sports fandom.

Communal consumption of sports events plays into the notion that fandom is supported by a collection of stories and identities. Watching a sporting event with an older relative creates common stories as the family has a shared experience. Watching sports together also allows the transmission of stories across generations, as the older relative can talk about past players or explain the game's nuances.

The trends that are reducing communal consumption are likely to continue as smartphones become standard and streaming supplants broadcast and cable television. However, while the shift towards Internet-based content distribution disrupts traditional communal consumption, it can also foster online communities. Communal consumption within families may be replaced with communal consumption within online communities. The rise of multiscreen consumption is especially common in sports. Game viewing threads can be found on platforms ranging from X (Twitter) to Reddit. However, these online communities are relatively anonymous. We are shifting from communal consumption in established and enduring families to communal consumption within temporary, anonymous social media-based communities.

- The likely result of diminished and changing communal consumption is a general weakening of sports fandom as real-life familial and friend fandom networks become less salient.

12.4.2 Pace of Consumption

The development of the Internet changed the pace of sports content consumption. The instant access provided by the Internet made the daily newspaper or weekly sports publication largely obsolete. Results are now instantaneous, and commentary is seconds away on social platforms. Sports consumption was previously more of a planned destination as the newspaper came each morning, Sports Illustrated came once a week, or the local sports report came on at 5:45 p.m. Technology has made the idea of waiting for sports content obsolete.

There has also been a shift in preferences for shorter content. For instance, social media has led to shorter attention spans as there are essentially endless choices and little effort is required to move to the next option. In such an environment, the content needs to hook the viewer in seconds and needs to be brief to retain the audience. Video games may also lead to shorter attention spans as sports video games take far less time than watching actual games.

Research on attention spans suggests that there has been a marked decrease in the amount of time people devote to online content. Mark (2023) reports that attention as measured by time spent on a given screen has dropped from about two and a half minutes in 2003 to about 47 seconds currently. Decreasing attention spans is a challenge for established sports leagues, as the average NFL game takes over 3 h (Rolfe, 2023), while the average EPL game in the 2022–2023 season only took about 98 min.

However, while 98 min may seem brief to NFL and MLB fans, the average TikTok video is between 21 and 34 s (Stokel-Walker, 2022). Stokel-Walker (2022) also report that internal TikTok survey data suggests that a significant number of TikTok audience members feel stressed by videos that exceed a minute. Given that TikTok skews towards younger generations, there would seem to be a growing disconnect between the length of traditional sports content and Generation Z preferences for content length. Sports leagues have responded to changing time preferences. Major League Baseball instituted a pitch clock in 2023 to reduce the length of games (Snyder, 2023), and the NFL created "Red Zone" as a broadcast platform that emphasizes scoring and highlights in short clips.

* Multi-hour games may be inconsistent with the preferences of younger and modern audiences. Sports organizations may need to redesign and create content to fit younger audiences' time preferences.

12.4.3 Platforms and Audiences

The development and growth of social media platforms and declining audiences for traditional media outlets are critical for sports and other fandom industries. From 1980 to 2000, the US population grew from about 220 million in 1980 to 250 million in 1990 and 280 million in 2000. During this period of the 1980s and 1990s, major network television events drew more than 75 million viewers. For instance, the *MASH* finale drew 106 million viewers, the "Who Shot J.R.?" Dallas episode attracted 83.6 million (Lowry, 1998), and the *Seinfeld* finale in 1998 had a viewership of 76.3 million (Lowry, 1998). During this era (1980 to 2000), the Super Bowl attracted similar-sized audiences, with a high of ninety-four million in 1996 and a low of seventy-four million in 1990 ("Super Bowl television ratings, 2023). In contrast, in 2023, with a US population of about 340 million, only NFL programming attracted average prime-time audiences exceeding 15 million, and the top-ranked non-sports programming was NCIS, with an average viewership of 9.86 million (Porter, 2023). The relevant point is that, with the exception of the NFL, traditional television viewership has dropped significantly since 2000.

While traditional media has experienced shrinking audiences, technological advancements have led to significant growth in online media. The key technological development was the spread of smartphones and tablets. Smartphone penetration reached 85% by 2021 versus only 35% in 2011 (Pew Research, 2021). Smartphones are critical because they have supported the growth of social media networks. The growth of social networks is especially prevalent with younger demographic cohorts. For example, Pew Research reports that over 90% of teenagers used YouTube in 2023 (Anderson et al., 2023). The rates for TikTok and Instagram were 60% and 59%, respectively (Anderson et al., 2023).

Furthermore, individual athletes and teams have been able to cultivate massive audiences on social media platforms. As of mid-2023, LeBron James had over 158 million Instagram followers. In contrast, the Los Angeles Lakers had about 23 million, ESPN had about 26 million, and the NBA had slightly more than 84 million. This is significant because a single athlete has a larger social media platform than the league he plays in, the team he plays for, and the most significant sports network. In fact, James' following exceeds the sum of the league's, team's, and primary media outlet's followings. Moreover, the social media accounts dwarf the viewership of most traditional media programming, as the average viewership of the 2023 NBA finals was 11.65 million viewers (Adgate, 2023).

- Technological advancements have created a decentralized media environment, with traditional media channel's audiences shrinking and newer social media channels growing. Connection with the next-generation of sports consumers will require partnerships with and content designed for growing media outlets.

12.5 Marketing

The third element of the fandom evolution figure (Fig. 12.2) is marketing. Fandom is passion and engagement for cultural entities, so fandom reflects what a population cares about in terms of sports, entertainment, music, and other cultural categories. Notably, having people, or a segment of people, care about a cultural product means that there is likely an opportunity to make money. A critical aspect of modern fandom is that it is increasingly actively managed with an emphasis on growing profits or revenues. The active management of fandom is an essential observation for considering how sports and other types of fandoms will evolve. Future fandom will be influenced not just by technological changes and demographic trends but also by the decisions made by sports, entertainment, and other organizations about how to attract and monetize fans. In this subsection, several relevant marketing trends are highlighted, including the following:

1. Increasing Sponsorships.
2. Internationalization and Consolidation.
3. Shifting Control.
4. Blurring Categories.
5. Gambling.
6. Algorithm-Driven Content.

12.5.1 Increasing Sponsorships

While many sports may be becoming segment or niche products, sports may also be positioned for growth in sponsorship activity. This contradictory statement of sports audiences shrinking but also becoming more attractive to sponsors and brand partnerships may be true because non-sports audiences are shrinking at a faster rate than sports audiences. General media fragmentation is leading to smaller audience sizes for many cultural products. Broadcast and cable television, magazines, and newspapers are all experiencing significant declines.

The general decline in mass audiences leaves advertisers scrambling for content with significant audiences. Sports may benefit from this trend in two main ways. First, as broadcast, cable, print, and local audiences have declined, advertisers have shifted to new media, such as social media content and podcasts. These new media are highly fragmented as there are limited barriers to entry for a new influencer or podcaster. The implication is that average audience sizes tend to shrink across traditional and new media. In September 2023 (the week prior to the NFL season), the audience sizes for cable sports talk shows ranged from a high of 525,000 viewers for ESPN's PTI (Pardon the Interruption) show to 149,000 for the tenth-ranked Undisputed on Fox Sports 1 (Burack, 2023). A viewership of 149,000 equates to about 0.045% of the US population. This is a pertinent calculation because it simultaneously shows how difficult it is to attract significant audiences in the modern media landscape and how few fans a sport needs to attract to entice advertisers.

Sports entities are well-positioned to maintain sizeable audiences. Even if a sport slips from mainstream status, the core sports audiences are still sufficiently large to attract advertisers and sponsors. Even second-tier sports may provide sufficiently large audiences to attract sponsors in an increasingly fragmented media landscape. For instance, women's sports like the WNBA or collegiate softball may benefit from a media environment with highly fragmented audiences. While these sports have relatively small fan bases and viewership, in an increasingly fragmented media landscape, a sport reaching perhaps a third or half of 1% of the US population may be sufficiently large to attract sponsors. For example, the 2023 Women's College World Series softball tournament drew 1.6 million viewers, with a peak of 2.3 million (Christovich, 2023). Women's softball may be a niche sport, but in comparison to other media audiences, it attracts a robust audience that will be attractive to sponsors.

Likewise, the growth of social media platforms and influencer marketing may position athletes for more sponsorship opportunities. Beyond the superstar athletes with mega followings, even less prominent sports figures can attract substantial social media followings. The structure of fandom means that athletes have natural audiences through their connections to their teams' fan bases. Becoming the quarterback for the Dallas Cowboys or Alabama Crimson Tide automatically grants the athlete a substantial fanbase. While influencers must build audiences through the production of content, athletes and teams build social audiences through established fandoms and athletic accomplishments.

* Fragmenting media audiences may create additional opportunities for (1) high fandom equity sports brands that can provide exposure to large audiences and (2) second-tier sports with smaller but engaged fandoms.

12.5.2 Internationalization and Consolidation

An important consequence of technology and social media trends is that it is becoming increasingly easy for fandom to be less tied to geography. Traditionally, most media coverage (local TV, newspapers, radio) would focus on the local clubs. The Internet now makes it possible for fans to become immersed in the narratives and lore of any team or athlete across the planet.

In fact, as local media declines and social channels grow in importance, it may become easier to follow high-profile teams and international stars than local sports figures. National and international-oriented media are far more likely to cover superstars and top teams than non-elite teams or players in second-tier markets. In addition, top NBA and International soccer stars can generate social followings that dwarf the reach of local media channels. These stars and influential team brands then tend to dominate social media algorithms.

The concentration of media attention on high-profile sports entities and the accessibility of worldwide audiences provided by the Internet are creating a winner-take-all environment in sports (Frank & Cook, 2010). Only one league can be the best in each sport, and fandom will tend to follow the league perceived as the best. These are the forces behind efforts to create soccer super leagues (Kirkland & Faez, 2023), international golf tours (Pells, 2023), and conference reorganizations in American collegiate football.

There are also concerted efforts to expand domestic leagues into other international markets. The quintessentially American NFL played multiple games in London in 2023 and has a "Global Market Program" that assigns teams to foreign markets for marketing and fan engagement activities (Kaplan, 2023). For example, the NFL program has assigned the Pittsburgh Steelers to Ireland and the Atlanta Falcons to Germany. While the NFL has targeted Europe, the NBA has also made significant investments in China. ESPN has estimated that NBA owner's investments in China are more than $10 billion (Fainaru-Wada & Fainaru, 2022).

* The transition from local media to social media and international media that concentrate attention on stars creates winner-take-all incentives for sports. The future will see further international expansion and efforts to collect high fandom equity sports entities into super leagues.

12.5.3 Shifting Control

Technology trends and the shift from traditional to social media are changing the dynamics of content distribution. As distribution control shifts from traditional media organizations and leagues to individual teams and athletes, there will likely be a shift in control over content development and content marketing. Traditional media becomes less important when teams and athletes can reach millions through in-house controlled channels.

The growth of player and team channels is a product of the "winner-takes-all" trends in media. Star athletes are increasingly likely to have massive social platforms; as of the summer of 2023, four soccer players had more than 100 million Instagram followers, with Lionel Messi at over 400 million and Cristiano Ronaldo approaching 600 million (Thomas, 2023). In US sports, LeBron James has far more Instagram followers than the Los Angeles Lakers or the NBA. When athletes have social platforms that outpace media and leagues, there will eventually be a shift in control and power. There has been a general trend toward athlete empowerment, but when an athlete can reach an audience that exceeds the viewing audience for the Super Bowl, the shifts in power are likely to become more pronounced.

The essential truth of sports is that teams and athletes are the content producers, and the media environment is evolving to empower content creators. Athletes and teams, particularly superstars and iconic teams, will have increasing opportunities to develop and distribute their own content directly to fans without the traditional media acting as a filter. We have already seen the consequences of players beginning to operate as brands as players have made movies (e.g., Michael Jordan, LeBron James, Kyrie Irving, Shaquille O'Neal) or made moves to teams that promised brand-building opportunities (e.g., LeBron James, Lionel Messi). The future will likely see players directly making content through their production companies and distributing it through social channels.

The discussion related to Collective Bargaining Agreements in Chap. 10 is also relevant to this trend. Future CBAs will likely need to consider the implications of teams and athletes acting as content producers or media companies. In the future, a relatively small set of athletes and teams will have sufficient social media influence to monetize the value of fandom at a much greater rate than others. Future CBAs may need to consider the implications of social media influence on competitive balance. If signing with a specific team leads to significant growth in social media following and the ability to monetize an athlete's brand, then rules regarding salary caps may become less relevant. NIL (Name, Image, Likeness) rules in college football are a case in point. While colleges are still prohibited from directly paying collegiate athletes, athletes now regularly choose schools or transfer to schools based on potential NIL earnings (Wallace, 2023).

- Market power and influence will continue to shift towards sports content producers. Superstar athletes and iconic teams will have increasing opportunities to become content producers and distributors.

12.5.4 Blurred Categories

In previous eras, business success was about making the most reliable car or the tastiest cookie. This emphasis on single products was largely true in entertainment, as great books, epic films, and games only occasionally crossed paths. In the current era, entertainment properties are relentlessly exploited and monetized to create products in new categories. A book series like *The Witcher* becomes a hit video game that becomes the basis for a streamed television series. The Marvel Comics Universe provides the building blocks for the Marvel Cinematic Universe which is the genesis for content for Disney's streaming platform. Along the way, the comic characters are featured in video games, toys, and apparel. The marketing innovation is that entertainment brands with significant fandoms are

12 The Future of Fandom and Fandom Analytics

especially extendable brands because fans will cross categories for the objects of their fandom.

Sports brands have the same properties that allow for the extendibility of entertainment properties. Sports brands come with built-in and highly engaged fan bases. Sports narratives contain heroes, villains, and dramatic peaks. Sports brands also occupy a cultural space that facilitates awareness and free media coverage.

These traits make sports documentaries and extensions into films a promising form of entertainment. Michael Jordan has been one of our core examples throughout the book. Since 2020, Jordan's career has been the source of material for ESPN's highest-ever rated documentary, *The Last Dance* (Hehir, 2020), and his marketing successes are the basis for the movie *Air* focused on the Air Jordan phenomena (Affleck, 2023). Jordan is not unique, as many other real-life sports figures and organizations examples have provided source material for movies and television. Netflix's *Drive to Survive* docuseries on Formula 1 translates the excitement and drama of racing to episodic television, and the NFL has partnered to create documentary content (Hard Knocks).

Sports content also inspires a desire to participate and engage. These traits make sports popular source material for video games. The NFL provides the core content for the Madden video game series, which has sold more than 130 million copies as of 2022. Notably, FIFA produces the most watched athletic event on the planet, and the FIFA video game is the number one ranked sports video game at 260 million copies as of 2022.

The extension of sports stories into documentary series or sports leagues into video games is well-established. However, we should expect more of this activity in a fragmented media market. Sports produce fascinating stories and bring with them an engaged fandom. Any cultural entity that continually creates compelling content and has an established audience is a prime candidate for extensions into multiple categories.

* Sports brands have the potential to extend into related media categories. The core sports product constantly supplies stories, stars, and established fandoms. Sports organizations should shift focus to become more general content producers.

12.5.5 Gambling

Sports gambling and fantasy sports are rapidly growing industries. The US Supreme Court effectively legalized sports gambling in 2018, and many states had authorized some form of sports betting by 2024. Relaxation of gambling restrictions has created opportunities for firms to create daily fantasy sports betting sites where fans can bet on items as varied as whether a specific player will score 20 points in an NBA to the fastest pitstop during an F1 race (Hennion & Maher, 2023). Data suggests that gambling has become extremely popular as Pew Research (Gramlich, 2022) has found that 19% of the US population bet on sports in 2021 and the daily fantasy sector is reported to have more than 60 million participants as of 2023.

The Next-Generation Fandom Survey includes questions related to gambling. An interesting result from the survey is the correlation between responses about an individual's sports fandom and the individual's interest in sports betting. The correlation between sports fandom and interest in gambling was 0.37 (Lewis, 2023). Multiple explanations may be offered for the strong link between gambling and fandom. Perhaps, gambling may enhance or makes sports consumption more exciting. In this scenario, gambling improves the sports consumption experience, making sports more appealing. Alternatively, we could explain the correlation with the idea that sports consumption may lead to gambling. Perhaps, the excitement of sports leads fans to want to become more connected or involved in sports contests, so they seek out gambling, or sports fans wish to demonstrate their expertise through winning gambles. A third possibility is that interest in sports and interest in gambling may be driven by some unobserved factor, such as a need for excitement. Teasing out the direction of the casual relationship is an important future topic, but the correlation indicates that gambling and sports have a potentially positive relationship that may be used to either create revenues through gambling products or to use gambling to foster fandom. Either way, legalized gambling promises revenue opportunities for sports organizations.

The growth of gambling and the correlation between interest in gambling and sports fandom are interesting data points for the sports industry. From a psychological standpoint, gambling may enhance sports enjoyment. As we have noted, the sports narratives that often underlie fandom may feature thrilling stories of close matches or come-from-behind victories. Economists have also proposed the "uncertainty of outcome hypothesis" that conjectures that consumers enjoy more even matches. Gambling seems to have promise as a tool for increasing fan engagement.

Gambling may enhance fan engagement in several ways. First, sports gambling can increase arousal and engagement by adding to a fan's commitment to a game or outcome. Fans often feel like they win or lose when their team wins or loses, but gambling makes the connection explicit and creates real economic consequences. The idea is straightforward as placing a wager on a team financially aligns a fan's interest with the team or player, as the wager is "skin in the game" (Taleb, 2018). Aligning the fan's financial interests with a team's performance also temporarily solidifies the "We" aspect of the fan-team relationship. Second, gambling can reinforce uncertainty. When gambling lines are set to equalize the amount wagered on each side of a game, gambling can provide an element of uncertainty. For instance, the daily fantasy industry uses data to set wagers that are also approximately 50–50 chances. Gambling can, thereby, add uncertainty to sports events that may not be even matchups between the participating teams.

However, while sports gambling may increase engagement, gambling's overall impact on sports fandom is unknown, and negative effects of gambling can be hypothesized. Sports fandom is the outcome of a complex set of experiences and relationships that lead to fans gaining social value from being connected to their sports teams and fandom communities. The traditional sports fan is exposed to the team by family and local media and roots for the same team from early childhood to the end of life. Notably, the traditional fan roots for the home team, regardless of team quality. It is an open question how gambling and fantasy sports will impact this type of devoted fandom. How does the fan feel when his fantasy player has an outstanding performance that leads to a defeat of the home team? Does the fan root for his favorite team or for his fantasy team? There are also important questions about the long-term effects of sports gambling on fandom. Over time, does prolonged gambling lead to a shifting of interest from being a fan to an interest in optimizing gambling returns? Sports gambling is growing, and technological advances will likely lead to increasing opportunities to gamble in real time on events like free throws or penalty kicks. The long-term impact of sports gambling on fandom is unknown as we can conjecture both positive and negative effects.

Perhaps, the danger for sports organizations is that it will be difficult to resist investing in gambling initiatives because of the ever-increasing need to keep pace with the revenues of other teams. The one certainty about gambling is that it has the potential to create current-period revenues. The gambling segment is sufficiently large and motivated that gambling revenues may quickly become necessary for sports organizations to keep pace with rivals. However, the long-term consequences of increasing gambling on teams' fandom assets (brands and fans) are largely unknown. Sports organizations may need to embrace gambling without knowing the long-term consequences on fandom equity and fandom lifetime value.

- Sports gambling is an enticing proposition for sports leagues as it promises revenues and can seemingly inspire fan engagement. The big questions are whether gambling erodes core identity-based fandom and if the gambler segment is expandable.

12.5.6 Algorithmic Marketing

A trend combining marketing and technology is the continued development of algorithms suggesting (and hiding) content. Social media and streaming platforms all utilize recommendation systems to suggest content to users. These recommendation systems are driven by user data. As users consume content via platforms, content distributors can collect user behaviors and preferences data. Data on user behaviors may be used to recommend or suggest additional content.

Advancing machine learning and artificial intelligence systems have the promise to identify recommendations that will maintain a viewer's attention. Automating the recommendation process has significant implications for sports and entertainment fandom. In previous eras, sports content was largely curated by media and leagues. These entities decided what games to broadcast and what athletes to feature. In the future, content curation may be increasingly driven by algorithms.

It is difficult to forecast where this trend leads. Faster computers and richer data sets will allow social and streaming platforms to predict preferences more accurately, but algorithms can also shape preferences by selecting the teams and athletes to which an individual is exposed. Algorithms may also be developed to enhance customer relationships or to promote certain types of content effectively. In other words, while it is easy to forecast more powerful recommendation engines, it is impossible to predict how they will be used.

Algorithmic marketing may also need to be a topic for future collective bargaining agreements. Minimum promotion policies may need to be specified so that all teams are featured in the league's social media and the social media of the league's broadcast partners. Suppose ESPN is a partner with the NBA. ESPN's social media virality might be maximized by focusing on a small set of the league's most popular players. However, this might create competitive imbalances as players on less popular teams are denied social media exposure. Without constraints or rules on social media promotions, there will be an increasing tendency for winner-take-all or star-focused outcomes.

* Content recommendation algorithms will continue to play a significant role in guiding viewing decisions. Marketing algorithms creating curation or filtering content will become increasingly important for fandom development.

12.6 Fandom Focused Organization

On one level, the message of the book is simple. Sports fandom is created when teams and players create shared memories for fans. Michael Jordan winning championships with last-second shots in front of packed arenas and massive TV audiences gives people a shared, thrilling experience. Max Verstappen's racing style, victories, and *Drive to Survive* publicity have made him the most popular driver in Formula 1 (Vaughn, 2021).

The stories are simple on the surface. Jordan is the greatest player of all time and a uniquely spectacular athlete. He won six championships while also retiring at the peak of his career and returned the US team to the Olympic Gold medal podium. Verstappen was a wunderkind driver making his debut at just 17, and he has become an all-time great by supplanting the legendary Lewis Hamilton. Jordan's and Verstappen's performances are the main ingredient that makes fandom possible. However, there is more to the Michael Jordan and Max Verstappen stories. The context of their stories and the organizations they work for are important aspects of their stories and resulting fandom.

In the year before Michael Jordan's arrival, the Chicago Bulls achieved a record of 27 wins and 25 losses. In Jordan's first season, the team improved to 38 and 44 and lost in the first round of the playoffs. It was not until Jordan's seventh season that the Bulls won an NBA championship. The only player on the Bulls roster during Jordan's rookie season and the team's first championship was Michael Jordan. Jordan is the clear cause of the Bulls' success, but the organization did need to remake the entire roster to support Jordan's stardom.

Jerry Krause is the controversial figure behind the Bull's championship teams during the 1990s. Krause may be viewed as the architect of the Bulls dynasty. Krause brought in key players such as Scottie Pippen and Dennis Rodman and made strategic coaching changes that ultimately led to the Bulls' success. He also had a knack for finding role players, such as Toni Kukoč and Steve Kerr, who became integral parts of the team. Throughout his tenure as the Bulls' general manager, Krause made bold moves that paid off, including hiring Phil Jackson as head coach and deciding to trade Charles Oakley for Bill Cartwright.

Michael Jordan's rise to superstardom was greatly aided by the marketing efforts of Nike and other commercials. Jordan's iconic Air Jordan sneakers, which were released by Nike in 1984, became a cultural phenomenon and helped cement his status as a global icon. The advertising campaigns that accompanied the release of the sneakers helped position Jordan as an aspirational figure by featuring Jordan's basketball skills and charisma. Jordan's endorsements with brands such as Gatorade and McDonald's further elevated his profile and made him a household name.

These marketing efforts effectively transformed Jordan into a cultural icon and helped catapult him to unprecedented fame and success.

Max Verstappen has become Formula 1's most popular driver, but like Jordan, Verstappen's success is the outcome of the combined efforts of a larger organization. A Formula 1 driver's success is dependent on their team's abilities to create a competitive car and an effective support organization. Christian Horner has been the team principal of the Red Bull Formula 1 team from 2005 to the time of this writing. Horner is the architect of the team and was responsible for signing Max Verstappen as Red Bull's lead driver. Horner also plays a crucial role in developing new cars (RB16B) and decisions like switching to Honda engines (Hughes & Piola, 2021). Horner has been the consistent factor in Red Bulls successes before and during Verstappen's time at Red Bull.

Red Bull's Formula 1 team has also successfully secured lucrative marketing deals and sponsorships. The team has partnered with some of the biggest names in the industry, including Aston Martin, Puma, and Honda, to promote their brand and products. These partnerships have contributed to the team's financial results and fund development efforts that support the racing program. Overall, the team's marketing strategies have been instrumental in elevating the Red Bull brand to new heights in the highly competitive world of Formula 1 racing.

Michael Jordan is one of the most famous and beloved athletes of all time. Max Verstappen is a global star who is beginning to expand his popularity beyond his sport. Jordan and Verstappen are the stars, but their successes were supported by organizations—organizations that helped build competitive teams either through finding the right power forward or the right engine manufacturer. Verstappen and Jordan have also benefited from partnerships with and promotions by incredibly powerful marketing organizations.

12.6.1 Fandom Organization Mission

The Fandom Analytics Framework (Fig. 2.1) presents an innovative framework for analyzing and managing fandom. The framework also encompasses a philosophy of fandom that considers the roles of stories, social identity, marketing science, and sports analytics. This chapter discusses several current technological and demographic trends that are changing how fandom operates in the modern world. Changing managerial philosophies and capabilities combined with an evolving cultural landscape suggest a need to revisit the organizational structures used to manage sports and other fandom-oriented organizations to meet current and new fandom challenges.

The starting point for this discussion is the observation that traditional stewards of fandom, the marketing department, may not be the right group for the future. Marketing departments have consumer expertise but, in sports, lack the ability to create fandom independently. What is needed is an organizational structure that is directly aligned with the sports organization's paramount goal of creating fandom.

Describing fandom as the ultimate goal may strike sports executives and fans as sacrilege as sports organizations usually focus on winning. However, winning and fandom are closely linked as fandom creation is overwhelmingly driven by winning. The fan wants the team to win, so specifying the organization's goal to be creating fandom is aligning the organization's goals with maximizing customer satisfaction. The slight adjustment in philosophy is that the organization's goal is not just to win but to win in a way that maximizes long-term fandom.

The starting point for this objective is to define the organization's goal as the maximization of the value of its fandom. The difference between a traditional sports organization with an agenda that balances winning goals with profitability objectives and a fandom-focused organization is subtle. In both cases, there is an emphasis on financially efficient winning, but in the case of fandom-focused organizations, there is a shift to an emphasis on why a team wants to win: to create a robust and valuable fandom.

It is also useful to directly specify the updated organization's vision through a mission statement. The following mission statement explicitly identifies fandom as the definitive goal and links winning to fandom. The mission statement is also "overwritten" to specify all the elements a fandom-oriented organization may wish to make explicit.

* Our organization is devoted to sustained excellence on the field (court, track, etc.) and the development of a passionate fandom and culturally relevant brand. Our athletic objectives are sustained excellence and championships. Through consistent, exciting play and winning, we will provide experiences that create a brand that connects members of the fandom community and creates a passionate, enthusiastic, and loyal fan base. Through championships and a robust fan base, our ultimate goal is to develop a beloved sports brand that is both economically valuable and provides a powerful platform for attracting future talent and fans. Our business should operate as a virtuous cycle where winning creates the stories that bond fans, and this fandom results in an economically and culturally powerful brand that helps us attract elite athletic talent.

A primary value of the mission statement is as communication tool. The mission statement emphasizes the connection between winning and fandom development. The mission statement also explicitly identifies the development of a valuable and culturally relevant fandom (brand) as the overarching objective. This is critical as it focuses the entire organization including general managers on fandom.

12.6.2 Organizational Structure

We started this chapter with examples from basketball. Michael Jordan arrived at a struggling Chicago Bulls franchise in the mid-1980s. The Bulls' attendance in the year before Jordan's arrival was just 6365 fans per game (Sengupta, 2023). By 1988, the average attendance was 17,794. Fast forward to the current era, the Bulls led the NBA in attendance in the 2022–2023 season despite failing to make the playoffs. The Bulls went from being a struggling NBA team in the early 1980s to an elite NBA brand that can lead the league in attendance even when they are not competing for championships. Who was the Bulls' Chief Marketing Officer during the 1980s?

One of the themes of the *The Last Dance* documentary was that General Manager Jerry Kraus wanted to dismantle the team and move on to a new generation of talent. Kraus had a track record of success in acquiring supporting stars, role players, and coaches. In hindsight, Kraus' desire to rebuild the team seems crazy. Michael Jordan is regarded by many as the greatest player of all time, a national hero, and an iconic marketing figure. Michael Jordan was also a fandom-creation machine. Dismantling a Michael Jordan-led team and pushing Jordan out of Chicago is one of the most fascinating sports management decisions ever made.

Changing the philosophy of the organization necessitates changing the organizational structure. The changed organization should be aligned with the new philosophy. Figure 12.3 shows a simplified version of a fandom-focused organizational structure. The key element of the new structure is simultaneously minor and radical. In contrast to a traditional sports organization where the General Manager is essentially the primary executive in charge of sports decisions, a new position of Chief Sports and Fandom Officer is created.

The logic for this new position is that fandom is the goal, and sports operations are the primary means to achieve the goal. Therefore, oversight of the sports function should also include oversight of fandom equity. The organizational structure that shifts oversight of marketing to the Chief Sports Officer is innovative but may meet with resistance from both marketing and sports executives. The existing General Manager may

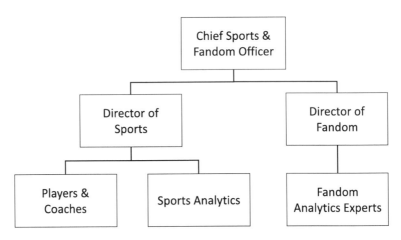

Fig. 12.3 Fandom-focused sports organization

not wish to report to an executive concerned with non-sports activities or to take on those responsibilities. Likewise, the existing marketing department may feel like the new structure encroaches on their territory.

Creating a fandom-focused organization requires at least three elements. First, the organization needs to specify and promote a philosophy that places fandom at the center of the organization's long-term goals. This element requires explicit communication and leadership support for the organization's refined mission. Second, the organization needs to be structured to align winning and fandom goals. Winning and fandom are so closely interrelated that this is a minor issue. The organization mainly needs to adopt a longer-term and more multidimensional orientation in terms of performance evaluation. For example, a general manager or coach should be evaluated based on the state of the team and the fandom. Third, the organization needs to create of an interdisciplinary team of analysts that can understand and monetize the nuances of fandom. The next section discusses core fandom competencies in the context of fandom analytics and the trends that are driving future fandom.

The adoption of any new organizational philosophy or structure may encounter resistance to change. The appropriate perspective on the proposal for a fandom-focused organization is similar to the organizational transformations that occurred related to analytics. As analytics have become more common, the path to the General Manager role has broadened to include executives with more business and quantitative skills and perhaps less playing experience. Just as sports executives have adapted to needing to use a broader set of analytical tools, the proposal is essentially for the sports executive to adopt a broader business perspective. In the following subsections, the skill sets and organization of several components of the fandom department are described.

12.7 Organizational Capabilities

As fandom evolves in response to technology, demographic, and marketing changes, sports organizations need to refine their capabilities. In particular, there will be increased needs for storytelling skills, fan identity and relationship building capabilities, quantitative marketing expertise, and refined sports analytics approaches that integrate sports performance and fandom goals.

12.7.1 Storytellers

The fandom-focused organization requires storytelling expertise through staff who can identify and produce fan-building narratives. The fandom-focused organization must be able to identify the stories and produce and distribute content. In previous eras, content was the province of local and national media. In a social media world, storytelling and distribution become a paramount responsibility of the sports organization. However, storytelling is a challenging function for non-creative organizations. Marketing and communications staff often start with a brand and then try to tell stories that support the brand vision. In sports, storytelling should strive for content that will inspire fans. The athletic accomplishments are the foundation of the sports brand rather than any brand message scripted by MBAs.

The trends towards social media channels' control by sports organizations heighten the importance of developing in-house storytelling capabilities. A challenge is that storytelling is independent of the medium. Stories can be told with Tweets, video clips, or longer-form articles and extended video pieces. As media shifts from traditional channels to social channels, fan-driven organizations gain greater control of storytelling but also greater responsibility.

The emphasis on stories from the athletic field rather than the advertising creative executives is a double-edged sword. On the plus side, the organization benefits because the brand story is based on reality and is, therefore, authentic. The challenge is that the organization loses some freedom as they are restricted by the team's past and present performances.

Developing in-house storytelling capabilities can also provide a competitive advantage in terms of recruiting. The stories organizations tell about their players can help build players' brands and earning potential. An organization that helps turn its players into stars with passionate fan bases can gain an advantage in salary-capped leagues. This is an important aspect of the proposed fandom-focused organization as the sports performance and fandom building functions should work in conjunction.

12.7.2 Fan Psychologists

The fandom-focused organization also requires expertise on fan psychology. Many teams have hired sports psychologists to assist athletes with stress and mental challenges. Psychologists may also be useful from the fandom side to understand how fans connect to teams. Developing the stories that underlie fandom is critical because these narratives create the subcultures that provide fans with social identity and group membership benefits.

Consumer psychology expertise is a foundation of modern marketing. Brands strive to understand the key aspects of consumer psychology that influence consumer decisions. In sports and other cultural categories, the role of consumer psychology is especially pronounced. While consumers can be thought of as having relationships with their favorite brands, brand loyalty becomes a foundational element of consumers' social identities only in a few categories, such as sports.

The differing roles of fandom in social identity construction are a powerful basis for segmentation. As discussed in Chap. 4, several psychological traits related to group membership are relevant to fandom and social identity. A segment that scores high in Identity Intensity (We Win), the trait of feeling like a team victory is also a personal victory, has a different set of motivations or needs than a segment scoring high in the "Reflected Glory" trait. A segment scoring high on the "My Own Thing" or Individualism trait represents another set of challenges.

Consumer behavior expertise may also be useful for mapping the process through which fans evolve across psychological segments. Is it possible to convert casual "Reflected Glory" fans to hardcore "We Win" fans? If it is possible, what are the types of stories or narratives that can lead to more committed and economically valuable fans?

The future fandom-focused organization needs an explicit focus on building fandom communities that lead fans to use sports fandom to create social identities. In an era of challenging demographic changes and social fragmentation, sports are less likely to enjoy organic fandom. Sports organizations need to foster the connection of fans to teams so that fans are identified as part of the team.

12.7.3 Marketing Scientists

The fandom-focused sports franchise also requires established marketing competencies supported by analytics. In particular, quantitatively oriented branding and customer-focused marketing is needed. The marketer's creativity and caution are also needed to find branding partnerships to extend the value of fandom. Data scientists and statisticians are needed to support the marketing side of fandom.

The call for quantitatively oriented marketing is nontraditional for the fandom realm. Fandom is usually the province of more creative-oriented marketers. In fandom-driven categories, the creative elements of marketing are primarily accomplished through storytelling and narratives constructed around the team's athletic performances rather than through branding and marketing communications programs. The creativity is in telling the story of a last-second victory, not in coming up with amusing advertising.

Quantitative marketing is growing in prevalence in general and within sports. But still, many organizations struggle with understanding and maximizing the value of marketing data. The fandom-focused organization needs competencies in brand equity measurement and customer lifetime value analysis. Collectively quantitative analyses of customer (fan) value and brand equity are vital to the fandom-focused organization because they can potentially link team quality (winning) with the long-term value of the fan base. Linking winning with long-team value can guide investment strategies in players and facilities.

Quantitative marketing capabilities are destined to become more critical given current technological and marketing trends. For instance, social media is changing the landscape in terms of data availability. Social media both increases the amount of data and produces text and image data that may require new technologies such as artificial intelligence to analyze.

The trends related to marketing such as gambling, blurring categories, and algorithmic marketing will all increase the amount of customer level data. There will be immense opportunities and challenges related to managing and optimizing Fan Lifetime Value.

The key insight for quantitative marketing capabilities is that sports success and fandom-focused marketing are completely intertwined. Winning games and championships leads to fandom attitudes that drive valuable behaviors such as social media posting and gambling. The fandom-focused organization should be structured to help optimize the value of fan relationships.

12.7.4 Sports Analytics

The fandom-focused sports organization needs a sophisticated sports analytics function. Sports analytics have grown in popularity and are now standard across many sports leagues. Data science and statistics are the essential foundation for sports analytics, and sports analytics are currently a core function for major sports organizations. Moving forward, the application of analytics to roster construction and game strategy is likely to become a prerequisite for on-field success.

The fandom-focused organization requires sports analytics that extend sports analytics techniques in two directions. First, the sports analytics function must explicitly include financial constraints and salary caps. Guaranteed contracts, rookie salary scales, and salary caps mean that roster optimization is a dynamic optimization problem where the analysts should consider the multi-year impact of investments in players on winning. Second, the future sports analytics organization needs to understand the link between on-field results and future revenues.

12.8 Final Thoughts

The goal of this final chapter has been to identify the factors that are driving the evolution of sports fandom and to extrapolate how current trends are likely to play out in the near term. Demographics, technology, and marketing will all play significant roles in how sports and other types of fandoms evolve. The future is partially uncertain as demographics, technology, and marketing can also be subjected to unexpected shocks. For example, political shifts or global conflict may abruptly reduce or reverse immigration. New technologies and innovative distribution channels may create unexpected opportunities for sports.

Barring any unforeseen societal upheavals or technological shocks, marketing's influence is the great unknown in future projections about sports fandom. Fandom is different from many other aspects of culture in that it is actively managed. The future of sports fandom is not set because sports leagues, teams, athletes, broadcasters, and other organizations have a say. Every major and minor professional league wants to grow its share and attract fans. As technology evolves, populations change, and distribution platforms grow or shrink in importance, sports organizations will adapt and respond. Teams and leagues can target different segments of customers, adapt their games for a new environment, and create new and innovative content. There is also the specter of government regulation and interventions. Gambling or social media regulations may have mixed effects on sports fandom.

Demographic trends portend an increasingly difficult environment for traditional sports fandom. Sports have traditionally been a cornerstone for shared culture, and sports organizations will face a new market as the United States and other Western nations become more diverse and traditional aspects of culture and family life change. In the United States, sports like soccer may grow, while sports like baseball may shrink.

Demographic trends place particular stress on one of the foundational elements of sports fandom: the ability to unify. Sports fandom has been a unifying force within families and for cities and nations. Sports' future as a unifying aspect of culture is uncertain. This is a critical issue for sports as sports have enjoyed a special cultural space because they attract a mass audience. If a sport loses its cultural centrality, then that sport may lose out on much of what has made sports special, such as free media coverage and ample sponsorship dollars.

Both global and American versions of football provide common cultural touchpoints in their respective regions. The 2023 World Cup reportedly drew 1.5 billion viewers or almost 20% of the global population. The Super Bowl typically draws about 100 million viewers and is the most-watched TV program in the United States annually. Messi and Ronaldo are renowned in London, Buenos Aires, and Tokyo. Tom Brady and Patrick Mahomes are famous from Boston to Los Angeles.

People are naturally driven to be able to connect with each other, and sports have traditionally provided shared points of reference. As technology trends lead to less communal sports consumption, it is likely that shared experiences will become less frequent. Outside of the Super Bowl or FIFA World Cup, there is little in the world of sports that reaches a broad, mass audience. The growth of social media has also changed sports' role as a unifier. Social networks now more easily extend beyond local areas. Combined with algorithms that reinforce popular content, people are more likely to be exposed to international superstars than local athletes. Sports may still act as a unifier, but the number of sports and athletes will shrink to a small elite group.

A consequence of these trends is that sports leagues will be in a race to become the dominant players in ever-widening regions. The quest for a soccer super league and conference realignment in US college football highlight the trend. The preceding point is related to the idea of globalization of sports. European football is dominated by several national leagues (EPL, La Liga, Bundesliga, Serie A, and Ligue 1). However, Deloitte estimates that the EPL generates about twice the revenue of the second-ranked league (Rumsey, 2023). In American college football, there has been a steady movement towards the two dominant conferences, the Big Ten and the SEC.

Revenues are largely synonymous with popularity and fandom. As fandom concentrates within a sports league, that league tends to gain economic and mind-share benefits that reinforce its advantages. The leagues that collect the global stars will likely attract the most fans, generating the most lucrative media and sponsorship deals. The sports marketplace will be increasingly dominated by a smaller group of elite teams and leagues. We are moving away from an era where teams' economic goals were focused on local market success to an era where consortiums of teams (or athletes) try to dominate national or global markets.

As the sports landscape changes, sports organizations need to align their goals and capabilities to meet new challenges and opportunities.

The traditional sports organization has had the overarching mission of winning. The economic mission of being a profitable enterprise is always present but has often been unstated. When the economic goals are acknowledged, it is common to think of sports organizations as having dual objectives to both win and generate profits.

The critical insight of this book is that fandom is an asset that flows from on-field success. As such, the dual objectives are more appropriately viewed as intermediate steps along a single goal. The goal is to maximize the value of fandom assets. The intermediate steps to maximize fandom are winning and short-term profits. The fandom framework illustrates how these intermediate steps are inextricably linked. The observation that the ultimate goal of the sports organization is a valuable fandom leads to the conclusion that the organization should be structured to achieve the final goal. The Chief Fandom Officer is responsible for the product that creates the fans and brands that make up the organization's fandom assets.

The next few years are likely to be a time of dramatic changes for sports organizations. Sports fandom is fading in younger demographic segments, but media rights and sponsorships are booming. Technology is expanding the opportunities to distribute content, but also shattering communal connections. Organizations have an ever-increasing set of tools for building engagement, but consumers are increasingly skeptical of marketing activities. It will be a challenging environment where success will be determined by organizations' abilities to adapt to a new environment without losing sight of the specialness of sports fandom.

References

Adgate, B. (2023). Viewing to the 2023 NBA Finals drop 6% from 2022. *Forbes*. Accessed February 3, 2024, from https://www.forbes.com/sites/bradadgate/2023/06/14/viewing-to-the-2023-nba-finals-drop-6-from-2022/

Affleck, B. (Director). (2023). Air [Film]. *Amazon Studios, Skydance Sports, Mandalay Pictures*.

Anderson, M., Faverio, M., & Gottfried, J. (2023). YouTube, TikTok, Snapchat and Instagram remain the most widely used online platforms among U.S. teens. Accessed December 15, 2023, from https://www.pewresearch.org/internet/2023/12/11/teens-social-media-and-technology-2023/

Binoy, A. (2022). What are the ppv buys for Jake Paul's boxing fights so far? *Sportskeeda.com*. Accessed November 2, 2023, from https://www.sportskeeda.com/pro-boxing/news-jake-paul-s-boxing-fight-ppv-buys

Budiman, A. et al. (2020). *Facts on U.S. immigration*. Pew Research Center. Accessed December 1, 2023, from https://www.pewresearch.org/hispanic/2020/08/20/facts-on-u-s-immigrants/

Burack, B. (2023). What to make of Pat McAfee's lukewarm ESPN debut viewership. *Outkick.com*. Accessed January 3, 2024, from https://www.outkick.com/what-to-make-of-pat-mcafees-lukewarm-espn-debut-viewership-bobby-burack/

Camarota, S., & Zeigler, K. (2023). In October 2023, the foreign-born share was the highest in history. *Center for Immigration Studies*. Accessed December 26, 2023, from https://cis.org/Report/October-2023-ForeignBorn-Share-Was-Highest-History

Christovich, A. (2023). WCWS Championship Series draws 1.6M viewers. *Front Office Sports*. Accessed January 3, 2024, from https://frontofficesports.com/wcws-championship-series-draws-1-6m-viewers/

Draper, K. (2023). PGA Tour and LIV Golf agree to merger. *NY Times*. Accessed November 1, 2023, from https://www.nytimes.com/2023/06/07/sports/golf/pga-liv-golf-merger.html

Fainaru-Wada, M., & Fainaru, S. (2022). ESPN analysis: NBA owners, mum on China relationship, have more than $10 billion invested there. https://www.espn.com/nba/story/_/id/33938932/nba-owners-mum-china-relationship-more-10-billion-invested-there

Frank, R. H., & Cook, P. J. (2010). *The winner-take-all society: Why the few at the top get so much more than the rest of us*. Random House.

Gramlich, J. (2022). As more states legalize the practice 19% of U.S. adults say they have bet money on sports in the past year. *Pew Research*. Accessed December 2, 2023, from https://www pewresearch.org/short-reads/2022/09/14/as-more-states-legalize-the-practice-19-of-u-s-adults-say-they-have-bet-money-on-sports-in-the-past-year/.

Hauser, M. (2009). Why is boxing slowly dying? Can it be saved? *Bleacher Report*. Accessed December 25, 2023, from https://bleacherreport.com/articles/127217-why-is-boxing-slowly-dying-and-can-it-be-saved

Hehir, J. (Director). (2020). The last dance [Documentary series]. *ESPN Films*.

Hennion, N., & Maher, T. (2023). How to bet on formula 1 racing. *Forbes*. Accessed January 3, 2024, from https://www.forbes.com/betting/formula-1/how-to-bet-on-formula-1/

Hernez, P., & Washington, C. (2021). Percentage and number of children living with two parents has dropped since 1968. U.S. Census. Accessed December 26, 2023, from https://www.census.gov/library/stories/2021/04/number-of-children-living-only-with-their-mothers-has-doubled-in-past-50-years.html

Hughes, M., & Piola, G. (2021). Tech Tuesday: How Red Bull and Honda cleverly transformed 2020's RB16 into the title-winning RB16B. *Formula1.com*. Accessed December 22, 2023, from https://www.formula1.com/en/latest/article.tech-tuesday-how-red-bull-and-honda-cleverly-transformed-2020s-rb16-into-the.1iHxI46LM8z3t1fXX7SQBg.html

Kaplan, D. (2023). NFL around the world: League announces teams adding more global markets. *The Athletic*. Accessed December 29, 2023, from https://theathletic.com/4543000/2023/05/23/nfl-global-markets-germany-ireland/

Kirkland, A., & Faez, R. (2023). 64 clubs, 3 divisions: Super league's new plan after ruling. *ESPN*. Accessed December 29, 2023 from https://www.espn.com/soccer/story/_/id/39160077/64-clubs-3-divisions-super-league-new-plan-ruling

Lewis, M. (2021). Name, image and likeness: Politics tackles NCSS's attempts overdue changes. *Fansided*. Accessed December 25, 2023, from https://fansided.com/2021/01/13/ncaa-name-image-likeness-politics/

Lewis, M. (2023). Millennial passion, disengaged boomers, and evolving Generation Z: Next Generation Fandom Survey 23. Fandomanalytics.com. Accessed December 2, 2023, from https://www.fandomanalytics.com/post/millennial-passion-disengaged-boomers-and-evolving-generation-z-next-generation-fandom-survey-23

Lowry, B. (1998). "Seinfeld's" finale ends up in sixth place of all time. *Los Angeles Times*. Accessed December 29, 2023, from https://www.latimes.com/archives/la-xpm-1998-may-16-ca-50143-story.html

Mark, G. (2023). *Attention span: A groundbreaking way to restore balance, happiness and productivity*. Harlequin.

Matthews, W. (2017). Boxing struggles, but it has a culture in its corner. *New York Times*. Accessed December 25, 2023, from https://www.nytimes.com/2017/05/05/sports/boxing-julio-cesar-chavez-jr-saul-alvarez-hispanic-fans.html

Pells, E. (2023). In 2023, the Saudis dove further into sports. They are expected to keep it up in 2024. *The AP*. Accessed December 26, 2023, from https://apnews.com/article/liv-saudis-golf-sportswashing-063c639305121c034b8dceaab24f26b3

Pew Research. (2021). Mobile fact sheet. Pew Research Center. Accessed November 5, 2023, from https://www.pewresearch.org/internet/fact-sheet/mobile/

Pew Research Center. (2022). How U.S. religious composition has changed in recent decades. Pew Research Center. Accessed November 5, 2023, from https://www.pewresearch.org/religion/2022/09/13/how-u-s-religious-composition-has-changed-in-recent-decades/

Porter, R. (2023). TV ratings 2022-23: Final seven-day averages for every network series. *Hollywood Reporter*. Accessed December 28, 2023, from https://www.hollywoodreporter.com/tv/tv-news/tv-ratings-2022-23-every-primetime-network-show-ranked-1235508593/

Raghuwanshi, V. (2023). Canelo Alvarez ppv buys—How many pay per views Canelo sol? *ITN WWE*. Accessed December 25, 2023, from https://www.itnwwe.com/boxing/canelo-alvarez-ppv-buys/

Rolfe, B. (2023). How long is a football game? Breaking down the time between the first and last whistle. *Pro Football Network*. Accessed December 29, 2023, from https://www.profootballnetwork.com/how-long-is-a-football-game-breaking-down-the-time-between-the-first-and-last-whistle/

Rumsey, D. (2023). Europe's big five soccer leagues seeing revenue near $20 billion. *Front Office Sports*. Accessed December 25, 2023, from https://frontofficesports.com/europes-big-five-soccer-leagues-seeing-revenue-near-20b/

Sengupta, T. (2023). Increasing the Bulls' attendance by 11000 in 4 years, Michael Jordan brought on a $5,000,000 per year hike in value for the team by 1990. *The Sports Rush*. Accessed November 5, 2023, from https://thesportsrush.com/nba-news-increasing-the-bulls-attendance-by-11000-in-4-years-michael-jordan-brought-on-a-5000000-per-year-hike-in-value-for-the-team-by-1990/

Snyder, M. (2023). Two months in, MLB's new itch clock is shortening games, speeding up action and bringing fans to the ballpark. *CBS Sports*. Accessed November 10, 2023 from https://www.cbssports.com/mlb/news/two-months-in-mlbs-new-pitch-clock-is-shortening-games-speeding-up-action-and-bringing-fans-to-the-ballpark/

Stokel-Walker, C. (2022). TikTok wants longer videos- whether you like it or not. *Wired*. Accessed December 29, 2023, from https://www.wired.com/story/tiktok-wants-longer-videos-like-not/

Summerscales, R. (2023). FIFA world cup final beats super bowl LVI by more than one billion viewers in tv ratings. *Sports Illustrated*. Accessed December 25, 2023 from https://www.si.com/fannation/soccer/futbol/news/how-fifa-world-cup-final-beat-super-bowl-lvi-in-tv-ratings

Super Bowl television ratings. (2023, December 5). In Wikipedia. https://en.wikipedia.org/w/index.php?title=Super_Bowl_television_ratings&oldid=1188406141

Taleb, N. N. (2018). *Skin in the game: Hidden asymmetries in daily life.* Random House.

Thomas, L. (2023). 11 Most followed footballers on Instagram. *Givemesports.com.* Accessed December 28, 2023, from https://www.givemesport.com/most-followed-footballers-instagram/#lionel-messi%2D%2D-476-million

Vaughn, M. (2021). Massive F1 fan survey reveals the most popular drivers, teams, and races. *Autoweek.* Accessed November 2, 2023, from https://www.autoweek.com/racing/formula-1/a38029048/massive-f1-fan-survey-ladies-love-lando/

Wallace, T. (2023). College football coaches are now in nil bidding wars. *Outkick.com.* Accessed January 3, 2024, from https://www.outkick.com/transfer-portal-nil-college-football-name-image-likeness-ncaa/

World Series television ratings. (2023, December 5). In Wikipedia. https://en.wikipedia.org/w/index.php?title=World_Series_television_ratings&oldid=1188487067

Zucker, J. (2021). Report: Floyd Mayweather vs. Logan Paul sold roughly 1M PPV buys, made $50M. *Bleacher Report.* Accessed August 8, 2024, from https://bleacherreport.com/articles/10005347-report-floyd-mayweather-vslogan-paul-sold-roughly-1m-ppv-buys-made-50m

Printed in the United States
by Baker & Taylor Publisher Services